Plugged In to God's Power

by Doug Beacham

PLUGGED IN TO GOD'S POWER by Doug Beacham
Published by Charisma House
A part of Strang Communications Company
600 Rinehart Road
Lake Mary, Florida 32746
www.charismahouse.com

Cover and interior design by Koechel Peterson

Library of Congress Catalog Card Number: 2001098942
International Standard Book Number: 0-88419-779-4

02 03 04 05 — 8 7 6 5 4 3 2 1
Printed in the United States of America

DEDICATION

AS I BEGIN THIS BOOK, THERE ARE SEVERAL THANK-YOU NOTES THAT I MUST SHARE:

Thank you to my wife, Susan, who for nearly thirty years has shown me what life in the Spirit is about, and to our children, Beth and Douglas, who inspire us with their joy, their service to God and humanity and their integrity.

Thank you to Lee Grady and the wonderful staff at Strang Communications who entrusted me with the opportunity to write this book. Their patience and support have been an act of grace in my life.

Finally, this book is a thank you and dedication to my parents. Both Susan and I were reared in homes of the International Pentecostal Holiness Church. To me, Guy and Elizabeth Reed ("Mama Lib and Daddy Buck") exemplify Spirit-filled, "salt-of-the-earth" people. By example and instruction, they taught their five girls prayer, sacrifice and excellence. A. D. Beacham, Sr. (Pete) and Marjorie have finished their race, and from their vantage point in heaven they now "see clearly" the Spirit's leading in the pastorate, denominational leadership, writing, teaching and, especially, in rearing three children. Thank you.

CONTENTS

Introduction

"I AM LOOKING FOR SOMEONE TO SHARE IN AN ADVENTURE THAT I AM ARRANGING, AND IT'S VERY DIFFICULT TO FIND ANYONE," Gandalf said to the hobbit Bilbo Baggins in the opening scene of J. R. R. Tolkien's *The Hobbit.*[1] Gandalf's surprise invitation to Baggins reminds me of what the Holy Spirit does in our lives. The Holy Spirit comes, unexpectedly from our perspective, reveals a hint about our destiny and invites us to come along for the adventure that is more than an adventure of a lifetime—as if this adventure will end. The Spirit invites us to "the lifetime adventure" that never ends.

But like Gandalf, the Spirit often finds it "very difficult to find anyone." There are many whom the Holy Spirit is wooing as they search for truth and meaning in life. But when the Spirit leads them to Jesus as "the way, the truth, and the life," they reject that way as too narrow and stumble at the door. There are many others who are born again, who are active in the church and who have had an encounter with the Holy Spirit—but they still live compartmentalized lives. We conveniently have our social, personal, workplace and religious lives neatly organized as pleasant rooms around a central enclave named Self. We don't mind the Holy Spirit having occasional visiting rights (especially if the music and speaker are really good), but He certainly should not impose Himself upon us by knocking down our self-built walls and insisting that everything be centered in one room where Jesus has the best chair.

This book is an invitation to two kinds of people. First, to those of you who are not Christians, it is an effort to invite you to a different kind of life. The Christian life is not about choosing a religion from a smorgasbord of religions. The Christian life is about life and the Spirit of life. I don't really expect this book to convert you. The very idea of being converted probably offends some of you, anyway. But I do pray

that the Spirit of truth will speak to you at some level through this book and help you better understand why many of us believe and act the way we do. Who knows, you just might want to find out more!

Second, this book is written for those who have experienced some things of the Holy Spirit and want to know what in the world has happened to them! You may be from a historic Pentecostal church, a contemporary Charismatic church or a Christian in a historic church group as Roman Catholic, Presbyterian, Methodist, Episcopalian, Lutheran or whatever, and you want to know more about life in the Spirit.

Whether you fit the description of the first group or second group described above, this book is not a scholarly presentation. It's an effort at speaking on a basic level about the Holy Spirit.

I hope this will not offend you, but the mental title for me in writing this book was *The Holy Spirit for Dummies.* Don't feel too bad about that; sometimes I still feel like a dummy in my walk with the Holy Spirit. We'll learn together about our wonderful Holy Spirit as we read.

Let me close this introduction with a final note about endnotes. I think they are important—sometimes they are the most important part of a book—but in this book, which is written in a more popular style, I've tried to be selective and not bog you down with references. I've also tried to document direct quotes and primary ideas from other sources. What I ask you to keep in mind is that in preaching and studying over thirty years, many ideas take root in your mind and spirit and become assimilated into your life. Over time you forget where they originated, but you know they are not original with you. I readily admit I've never had an original idea! The endnotes and additional resources at the end of this book are a guidepost to some of the writers who have influenced my life. Any undocumented ideas have not been intentional; if someone discovers their source, I will gladly give credit and thanks!

CHAPTER ONE

Who Is the Holy Spirit?

IN THIS CHAPTER YOU WILL DISCOVER THAT . . .

- Through the Holy Spirit is our primary way to relate to God the Father.
- The Holy Spirit communicates with us by speech, with will and through emotions.
- The Bible is our primary sourcebook about the Holy Spirit.

POWER. Power play. Power player. Power move. Power lunch. Power point. Power source. Power shortage. Powerful. Powerless. *Power.* You quake in anger because you lack it, or you strut your stuff because you have it.

But what about God's power? What's so special about God's power that I need it? Do any of the following responses ring a bell?

- "I'm a postmodern person, and I don't need the religious crutches hawked by the religious media."
- "I've been a Christian most of my life, but to be honest, I really don't feel or act any differently than my Buddhist friend in the next apartment."
- "I've tried to live a good life, but most of the time I feel that I fail God."
- "I'll never have enough power to be good enough for God."
- "I've had Christian experiences, and even did some of the 'gift stuff,' but I really feel pretty empty in life."
- "I need spiritual power? Hey, today I'm more worried about the power of my car battery! Give me a break! I don't have time for one more religious trip!"

Whether you want, understand or even care about power, God has determined that the primary way He will relate to you is through the presence and power of His Holy Spirit. So, if you want an encounter with the living God, you've got to come to terms with the Holy Spirit. Even under the blistering threats against his life, Israel's singing poet King David twice heard that "power belongs to God" (Ps. 62:11). Jesus said that His followers would receive power when the

But you shall receive power when the Holy Spirit has come upon you; and you shall be witnesses to Me in Jerusalem, and in all Judea and Samaria, and to the end of the earth.
—Acts 1:8

Holy Spirit comes upon them (Acts 1:8).

So, the Holy Spirit is about power. But what kind of power? Is the Holy Spirit nothing more than "the force" that was with Luke Skywalker? Is the Holy Spirit a particular "feeling" that makes us feel good? Some opinion polls indicate that 61 percent of Americans believe the Holy Spirit is "just a symbol of God's power or presence."[1] Is that all the Holy Spirit is?

God has determined that the primary way He will relate to you is through the presence and power of His Holy Spirit.

The best way to find out about the Holy Spirit and power is to return to the Bible. It's in the pages of the Bible that we discover important and interesting information about who it is that we're plugged in to when we are plugged in to the Holy Spirit.

Theology books that attempt to tackle the mysteries of God's nature abound. Actually, most are worth your time. However, since you're likely not reading this for a theology course, we're going to take a direct route with a biblical scenic view of God's nature. Since *theology* literally means "God talk," we're going to let God talk through His Word—the Bible. With a little help from our ancient and contemporary friends, we will discover what God says about His Spirit and His purposes in, for and through us.

GOD IN THREE PERSONS, BLESSED TRINITY

Do not pass Go. Do not collect any "get out of theology" cards. You have to start with monotheism, the truth that God is One: "Hear, O Israel: The LORD our God, the LORD is one!" (Deut. 6:4). As a faithful Jew, Jesus affirmed this same truth in Mark 12:29: "Jesus answered him, 'The first of all the commandments is: "Hear, O Israel, the LORD our God, the LORD is one."'" Thus Jews and Christians begin any dialogue about God on this fundamental revelation. For Christians, St. Patrick's "Breastplate" prayer captures this reality:

I arise today
Through a mighty strength, the invocation of the Trinity,

Through belief in the threeness,
Through confession of the oneness
Of the Creator of Creation.[2]

Christians believe that there is one God—the God of Abraham, Isaac and Jacob, the God of Israel. But Christians also believe that the Bible reveals that the one God exists in three Persons in perfect oneness, unity, love and will. The Bible does not teach, nor do Christians believe, in three separate Gods. There is one God, and He eternally exists in three distinct Persons: the Father, the Son and the Holy Spirit. All human analogies are inadequate—which makes sense since God is God, and we're not!

It took the Christian church about eight hundred years to work through the theological intricacies of the nature of the Triune God. The historic church resolved this in its confessional creeds by affirming that God is truly three distinct Persons in one substance. This personal substance, named *homoousia* in Greek, is the substantial unity of the Father, the Son and the Holy Spirit.

I know it sort of blows your mind. But it's really important. The failure to grasp this reality not only denies Scripture, but it also diminishes the reality of the atoning work of Jesus Christ on our behalf. (Read Matthew 3:16–17 where Father, Son and Holy Spirit are present at the same event.)

The reality of the Triune One means that love and communication are real. The Bible tells us, "God is love" (1 John 4:7, 16). But this is not love as an abstract philosophical concept. This is divine love, which exists in an eternal relationship between the Father, the Son and the Holy Spirit and which is manifested in our lives in how we love one another. (Read 1 John 3:16–17; 4:20–21.)

This is also true of communication. God has given us His Word because He wants to speak to us. He beckons us to prayer so we can speak to Him. The reality of divine-human communication is based on the reality of eternal communication between the Father, the Son and the Holy Spirit. Thus, when the Son, Jesus Christ, was born in Bethlehem, the Bible announces, "The Word became flesh" (John 1:14). For more insight, see Francis Schaeffer's discussion of the Trinity in *The God Who Is There* and *Genesis in Time and Space*.[3]

THE HOLY SPIRIT IS GOD

The above information provides a brief overview of some dimensions of the fact that God is One, yet nonetheless is three Persons. The Holy Spirit is usually called "the third" of these persons. The "third" does not imply any sequence

of creation or development regarding Jesus Christ or the Holy Spirit. With thoughts that cause our heads to spin, the Bible shows us that God has eternally existed as perfect Father, Son and Holy Spirit. We cannot talk about the Holy Spirit without talking about God. In other words, the Holy Spirit IS God. First John 5:7 specifically states of the Father, the Son (who is called "the Word") and the Holy Spirit that "these three are one." Jesus taught, "God is Spirit" (John 4:24). As noted above, Matthew 3:16–17 describes the voice of the Father and the Holy Spirit as a dove landing on the Son, Jesus, knee-deep in the Jordan River. All three are present, and all are One. (It's all right to take two aspirin and pray!)

As God, the Holy Spirit is everywhere and ever-present (omnipresent). (Read Psalm 139:7–10.) The Holy Spirit is all-knowing (omniscient). (Read Isaiah 40:13; John 16:13; 1 Corinthians 2:10.) The Holy Spirit is all-powerful (omnipotent). (Read Job 33:4.)

Through the Bible we discover that the Father, the Son and the Holy Spirit are all active in every phase of creation and redemption. In fact, the Hebrew word usually translated "God," *Elohim*, is plural and denotes the work of the one God in three Persons.

Question: Look up the following passages in Genesis and Isaiah. In the space provided, write what the "Us" intends in these verses:

Genesis 1:26

____

____

Genesis 11:7

____

____

Isaiah 6:8

____

____

In each of the texts, the New King James Version capitalizes the plural "Us," indicating the presence of the Triune God. The first passage shows that the Father, the Son and the Holy Spirit were at work together in the creation of humankind (the Hebrew *adam*, "man," refers to male and female). The Trinity's work in creation is clear in Genesis 1:1 with the plural for God being used: "In the beginning *Elohim* created the heavens and the earth." The Trinity's work in the course of human events is described in Genesis 11:8 with the Triune God's decision to frustrate humanity's efforts to elevate itself to the status of God. Isaiah 6 reveals the heart of the Father, the Son and the Holy Spirit in calling someone to go with the message of redemption.

So the Lord scattered them abroad from there over the face of all the earth, and they ceased building the city.
—Genesis 11:8

THE HOLY SPIRIT'S NAME AND IDENTITY

The reality of the Trinity is also why the Bible sometimes refers to the Holy Spirit as "the Spirit of God." (Read Genesis 1:2; 41:38; Exodus 31:3; 35:31; Matthew 12:28; Romans 8:9, 14.) Sometimes the Holy Spirit is called "the Spirit of [Jesus] Christ." (Read Romans 8:9; Philippians 1:19; 1 Peter 1:11.) First Peter 4:14 refers to the Holy Spirit as "the Spirit of glory and of God." There are times in the Bible when the Holy Spirit is simply called "the Spirit." (Read Genesis 6:3; Numbers 11:17; 1 Chronicles 28:12; Nehemiah 9:30; Job 26:13; Psalm 104:30; Matthew 4:1; 12:18, 31; John 3:34; 6:63; 7:39; Acts 6:10; Romans 8:13.) The phrase "the Spirit of the Lord" is found throughout the Bible (twenty-eight times).

In answering the question "Who is the Holy Spirit?", we have looked at the Spirit as an eternal member of the Godhead. That means that the Holy Spirit is not a created force or being. Like the Lord Jesus Christ, the Holy Spirit has existed and continues to exist eternally as God. (Read Hebrews 9:14 where the Spirit is called "the eternal Spirit.") We have seen that the Bible refers to the Holy Spirit by several different terms. But it is also important to note other characteristics of the Holy Spirit.

The Spirit is holy.

First, the Spirit is called "holy." The Spirit of God is holy. The Spirit is holy because He is God, and God is holy. (Read Leviticus 11:44–45; Hosea 11:9; 1 Peter 1:15–16.) This means that God is sinless and perfect in all His dealings with us. God's power is perfect in love, truth and every other attribute that belongs to Him. It means that the Holy Spirit will never lead us into error or sin. It means that everything the Holy Spirit is doing in our lives is always for the ultimate glory of God, and therefore His goodness can be trusted in every situation of life.

The Spirit is spirit.

Second, God's power is called the Holy "Spirit." What do we mean by "Spirit"? We know that every person is composed of "spirit, soul, and body" (1 Thess. 5:23; cf. Heb. 4:12). The human spirit is that part of our essential nature that lives eternally. (Read Genesis 2:7; Psalm 31:5; Ecclesiastes 12:7.)

Everything the Holy Spirit is doing in our lives is always for the ultimate glory of God.

We know that our human spirit is "dead in trespasses and sins" (Eph. 2:1). Our spirit must be made alive in Christ. (Read Ezekiel 18:31; Romans 8:15–16.) We know that there is a spirit of the world. Sometimes this is manifested in the "spirit" of a nation, a city, an army or a sports team.

It's clear, then, that the "spirit" is real. That's true whether of team spirit at a Saturday afternoon college football game or of the collective spirit of a nation celebrating its freedom. But it's also true that spirit is not the same as flesh and blood.

The word for *spirit* in both Hebrew and Greek *(ruach, pneuma)* refers to breath and wind. Like breath, the Holy Spirit is the source of eternal life. Like the wind, the Holy Spirit is invisible, immaterial and powerful. Jesus gave this comparison: "The wind blows where it wishes, and you hear the sound of it, but cannot tell where it comes from and where it goes"

(John 3:8). In John 4:24 Jesus said, "God is Spirit." God's essential nature is beyond the limitations and constraints of this physical universe. As Spirit, God is above all that is physical. God is able to reveal Himself in the physical realm. Thus, the phrase "Holy Spirit" describes all the goodness, grace, love and fullness of the eternal Spirit who created us and desires to redeem us for His glory.

THE HOLY GHOST

Many Christians still refer to the Holy Spirit as the "Holy Ghost." The older English translations based this on the Middle English *gost,* which was from the Old English *gast,* which was akin to the Old Saxon *gest* and the Old High German *geist.* The word *ghost* in modern English has come to signify something that is terrifying, the otherworldly presence of a deceased person. The modern use of ghost is like Haley Joel Osment's lines in *The Sixth Sense,* "I see dead people."

Some Christians draw a distinction between the Holy Spirit and the Holy Ghost. This is based on the King James Version of the Bible, which uses the terms interchangeably. That distinction is artificial because the Hebrew and Greek terms *(ruach, pneuma)* are the same regardless of the English usage. For most people today, the term "Holy Ghost" is archaic and fails to convey the biblical sense.

The Spirit is personal.

Third, the Holy Spirit is personal. While the Spirit is immaterial, we nonetheless use the personal pronoun "He" to refer to the Holy Spirit. Before we get nervous about sexism, let's remember what we're talking about. By referring to the Holy Spirit in the masculine we are consistent with the biblical revelation of God as "Father." This does not mean that God is a man or male. Male and female are categories of earthly existence that God Himself created (Gen. 1:27). God's fatherhood is an expression of His creative and protective power over this universe.

So God created man in His own image; in the image of God He created him; male and female He created them.
—Genesis 1:27

Because God is Spirit, it is biblically consistent to refer to any manifestation of the Trinity with the masculine pronoun. (Read John 16:13, where the neuter *Spirit* is clarified by the masculine pronoun: "He will guide you into all truth.")

A particular manifestation of the Holy Spirit—wisdom—is

given in the feminine and translated with the feminine. (Read Proverbs 3:13–18; 4:5–13.)

Don't get sidetracked on this issue and lose the primary focus of the personal pronoun—the Holy Spirit is a person. Thus, the Holy Spirit speaks to us, conveys the will of the Father and Son to us, intercedes for us to the Father and Son and responds to us with intelligence that is communicated to us. The Spirit communicates in several ways, including:

- By speech. Read Acts 8:29; 10:19; 15:28; Romans 8:27.
- With will. Read Genesis 6:3; Acts 16:6; 1 Corinthians 12:11.
- With emotions such as joy and grief. Read Isaiah 61:3; 63:10; Romans 8:26; Galatians 5:22; Ephesians 4:30.

THE HOLY SPIRIT IN THE OLD TESTAMENT

With the New Testament's emphasis on the Holy Spirit, it's tempting to think that the Holy Spirit has only been active since the Day of Pentecost in Acts 2 (about two thousand years ago). But that is not true. The Holy Spirit has been very active, including through spiritual gifts, since the beginning of the world. In this section we're going to examine the Holy Spirit's activities in the Old Testament, including the Spirit's role in the creation of the world, the Spirit's work in people, the Spirit's role in divine wisdom and the Spirit's role in prophecy.

The Holy Spirit and Creation

The second verse of the Bible introduces us to the Spirit of God "hovering over the face of the waters" (Gen. 1:2). This is the active presence of the Spirit moving over the unformed and dark earth, bringing order out of chaos. It is valuable to observe that the presence of the Spirit at Creation is connected to the voice of God who speaks into existence things that did not exist (Rom. 4:17; Rev. 4:11). Colossians 1:16 reveals that the Spirit's work at the beginning of the universe was also the work of the Son of God, and that it was Christ

...in the presence of Him whom he [Abraham] believed—God, who gives life to the dead and calls those things which do not exist as though they did...
—Romans 4:17

You are worthy, O Lord, to receive glory and honor and power; for You created all things, and by Your will they exist and were created.
—Revelation 4:11

Jesus who created all things and that "all things were created through Him and for Him." This does not show a contradiction, but rather the majestic unity of the Father, Son and Holy Spirit in every expression of God's work.

Furthermore, the Holy Spirit's creative work is described in terms of the wisdom of God. (Read Proverbs 8:22–31.) In particular, Proverbs 8:30–31 announces:

> *Then I [wisdom, the Holy Spirit] was beside Him [the Father and Son] as a master craftsman; and I was daily His delight, rejoicing always before Him, rejoicing in His inhabited world, and my delight was with the sons of men.*

Can you make this application in your life? The presence of the Holy Spirit in your life means that God, who created the world, also created you, and He wants to speak to you.

The second aspect of the Spirit's work in creation is directly related to human beings. God breathed into man's nostrils the breath of life, "and man became a living being" (Gen. 2:7). Think of it this way. The Potter took the clay, formed it to His pleasure and actually breathed His own life into it! Martin Luther wrote:

> We are vessels of God, formed by God Himself. This holds good not only for our origin but throughout our whole life; until our death and in the grave we remain the clay of this Potter.[4]

God's Spirit caused Adam to be alive differently from the other creatures God had created. It caused Adam to be alive to God with the capacity for intimate relationship with God. From the beginning, God created people to live in unity of body, soul and spirit through the Holy Spirit.

There are two important lessons for us from Genesis 2:7. First, in a certain sense we can distinguish between body, soul and spirit. But our capacity to distinguish should not keep us from understanding the fundamental unity of each person in body, soul and spirit. We are real personalities living in a real body. Our bodies are not evil houses that we ultimately seek to flee. Although they are made of dust, God nonetheless makes the human body. This is why the Christian faith affirms the resurrection of the body. In the resurrection this

earthly body will be raised as an incorruptible body. (Read 1 Corinthians 15:42–55.)

God formed man from the dust of the earth first and then breathed His Spirit into man, giving man his spirit. This combination of spirit and body resulted in the formation of man's soul. Although it was God's Spirit that gave life to man and made him a living being, man did not receive a spark of divinity within himself as if we ourselves are somehow divine. We are not divine. We are created beings. We were not created to be, nor shall we ever be, "gods." We are creatures who stand in a unique relationship with the Creator because He breathed His breath, the Holy Spirit, into us in such a way as to make us alive. Thus the Holy Spirit created the human spirit so we can be in this unique relationship with God.

Second, although all other animals are made from the same dust as humans and are also "living beings," no other creature had God place His mouth over its nostrils and breathe the breath of life. (Read Genesis 1:20–21, 24.) Humanity is qualitatively different from all other animals. In other words, we're at the top of the food chain! This has profound implications relating to environmental issues. Yes, we have a biblical responsibility to the earth and all creatures great and small. But that responsibility begins with the affirmation that human life is the highest form of life God created.

Human life is uniquely formed by God and has its destiny in God's purposes in the gospel.

This is one of the great truths of biblical religion that separate us from certain other world religions. Human life is more valuable than other forms of life. Human life is not a temporary home for a disembodied spirit that may have come from or is migrating toward another animal. Human life is uniquely formed by God and has its destiny in God's purposes in the gospel.

Question: Describe what it means to you that the Holy Spirit was active in Creation.

____

____

____

____

The Holy Spirit and individuals

The Holy Spirit worked in the lives of Old Testament characters similar to the same way He works in us today. In other words, the same Holy Spirit that worked in Joseph, Moses, David and Isaiah works in us! A few examples are given below.

Question: Read the passage, name the individual(s) and the specific name of the Holy Spirit in that text. In your own words describe how the Holy Spirit worked in that passage.

Genesis 41:38–39

___

___

___

▲▲▲▲▲▲▲

Exodus 31:1–6

___

___

___

▲▲▲▲▲▲▲

Numbers 11:24–29

___

___

___

▲▲▲▲▲▲▲

1 Samuel 16:11–13

___

___

___

▲▲▲▲▲▲▲

The Holy Spirit and wisdom

In the Exodus passage above you saw wisdom mentioned as a characteristic of the Holy Spirit. The Book of Proverbs contains several notable passages detailing how the Holy Spirit manifests Himself in wisdom.

- ▲ The Holy Spirit calls for men to live according to the fear of the Lord, which is wisdom. Read Proverbs 1:20–33; 2:5–10.

...for he is a prophet.
—Genesis 20:7

Aaron your brother shall be your prophet.
—Exodus 7:1

But since then there has not arisen in Israel a prophet like Moses...
—Deuteronomy 34:10

...Samuel had been established as a prophet of the LORD.
—1 Samuel 3:20

Now the prophet Gad said to David...
—1 Samuel 22:5

The king said to Nathan the prophet...
—2 Samuel 7:2

Then Elijah said to the people, "I alone am left a prophet of the LORD."
—1 Kings 18:22

And Elisha the prophet called...
—2 Kings 9:1

Then he sent Eliakim...to Isaiah the prophet.
—2 Kings 19:2

He...did not humble himself before Jeremiah the prophet.
—2 Chronicles 36:12

- The wisdom or presence of the Holy Spirit, through which the Lord made the earth, is mentioned. Read Proverbs 3:19–20.
- The Holy Spirit was present in the creation of the earth. Read Proverbs 8:22–36.
- The "house of wisdom," the presence of the Holy Spirit in preparing His abode in the human heart where God's power can be established and manifested, is described. Read Proverbs 4:1–12.

The Holy Spirit and the prophets

The Old Testament identifies many people who were known as prophets:

- Abraham (Gen. 20:7)
- Aaron (Exod. 7:1)
- Moses (Deut. 34:10)
- Samuel (1 Sam. 3:20)
- Gad (1 Sam. 22:5)
- Nathan (2 Sam. 7:2)
- Elijah (1 Kings 18:22)
- Elisha (2 Kings 9:1)
- Isaiah (2 Kings 19:2)
- Jeremiah (2 Chron. 36:12)
- Habakkuk (Hab. 1:1)
- Haggai (Hag. 1:1)

The prophetic books of the Old Testament provide significant insight into the ministry of the Holy Spirit. Here is a sampling from the Old Testament. Read the scripture portions listed from each book to understand better the ministry of the Holy Spirit.

1. **Isaiah**—The Holy Spirit is mentioned in connection with prophecies of the Messiah that were fulfilled in Jesus Christ (11:1–2; 42:1–9; 61:1–3). The Holy Spirit was at work in Israel's destiny (44:1–5; 59:19, 21). Isaiah also emphasized the presence of the Holy Spirit at Creation (40:12; 48:16). Israel's disobedience in the wilderness is understood as rebellion against

and causing grief unto the Holy Spirit because in the wilderness the children of Israel had the Holy Spirit within them (63:10–11).

2. **Ezekiel**—The Holy Spirit spoke through the prophet and gave the prophet visions of the future (11:5, 24). The Holy Spirit entered into the life of the prophet (2:2). The Holy Spirit creates a new heart and spirit in the repentant sinner (36:26–27). The Holy Spirit is able to raise the dead with new life (37:1–14).

3. **Daniel**—The Holy Spirit was dynamically active in the life of Daniel, enabling him to minister effectively in a worldly setting (4:8–9, 18).

4. **Joel**—Perhaps the most well-known reference to the Holy Spirit in the Old Testament, Joel 2:28–29, is a prophecy of Pentecost, which is described in Acts 2. Joel shows that the Holy Spirit will be "poured out" and all flesh will be impacted by this event.

5. **Micah**—Micah 3:8 reads, "But truly I am full of power by the Spirit of the LORD, and of justice and might." The power to speak divine truth comes only by the Holy Spirit. This truth manifests itself in justice and the strength to bring about justice.

6. **Zechariah**—The prophet affirmed that the Holy Spirit and grace are the only effective ways for godly change to occur in this world.

THE HOLY SPIRIT AND THE BIRTH OF JESUS CHRIST

Through the Holy Spirit, Isaiah prophesied that a "virgin shall conceive and bear a Son, and shall call His name Immanuel" (Isa. 7:14). That prophecy was fulfilled 750 years later with the birth of Jesus Christ. Luke 1:26–38 carefully describes how the Holy Spirit was involved in this miraculous birth. The angel Gabriel visited Mary, a young virgin betrothed to be married to a carpenter named Joseph who lived in the Galilean hill town of Nazareth.

The burden which the prophet Habakkuk saw.

—Habakkuk 1:1

The word of the LORD came by Haggai the prophet...

—Haggai 1:1

After getting over the shock of an actual visit from an angel, Mary listened to the message that she was going to have a son. Her immediate response was, "How can this be, since I do not know a man?" (Luke 1:34). Mary, like most of us, could not think of the Holy Spirit's power outside her limited frame of reference. That God could operate outside the normal boundaries of human experience was as foreign to her as it is to us. The answer was simply, "The Holy Spirit will come upon you, and the power of the Highest will overshadow you; therefore, also, that Holy One who is to be born will be called the Son of God" (v. 35).

This verse is important for several reasons. This account is simple and is unlike the sexual encounters among the gods in Greek and Roman mythology. There is nothing lewd or suggestive in the biblical account. Human sexual activity was created by God and is filled with His blessings within the context of marriage. But human sexual activity operates within the realm of earthly existence. What God needed to accomplish in this birth had to occur from the power of another realm of existence.

When the Holy Spirit comes upon us, He changes our wilderness experiences into fruit and life-bearing vitality.

The Holy Spirit came upon Mary. The expression in verse 35, "will come upon you," is used in several other places in the Bible. In the New Testament, it is used in Acts 1:8 to describe the Holy Spirit coming upon the disciples at Pentecost. Acts 1:8 is Jesus' word that His disciples will receive power when the Holy Spirit comes upon them. The Holy Spirit was divine power to generate new life, a different life, in Mary even as He brings new power to us in the baptism of the Holy Spirit.

There are two important Old Testament passages that use this same phrase. The first is 1 Samuel 16:13, where Samuel anointed David, and "the Spirit of the Lord came upon David from that day forward." The presence of the Spirit meant a significant change for the recipient. The second passage is Isaiah 32:15: "Until the Spirit is poured upon us from on high, and the wilderness becomes a fruitful field, and the fruitful field is counted as a forest." When the Holy Spirit comes upon us, He changes our wilderness experiences into fruit and life-bearing vitality.

When the Holy Spirit "came upon" Mary, through His power He brought about a change that only God could do. It was not a violation of the natural order, but rather the divine connection of the supernatural and the natural.

Luke further described the presence of the Holy Spirit upon Mary as "the power of the Highest" that "will overshadow" her (Luke 1:35). The "power of the Highest" is another term for the Holy Spirit. The Spirit's action in her life is expressed in a word with rich Old Testament overtones—"overshadow."

Question: In the passages below, describe how "overshadow," which can sometimes be translated as "cover" or "shelter," is used:

Exodus 40:34

____

____

▲▲▲▲▲▲▲

Deuteronomy 33:12

____

____

▲▲▲▲▲▲▲

Psalm 91:4

____

____

▲▲▲▲▲▲▲

Luke 9:34

____

____

▲▲▲▲▲▲▲

From insights gained from your study of the passages above, briefly describe how the Holy Spirit has "covered, sheltered and overshadowed" your life:

___

___

▲▲▲▲▲▲▲

THE HOLY SPIRIT AND THE BIBLE

Maybe the Bible is a new book to you. Perhaps in your perspective the Bible is a strange book or is more like a history of religions book. You may think that the Bible is inspired religious writing, but no more inspired than other religious books such as the Quran.

But we're approaching the Bible differently. We're looking at what the Bible says from what is in the Bible itself. For example, in 2 Timothy 3:16 the apostle Paul informs us that "all Scripture is given by inspiration of God." The word *inspiration* literally means "God-breathed."

Earlier in this chapter we saw from Genesis 2:7 that God breathed life into the clay form of Adam. The same Spirit of life that came into Adam also breathed life into the words of the people who wrote the Bible. This means that as the various writers composed, the Holy Spirit used their minds, cultural framework and varied experiences as the conduit by which God's promises and plans for humanity were revealed. The writers did not become robots who went into a trance and wrote mechanically. Rather, the Holy Spirit worked through them to express the Father's will and the Son's ministry.

This is why Christians call the Bible the *Word of God*. That term is applied to Jesus Christ, the Living Word of God (John 1:1, 14). But it is also rightfully applied to the books that for nearly two thousand years Christians have recognized as inspired by the Holy Spirit. The Bible gives objective, revealed truth of and from God.

Because this is the case, we can join with John Wesley and say:

> I want to know one thing—the way to heaven; how to land safe on that happy shore. God Himself has condescended to teach the way; for this very end He came from heaven. He

In the beginning was the Word, and the Word was with God, and the Word was God…And the Word became flesh and dwelt among us, and we beheld His glory, the glory as of the only begotten of the Father, full of grace and truth.
—John 1:1, 14

hath written it down in a book. O give me that book! At any price, give me the book of God! I have it: here is knowledge enough for me.[5]

As you have already noticed, the Bible is our primary sourcebook about the Holy Spirit. Anything else is speculation or limited by the shifting sands of human experience. That's why we cannot understand being plugged in to God's power unless we understand it within the context of the Bible.

The Bible does not attempt to answer all our questions. I have thousands of unanswered questions about God and His purposes. My prayer is that heaven has a huge videotape section so I can check out the details of the creation of the universe! The Bible does not claim to give exhaustive knowledge. But I have confidence that the Bible gives us true knowledge of those things essential for our salvation and fulfillment of our destiny in Christ. This confidence is based on the fact that "all Scripture is given by inspiration of God" (2 Tim. 3:16). The fact that the Holy Spirit is the power behind the writers means that the words are true, and they are life.

LET'S TALK ABOUT IT

▲ After reading this chapter, how has your view of the Holy Spirit changed?

▲ How does the reality of love and communication relate to the Christian doctrine of the Trinity?

▲ What does it mean that the Spirit of God is "holy"?

▲ What are the two primary ways that the Holy Spirit was active in Creation?

▲ Why are human beings different from other animals?

▲▲▲▲▲▲▲

▲ You described how the Holy Spirit worked in the lives of individuals. Which of those texts and individuals best illustrates how the Holy Spirit has worked in your life?

▲▲▲▲▲▲▲

▲ How does the biblical account of the birth of Jesus differ from mythological accounts of the Greek and Roman gods?

▲▲▲▲▲▲▲

TIME TO PLUG IN TO THE HOLY SPIRIT

Are you beginning to get a sense of what it means to be plugged in to God's power? Notice that being plugged in is not mainly about what you feel. It really starts with God's truth about Himself as revealed in the Bible. That means you can pray with absolute certainty because you pray according to the Word of God. If you pray according to your feelings, then you are a prisoner to your limited experience (and maybe to the pizza you ate last night!). So, as you prepare to move to the next chapter and look at what Jesus said about the Holy Spirit, why don't you pray something like this:

> *Holy Spirit, I come before You in humility of heart and intellect. There are a lot of things I don't understand. But I do understand that You really have been there in love and communication for all eternity. So I open my heart, my spirit, to You. Make Your Word, the Bible, alive to me as I have never known before. You said that You would give me the desires of my heart. So now my deepest desire is to know You and to know Your Word. Speak to me, and I will listen. Touch my heart, and I will be changed. Love me, and I will be free. In Your holy name I pray. Amen.*

CHAPTER TWO

The Holy Spirit, From Someone Who Knows Him Best

IN THIS CHAPTER YOU WILL DISCOVER THAT...

- Jesus lived on earth in constant communication with His Father through the Holy Spirit.
- The kingdom of God expands in greater spheres of impact as Spirit-filled disciples obey the Lord.
- The Holy Spirit always glorifies Jesus Christ.

WE KNOW THE PRESIDENT OF THE UNITED STATES BY NEWS REPORTS. We know good things about him from his spinmeisters and questionable things about him from political pundits. Sometimes we see what we think are his actions, but wonder if those acts are his or are from someone else in the administration.

If we really want to know the president of the United States, not only do we have to have a personal relationship with him, but we also must learn about him from those who really know him best—his parents, his siblings, his children and especially his wife.

It's sort of that way with the Holy Spirit. In the last chapter we discovered there is a lot to learn about Him from reading the Bible. There are a lot of folks who have had an experience with the Holy Spirit but not necessarily a relationship with Him. If we really want to know about the Holy Spirit, we need to listen to someone who has known Him and worked with Him a long, long time. That someone is Jesus Christ.

Our scenic tour of the Bible in search of the Holy Spirit takes us to the Gospel of John. Jesus told us more about the Holy Spirit in this Gospel record than in any other account. Here we discover a very personal relationship between Jesus and the Holy Spirit. Our personal tour guide on this part of our journey is Jesus Christ. In fact, you really cannot know the Holy Spirit unless you know Jesus.

Open your Bible to the Gospel of John, and we're going to follow this road, chapter by chapter, as we allow the terrain of the Holy Spirit to take us higher. Have a pleasant drive!

[John] said, "I am 'the voice of one crying in the wilderness: "Make straight the way of the Lord,"' as the prophet Isaiah said."

—John 1:23

You yourselves bear me witness, that I said, "I am not the Christ," but, "I have been sent before Him."

—John 3:28

He must increase, but I must decrease.

—John 3:30

THE HOLY SPIRIT REVEALS THE SON OF GOD

As we saw in the first chapter, everything related to the birth of Jesus was accomplished through the Holy Spirit. (Read Luke 1.) That included the birth of Jesus' cousin, John the Baptizer, better known as John the Baptist. (Read Luke 1:5–25, 39–45.) John, who was about six months older than Jesus, walked to the sound of the same drummer (the Holy Spirit) but with a different beat. He lived in the desert, dressed in camel's hair (not quite Armani) and frequented the local locusts and wild honey bistros.

However, John was a man of the Spirit of God. He knew his role as a forerunner of Jesus (John 1:23; 3:28). He knew that Jesus is the main feature (John 3:30). John also knew that the Holy Spirit was going to do something special in Jesus. "He [Jesus] will baptize you with the Holy Spirit and fire" (Matt. 3:11). John also knew how to recognize the presence of the Spirit. (Read Matthew 3:16; John 1:32–33.)

When both men were thirty years old, John was baptizing at the Jordan River when he saw Jesus standing in the crowd. Jesus came forward to be baptized, but John at first refused. But Jesus made John understand that there were issues of righteousness and obedience to the will of the heavenly Father that were necessary. (Read Matthew 3:14–15.) The Holy Spirit had already told John that he would recognize the Messiah by the presence of the Holy Spirit "descending and remaining upon Him" (John 1:33).

Like us, Jesus lived by the power of the Holy Spirit.

This is exactly what happened when Jesus was baptized in water. The Holy Spirit, in a visible form like a dove, descended from heaven and remained upon Jesus. (Read Matthew 3:16; Mark 1:10; Luke 3:22; John 1:32.) The remaining form symbolized that every aspect of Jesus' ministry was by the Holy Spirit. In other words, like us, Jesus lived by the power of the Holy Spirit. The gifts of the Spirit operated freely in Him as He walked in the Spirit.

SYMBOLS OF THE HOLY SPIRIT

The Bible uses six physical symbols to show how the Holy Spirit operates in the world.

1. *Dove*—A symbol of innocence and purity, the dove does not have gall. That is, there is no bitterness in the Holy Spirit. Doves also are loyal to their mate. The dove as a symbol of finding rest is introduced when Noah sent doves from the ark to discover if the flood had receded. (Read Genesis 8:8–12.) The Song of Solomon mentions the "voice of the turtledove," a voice Jewish interpreters understood as a symbol of the Holy Spirit and redemption (2:12).

   The dove is used to symbolize the presence of the Holy Spirit descending from heaven and remaining (with the sense of abiding) upon Jesus. The *remaining, abiding* theme reflects the Holy Spirit's faithfulness to us. It is an important theme to Jesus as He commands us to "abide" in Him (John 15:4–7, 9–10).

2. *Wind, Breath*—We have already seen that the Hebrew and Greek words for *spirit (ruach, pneuma)* mean "wind" or "breath." Jesus used this same metaphor to illustrate the freedom of the Holy Spirit. (Read John 3:8.) The sound of the wind was evident when the disciples received the baptism of the Holy Spirit at Pentecost. (Read Acts 2:2.) The Holy Spirit as breath is found in the creation of man, the restoration of Israel symbolized in the vision of the dry bones and when the risen Jesus breathed on the disciples. (Read Genesis 2:7; Ezekiel 37; John 20:22.) The primary meaning of this metaphor is life and freedom.

3. *Fire*—John the Baptist knew that Jesus was going to baptize people with the Holy Spirit and fire to consume evil. (Read Matthew 3:11–12; Luke 3:16–17.) This symbol was introduced in the Old Testament where the "spirit of burning" consumes evil and results in the illumination of fire (Isa. 4:4–5). When the Holy Spirit came at Pentecost, He came upon each disciple as "divided tongues" of fire (Acts 2:3). The primary meanings of this metaphor are purification, illumination and empowerment.

4. *Water*—The prophet Isaiah prophesied that the Lord God "will pour water on him who is thirsty; I will pour My Spirit on your descendents" (Isa. 44:2–3). The theme of running (or living) water is used by Jesus to illustrate the refreshing and life-giving quality of the Holy Spirit. (Read John 4:10; 7:37–39.) The Bible refers to the river of life that symbolizes the flow of the Holy Spirit. (Read Ezekiel 47:1–9; Zechariah 14:8; Revelation 22:1–2.)

5. *Seal*—The Holy Spirit is called a "seal" in Ephesians 1:13 and 4:30. This seal reflects an official impression or stamp that authenticated the legitimacy of an action by someone in authority. The seal is the Holy Spirit, and the sealer is Jesus

Christ. Thus the presence of the Holy Spirit in our lives marks us as belonging to Christ. This means we are under Christ's ownership and protection.

Additionally, a seal functioned as a guarantee (Greek, *arrabon*) of something that is to be completed. (Read Ephesians 1:14; 2 Corinthians 1:22.) The presence of the Holy Spirit means that God's destiny for us in this life, in heaven and in the resurrection will be accomplished.

6. *Oil*—A symbol for anointing, oil describes the covering of the Holy Spirit. When the prophet Samuel anointed David with oil the Holy Spirit came upon the young leader. (Read 1 Samuel 16:12–13.) Jesus was anointed with the Holy Spirit to fulfill prophecy. (Read Isaiah 61:1–2; Luke 4:18.)

And John bore witness, saying, "I saw the Spirit descending from heaven like a dove, and He remained upon Him . . . And I have seen and testified that this is the Son of God."
—John 1:32, 34

The fact that the Holy Spirit remained upon Jesus marked Him as the Son of God (John 1:32, 34). While Jesus is the unique, beloved, only begotten of the Father, we share as God's children as the Spirit lives in us. (Read Matthew 3:17; John 3:16.) The apostle Paul understood this truth and proclaimed, "As many as are led by the Spirit of God, these are sons of God," and "The Spirit Himself bears witness with our spirit that we are children of God" (Rom. 8:14, 16).

The Holy Spirit became visibly present in the life of Jesus at His baptism. At that point, the power of the Holy Spirit was released in a different measure in Jesus' life. Jesus left the Jordan River "full of the Holy Spirit," and the Spirit led Him into the wilderness to be tempted by the devil. (Read Luke 4:1–13.) Mark 1:12 vividly describes the activity of the Spirit in this episode as driving Jesus into the place of temptation. This does not mean that God tempts us to sin (James 1:13). However, Jesus had to face genuine temptation and genuinely overcome it. (Read Hebrews 2:14–18.) This was necessary because as the second Adam (the second man on earth ever directly created by God), Jesus had to face Adam's temptation and prevail in order to establish righteousness. (Read Romans 5:12–21.)

Immediately the Spirit drove Him into the wilderness.
—Mark 1:12

Let no one say when he is tempted, "I am tempted by God"; for God cannot be tempted by evil, nor does He Himself tempt anyone.
—James 1:13

While the Holy Spirit will never tempt us to sin, the Holy Spirit may drive us to the place where we learn to be totally dependent upon Him. We have places of pride, insecurity and lust that can only be recognized and removed in the wilderness places of life. So the struggles you are facing may not be from the devil at all. If you're a Christian, it is very likely that the Holy Spirit is behind some of the problems you have. His purpose is to get your attention so that God's purposes in your life can be accomplished.

What happens when you come out of this wilderness season of life? You have greater power in the Holy Spirit! That's what happened with Jesus: "Then Jesus returned in the power of the Spirit" (Luke 4:14). Getting plugged in to God's power probably means you're going to face some tough times. Don't fight it, but accept that God is at work in your life so you can plug in to His power. This is pretty serious stuff for learning about the Holy Spirit. It means that once the Spirit comes to live in your life, He desires to remain and is there even in difficult times. He's even there when you don't feel Him. If you're walking through a dark night of the soul, don't give up. You're going to come out on the other side stronger in the Lord.

Getting plugged in to God's power probably means you're going to face some tough times.

Question: Stop reading for a few minutes, and take time to write about any wilderness in your life. What do you think the Holy Spirit is up to in this?

____

____

▲▲▲▲▲▲▲

THE HOLY SPIRIT AND THE KINGDOM OF GOD

An example of how Jesus ministered in the power of the Holy Spirit and established the kingdom of God is in Luke 11:20. We know that Jesus touched people as part of His way of establishing divine-human contact. In the Luke passage, Jesus cast out demons and announced that His power over demons was due to "the finger of God." This expression is from two passages in Exodus. The first describes Egyptian magicians who recognized that God's power is superior and qualitatively different from their power. (Read Exodus 8:19.) The second is when God gave Moses the Ten Commandments "written with the finger of God" (Exod. 31:18). This is a vivid picture of the Holy Spirit being the divine instrument that the Father uses to connect with the physical world.

But if I cast out demons with the finger of God, surely the kingdom of God has come upon you.
—Luke 11:20

Both Exodus references to the "finger of God" are significant in comprehending Luke 11:20. Jesus was accused of being an instrument of demonic powers. (Read Luke 11:14–19.) But His power is qualitatively different from that of the realm of darkness. Jesus' power is also the power of divine righteousness in that God acts in accordance to what He has revealed to humanity. The acts of the Holy Spirit mean that God can be trusted.

This manifestation of the Holy Spirit in the ministry of Jesus shows that the kingdom of God is a present reality. The kingdom of God refers to the sphere of God's rule. The Holy Spirit is the divine instrument for extending that sphere from the spiritual to the physical realm. God is conquering the earth through the redeeming blood of Jesus and the power of the Holy Spirit.

This is what makes John 3:3–8 so important. (Read John 3.) It's more than an evangelistic "you must be born again." It is the reality of entering the sphere of God's dominion over every part of your life by being born "from above" (the literal meaning of the phrase "born again" in John 3:3). We are born from the flesh. But because of sin's devastating effects upon fleshly existence, our destiny is death. When we are born of the Holy Spirit by faith in Jesus Christ, we enter into a new destiny, a destiny of the eternal and righteous rule of God. When the "finger of God" transforms our lives, we receive a qualitatively different power from the power of sin. This power is the power of righteousness through Christ Jesus.

When we are born of the Holy Spirit by faith in Jesus Christ, we enter into a new destiny, a destiny of the eternal and righteous rule of God.

The conclusion of John 3:27–36 is a speech by John the Baptist concerning his ministry and the ministry of Jesus. John's baptism was one of repentance from sin with a focus on turning from evil and doing good deeds. (Read Luke 3:7–14.) It was a baptism of water that had an effect but still did not touch the deepest place of the human heart. Jesus' baptism was of water *and* the Holy Spirit and fire, which brought spiritual transformation in the deepest places of our lives. John knew that "He [Jesus] must increase" as John decreased (John 3:30).

The reason was because the words of Jesus, as the eternal Son of God, were "grace and truth" (John 1:14). Jesus' words are the "words of God" (John 3:34). Jesus spoke the word of God because Jesus lived in the fullness of the Holy Spirit. Jesus was given the Spirit without any limitations, "for God does not give the Spirit by measure" (John 3:34). Jesus' triumph in the wilderness over sinful temptation meant He lived in constant communion with His Father through the Holy Spirit. That is why Jesus spoke what He heard the Father speak and did what He saw the Father do. (Read John 5:19; 8:28.) Jesus' words are the words of the Spirit, and because of that "they are life" (John 6:63). No other religious figure, no other person, no other idea or philosophy has that capacity. Only Jesus speaks life-giving Spirit to lost and fragmented humanity. Talk about power!

When Jesus was born in Bethlehem to the virgin Mary, He gave up His privileged status in heaven. (Read 2 Corinthians 8:9; Philippians 2:5–8.) The dimension of the fullness of the Spirit that Jesus had shared through eternity was set aside so that Jesus and the Spirit could work together to accomplish salvation and prepare us to receive the power of the Holy Spirit.

LET THE RIVER FLOW

Our scenic tour through the Gospel of John moves to an out-of-the-way well in Samaria and then to a huge fall festival in Jerusalem. (Read John 4 and 7.) What connects both sites is the common theme of living water and the Holy Spirit. "Symbols of the Holy Spirit" on page 21 gives an Old Testament background to this theme.

The encounter in Samaria has an additional Old Testament and water connection (John 4). This connection is with "Jacob's well" that was at the Samaritan village of Sychar (John 4:5–6). Jacob, one of Israel's founding fathers, was a man blessed by God but also a man who wrestled with God. (Read Genesis 25–35.) There were times he lived isolated from his kinfolk. This is not unlike the woman Jesus met at Jacob's well. She lived isolated from the community. Her past and present were marred by broken marital relationships. Her isolation and embarrassment were so strong that she had to go to the well for water in the heat of the day alone so as to avoid the caustic remarks of other women. But more than that, she was a Samaritan and was considered a "half-breed" by Jews. She was a social, religious and personal outcast.

But one day the river started flowing right beside her. In an episode filled with insight on how Christians can sensitively meet people, Jesus did not condemn her but offered living water. He spoke of the Holy Spirit (and perhaps Himself) as "the gift of God" and pointed her to Himself as the One who could provide that gift (John 4:10). She wanted to know if Jesus was greater than Jacob. Jesus did not get into a debate with her but simply said, "Whoever drinks of this water [at Jacob's well] will thirst again, but whoever drinks of the water that I shall give him will never thirst. But the water that I shall give him will become in him a fountain of water springing up into everlasting life" (John 4:13–14).

How many of us have drunk from the wells of religion, social prestige, drugs, sex, money and worldly power, only to discover we were satisfied for just a brief time? Jesus describes the Holy Spirit in terms that promise and deliver time after time.

Question: In John 4:14, Jesus said four things that you need to consider:

- *When you drink from the Holy Spirit you will never thirst again.* That's a pretty strong statement. Do you agree with it? What kind of quenching of thirst does the Holy Spirit give so that you're not thirsty again?

  ____

  ____

▲▲▲▲▲▲▲

- *The Holy Spirit is a gift that Jesus gives.* At the beginning of this chapter I mentioned that you couldn't know the Holy Spirit unless you know Jesus. Do you agree with that statement? Is there a Holy Spirit that does not come from Jesus?

  ____

  ____

▲▲▲▲▲▲▲

- *Jesus said that the Holy Spirit is in you a "fountain of water springing up."* A fountain denotes a source that flows from sight unseen. It implies an unlimited flow of water. More than that, it is not a small trickle, but a stream of water that springs into the air. It means the Holy Spirit is visible and alive. The Holy Spirit in your life is not a passive experience. The Spirit's presence is the life of God active, dynamic, creative and real in your mind, emotions, will, body and spirit. Describe how you have experienced the Holy Spirit "springing up" or "flowing" in your life.

  ____

  ____

▲▲▲▲▲▲▲

- *The presence of the Holy Spirit will spring up in your life into everlasting life.* This certainly refers to the Spirit's work in salvation in our lives. But it also means that the power of everlasting life, the power to make an eternal impact on someone's life, is real today. In your view, what does "everlasting life" mean on a day-to-day basis?

  ____

  ____

▲▲▲▲▲▲▲

The river of the Spirit flowed everywhere with Jesus. To paraphrase Sting, "Every breath you take, every move you

make, every step you take, I'll be flowing with you." The river of the Spirit that bubbled forth for an outcast woman made its way to the temple precincts of Jerusalem. Sometime near the end of September and the beginning of October, Jesus made His way to the Feast of Tabernacles. (Read John 7:2; Leviticus 23:33–36, 39–43.) Also called the Feast of Booths, this seven-day celebration commemorated Israel's deliverance from Egypt and their time of provision while wandering in the wilderness.

The theme of flowing water dominated this festival. Because it was celebrated in the autumn harvest, rain was prayed for and seen as a blessing for the crops to come the following year. Even today modern Jordanian Arabs watch carefully to see if it rains during Tabernacles as a sign of weather patterns for the coming year.[1] Each day of the feast, priests went to the fountain of Gihon near the temple and in a worshipful procession brought back a golden pitcher with water that was poured out at the altar. On the seventh day the priest walked around the altar seven times and as the climax of the feast poured the water upon the altar.

On the last day, that great day of the feast, Jesus stood and cried out, saying, "If anyone thirsts, let him come to Me and drink. He who believes in Me, as the Scripture has said, out of his heart will flow rivers of living water."

—John 7:37–38

Those who believe in Jesus as the Messiah and Son of God will have the Holy Spirit flowing out of their heart as living water.

It was at this moment that Jesus stood in the temple court and proclaimed that He was the source of this living water. Jesus announced that the spiritually thirsty can come to Him and drink (John 7:37). Those who believe in Jesus as the Messiah and Son of God will have the Holy Spirit flowing out of their heart as living water (v. 38). John 7:39 further clarified these words of Jesus: "But this He spoke concerning the Spirit, whom those believing in Him would receive; for the Holy Spirit was not yet given, because Jesus was not yet glorified." The reference to the Holy Spirit "not yet given" is a reference to Pentecost in Acts 2. Jesus had to pay the price of atonement on the cross, rise from the dead and ascend to heaven before the Holy Spirit could come in personal power upon the disciples.

The idea of drinking from the Holy Spirit so that He

continually flows through us as rivers of living water is provocative. Jesus used the plural, *rivers* of living water. This means that the Holy Spirit is multifaceted in His operations. From 1 Corinthians 12:4 we know there are "diversities of gifts," but each comes from the same Holy Spirit. The Book of Revelation mentions the "seven Spirits of God," denoting a sevenfold way that the Holy Spirit manifests Himself. (Read Revelation 1:4; 3:1; 4:5; 5:6.) The Holy Spirit flows as rivers of living water touching every aspect of our lives and God's destiny for us. In other words, we are made complete as the Holy Spirit flows through us.

In later chapters we'll explore more of the "streams of the Spirit" that make up this powerful supernatural life of God that lives in us.

WHAT DID JESUS LEAVE BEHIND?

The stories of the men and women on United and American Airlines flights on September 11, 2001 are compelling. Those people knew they had but minutes to live. In their final minutes they called their families with messages of love and faith. What would you do if you knew you had just minutes or hours to live? We cannot understand Jesus' teachings about the Holy Spirit in John 14–16 unless we remember that everything He said and did was in the span of a few brief hours on the Thursday night that He was betrayed. This is Jesus' most extensive teaching about the Holy Spirit. Jesus first left the teaching, and then He sent the Holy Spirit on Pentecost to His disciples. He had promised them, "I will never leave you nor forsake you" (Heb. 13:5). Jesus kept His word.

The final night began in the upper room, possibly the same room where the Holy Spirit fell fifty days later. Jesus first washed the disciples' feet, and then they partook of the Last Supper. (Read John 13:1–27.) At the close of the supper Jesus dismissed Judas to prepare the ultimate betrayal.

In this setting in the upper room, around a Passover table with eleven disciples present, Jesus talked about the Holy Spirit. The impact of each reference is magnified by the situation. We are going to take a closer look at each of Jesus' references.

1. John 14:12

Most assuredly, I say to you, he who believes in Me, the works that I do he will do also; and greater works than these he will do, because I go to My Father.

It's almost scandalous, but we'll do greater works than Jesus because His going to the Father meant the Holy Spirit coming into us. What does "greater" mean here? The quality of the works can never exceed what Jesus did in His ministry and on the cross for all humanity. It refers to the quantitative dimension of Christ's works through us. The kingdom of God expands in greater spheres of impact as Spirit-filled disciples obey the Lord.

The kingdom of God expands in greater spheres of impact as Spirit-filled disciples obey the Lord.

Question: How has the kingdom of God expanded in the spheres of influence of your life?

▲▲▲▲▲▲▲

2. John 14:16

And I will pray the Father, and He will give you another Helper, that He may abide with you forever.

The Greek word for *prayer* in this passage is used when the petitioner is on equal footing with the person to whom the request is made. Jesus was aware of His eternal relationship with the Father and knew that this request was in God's heart from eternity.

This "other Helper," the Holy Spirit in personal power, was present at the throne of the Father awaiting this moment. Jesus spoke of the Holy Spirit as "another." Jesus meant that the Holy Spirit was different from the Father and Son but was the same (another reference to the historic Christian understanding of the Trinity). The word *Helper* is the Greek *parakletos*. Often referred to as the *Paraclete*, this term for the Holy Spirit was used by Jesus four times on this final night. It literally refers to someone who is called to one's side and denotes the availability and capability to give assistance. The term was a legal term describing a lawyer.

(Read 1 John 2:1, where it is translated as *Advocate.*)

Jesus promised that the Holy Spirit would be manifest to us as a divine comforter, just as Jesus had brought comfort to hurting people in His ministry. The Holy Spirit is with us "forever," an expression focusing on the unlimitedness of His presence with us.

Question: How has the Holy Spirit been a Comforter, a Helper, to you? As you write of an experience, give thanks to Him.

___

___

▲▲▲▲▲▲▲

3. John 14:17

> *The Spirit of truth, whom the world cannot receive, because it neither sees Him nor knows Him; but you know Him, for He dwells with you and will be in you.*

Jesus called the Holy Spirit the "Spirit of truth." The Holy Spirit bears witness to Jesus, who is "the way, the truth, and the life" (John 14:6). Everything the Spirit testifies about Jesus is true. An evidence of the Holy Spirit in a situation is the presence of truth. Where there are deceptions, half-truths, cover-ups and lies, the Holy Spirit is not present except to expose and bring truth to light.

Genuine worship of the living God occurs "in spirit and truth" (John 4:23–24). The Holy Spirit is a true witness of who Jesus is (John 5:32). In contrast to Jesus, Satan "is a liar and the father of it" (John 8:44). In the church, the Holy Spirit expects believers to tell the truth. (Read Acts 5:3–11.) We purify our "souls in obeying the truth through the Spirit" (1 Pet. 1:22). By hearing the Word of God we can know the spirit of truth and the spirit of error (1 John 4:6).

The world cannot receive the Spirit of truth because the world cannot see Him or know Him. The world lives by the father of lies because it wants to do the desires of Satan. The world lives by the spirit of murder and self-will. (Read John 8:44.)

But those who have been born again by the Holy Spirit

There is another who bears witness of Me, and I know that the witness which He witnesses of Me is true.

—John 5:32

We are of God. He who knows God hears us; he who is not of God does not hear us. By this we know the spirit of truth and the spirit of error.

—1 John 4:6

know Him because "He dwells with you and will be in you" (John 14:17). Because He dwells in us we are able to discern truth from error as He leads us into the Word of God.

Question: As you reflect on this issue of the Holy Spirit and truth, can you identify ways that you have allowed Satan to deceive you?

---

4. John 14:18

I will not leave you orphans; I will come to you.

The issue of being left orphans, that is, alone without our heavenly Father, is addressed in the context of the Holy Spirit. This truth is picked up by the apostle Paul in Romans 8:14–17:

As the one who stands with us, the Holy Spirit teaches us all things pertaining to godliness.

For as many as are led by the Spirit of God, these are sons of God. For you did not receive the spirit of bondage again to fear, but you received the Spirit of adoption by whom we cry out, "Abba, Father." The Spirit Himself bears witness with our spirit that we are children of God, and if children, then heirs—heirs of God and joint heirs with Christ, if indeed we suffer with Him, that we may also be glorified together.

Without Christ, the father of lies has us bound in deception. But in Christ we discover our true Father and His loving intentions for us.

5. John 14:26

But the Helper, the Holy Spirit, whom the Father will send in My name, He will teach you all things, and bring to your remembrance all things that I said to you.

We are not orphans because the Holy Spirit lives in us and establishes the reality of our sonship with the Father. As the one who stands with us, the Holy Spirit teaches us all things pertaining to godliness. This is made clear by the apostle Peter when he writes that "divine power [the Holy Spirit] has given to us all things that pertain to life and godliness, through the knowledge of Him who called us by glory and virtue" (2 Pet. 1:3; cf. verses 4–11).

The Holy Spirit not only teaches us all things pertaining to godliness, but He also brings to our remembrance what the Lord Jesus has said. Originally this was meant for the apostles who proclaimed and wrote the Gospel records. The Holy Spirit brought to their remembrance the specific things and ways they recorded the deeds and sayings of Jesus. For us today, the Holy Spirit takes the portions of the Bible that we have studied and memorized and brings them to our remembrance when they are most needed. The importance of memorizing the Word is emphasized in Psalm 119:11: "Thy word have I hid in my heart, that I might not sin against thee" (KJV). The word *hid* actually means to treasure something. The psalmist understood that as he treasured the Word of God in his heart, he gave the Holy Spirit an instrument by which his life could be guarded from sin.

Question: How do you "treasure" the Bible in your heart? Do you give the Holy Spirit something to work with in bringing God's Word to your memory? Can you describe an episode where the Holy Spirit brought a passage of Scripture to you in a difficult time?

▲▲▲▲▲▲▲

6. John 15:26

But when the Helper comes, whom I shall send to you from the Father, the Spirit of truth who proceeds from the Father, He will testify of Me.

The Holy Spirit testifies two absolutely essential things concerning Jesus Christ:

- ▲ Jesus is Lord (1 Cor. 12:3)

**No one can say that Jesus is Lord except by the Holy Spirit.
—1 Corinthians 12:3**

Every spirit that confesses that Jesus Christ has come in the flesh is of God, and every spirit that does not confess that Jesus Christ has come in the flesh is not of God.

—1 John 4:2–3

▲ Jesus is the Son of God (1 John 4:2–3)

There is no room here for religious syncretism or compromise. The Holy Spirit will not proclaim another god, ideology or viewpoint. The Holy Spirit is politically correct only in terms of the truth of the kingdom of God.

7. John 16:7–11

Nevertheless I tell you the truth. It is to your advantage that I go away; for if I do not go away, the Helper will not come to you; but if I depart, I will send Him to you. And when He has come, He will convict the world of sin, and of righteousness, and of judgment: of sin, because they do not believe in Me; of righteousness, because I go to My Father and you see Me no more; of judgment, because the ruler of this world is judged.

In the final hours of His earthly ministry, Jesus lovingly and carefully told the disciples that He must go away so that the Holy Spirit could come. When the Holy Spirit came, He not only testified of Jesus, but He also performed, and continues to perform, three specific acts. Each of these actions is best seen in light of the trial that Jesus will face in the following hours, which will be anything but righteousness and true judgment. Instead, the Holy Spirit will initiate a true judgment and justice in the world.

The Holy Spirit convicts of sin. To convict someone is to find them guilty of a charge against them—in other words, to prove a case. It can mean that light is brought to bear so that something is exposed. In this sense it is part of the truthful dimension of the Holy Spirit in our lives. The Spirit "refutes" the deceptions by which we so easily live. The Spirit does not condemn us, but He draws our attention to the reality of our need so we can experience the reality of Christ's provision. The primary sin the world commits is its failure to believe in Jesus as the Messiah and Son of God. All other sins occur as a result of this failure to recognize the presence of the Son of God.

The Holy Spirit convicts of righteousness. Righteousness is a characteristic of God. God is righteous because He acts in accordance with His revealed Word. While there are dimensions of God's nature and His acts that we cannot fathom, those dimensions are not out of harmony with what God has revealed regarding Himself. That is why we are confident of God's promises. Jesus gave an interesting reason why the Holy Spirit convicts the world of righteousness: "Because I go to My Father and you see Me no more." The fact that Jesus arose from the dead and returned to His Father vindicated His mission on earth. As the sinless Son of God, Jesus was faithful to His redemptive mission. This faithfulness proved the righteousness of God.

The Holy Spirit convicts the world of judgment. The Holy Spirit convicts the world of judgment, "because the ruler of this world is judged." Earlier Jesus said, "The ruler of this world will be cast out" (John 12:31). The ruler of this world is Satan, and his time of judgment has come in the death of Jesus. This judgment upon Satan is actually Satan's condemnation. Satan's dominion over the believer is broken.

As we follow the witness of the Holy Spirit in Scripture, we will be led into truth.

8. John 16:13–15

However, when He, the Spirit of truth, has come, He will guide you into all truth; for He will not speak on His own authority, but whatever He hears He will speak; and He will tell you things to come. He will glorify Me, for He will take of what is Mine and declare it to you. All things that the Father has are Mine. Therefore I said that He will take of Mine and declare it to you.

Jesus' final words about the Holy Spirit on this final night give further insight into the ministry of the Holy Spirit. The Spirit of truth will guide us into all truth. The word *guide* means someone who leads the way. As we follow the witness of the Holy Spirit in Scripture, we will be led into truth.

The Holy Spirit does not act independently of the divine will established in eternity. No one can claim inspiration of the Holy Spirit for actions, words or attitudes that are contrary to Scripture. The Holy Spirit will not point to another Christ or to another testament of Jesus Christ. When the Holy Spirit speaks to us, He speaks what He has heard in the presence of the Father and Son. The Holy Spirit informs us of what is to come through the gifts of prophecy, discernment and knowledge. The Holy Spirit always glorifies Jesus Christ. The Spirit as God is worthy of our worship. But our worship

through the Holy Spirit always leads us to Jesus Christ as revealed in the Bible.

LET'S TALK ABOUT IT

▲ This chapter began by discussing that we cannot know the Holy Spirit without knowing Jesus. After reading this chapter and studying the Gospel of John, what insights have you learned about Jesus? About the Holy Spirit?

____

____

____

▲▲▲▲▲▲▲

▲ Which of the symbols of the Holy Spirit mean the most to you?

____

____

____

▲▲▲▲▲▲▲

▲ Has the Holy Spirit ever led you into a wilderness situation? Describe how you became stronger as you came through it.

____

____

____

▲▲▲▲▲▲▲

▲ In this chapter we learned that when the "finger of God" transforms our lives, we receive a qualitatively different power from the power of sin. This power is the power of righteousness through Christ Jesus. Describe how the "finger of God" has transformed your life.

____

____

____

▲▲▲▲▲▲▲

▲ Jesus said that the Holy Spirit would flow through us like "rivers" of living water. Can you identify different ways that the Holy Spirit "flows" in your life?

____

____

____

▲▲▲▲▲▲▲

TIME TO PLUG IN TO THE HOLY SPIRIT

This has been quite a journey through the Gospel of John. Four major themes emerged:

- ▲ The Holy Spirit reveals the Son of God
- ▲ The Holy Spirit and the kingdom of God
- ▲ Let the river flow
- ▲ What Jesus left behind

These are very important themes. Probably one or more of these themes really spoke to your life.

It's hard to pick one over the others since they tend to run together. However, what really impresses me is the fact that on His last night Jesus neither panicked nor was confused, but He was crystal clear about the Holy Spirit. Jesus knew that the disciples were going to have some hard days when He died. But Jesus also knew that the disciples were going to experience the greatest joy of their lives when the Holy Spirit came in power.

Whatever you're going through, don't give up. Even if it's the valley of the shadow of death, don't give up on what God's ultimate purposes are in your life. Pray these words:

Holy Spirit, show me the love of Jesus. Touch my life with His grace, peace, mercy and hope. Search my heart for hidden places of sin, and establish Your Word as life for me. Come, Holy Spirit; show me the love of Jesus. Amen.

CHAPTER THREE

How the Holy Spirit Makes New Creatures

IN THIS CHAPTER YOU WILL DISCOVER THAT . . .

- ▲ The Holy Spirit is busy as God's evangelist in the world.
- ▲ When you confess that Jesus Christ is Lord and ask forgiveness of your sins, the Holy Spirit comes to live in your spirit.
- ▲ The Spirit is building a community of people from every nation and generation as a showcase for the glory of God.

SEVERAL YEARS AGO I WAS A PASTORAL CANDIDATE AT A PENTECOSTAL CHURCH. At that time my five-year-old son had a slight speech impediment, which was corrected by therapy. On the night of the church's decision and call, several people came by the house with excited congratulations. My son had already gone to bed, and after some of the visitors had left I went to kiss him goodnight. He had heard the noise and looked at me. Trying to say "preacher," he said, "Daddy, are you the new creature?"

I smiled and replied, "Yes, I'm the new preacher, and I really need to be the new creature, too."

Besides remembering that incident for the humor, I've remembered it because it reminds me of our constant need for the Holy Spirit to complete that good work that has started in our life. (Read Philippians 1:6.) In fact, the apostle Paul's observation in Philippians 1:6 is a good starting point as we reflect on the work of the Holy Spirit in our personal redemption.

WHAT IT MEANS TO BE SAVED

The biblical understanding of salvation is more comprehensive than what is often implied in contemporary evangelism. Salvation is more than our response to an altar call by coming forward, confessing Christ, signing a commitment card for follow-up and leaving the service feeling a little less guilty about life. *Salvation* describes everything that God does in our lives through the Holy Spirit. This begins with the Holy Spirit's seeking us prior to our conversion, through the reality of our being born again, through the joys and struggles of growing in God's grace, even through the reality of death to the day of resurrection.

The basic idea of the Hebrew word for salvation is "spaciousness, room." This runs counter to the idea that to follow Christ we have to give up really living. Entering the kingdom of God is like coming upon what looks like a small place with a little door but discovering the inside is huge. In his series *The Chronicles of Narnia*, C. S.

Lewis described entering into heaven like this: "The further up and the further in you go, the bigger everything gets. The inside is larger than the outside."[1] That's also a good way to think of the new life we have in Christ.

Many Christians struggle after their initial conversion because they think all their problems are solved, or they think they have to work harder to get to heaven. Actually, neither is the case. As to your problems, the Holy Spirit will probably bring many of them to greater intensity so they can be recognized properly and redeemed or removed. As to working harder, you didn't work to be born again; that came by the grace of God as you believed in Jesus as your Savior. Now the Holy Spirit is at work in you, re-creating and reshaping your life to conform to your destiny. The Holy Spirit asks you to cooperate with Him. In that way, you "work out your own salvation" with a holy awe and regard for the grace of God (Phil. 2:12).

The apostle Paul called the comprehensive work of salvation a "good" work. We use the word *good* loosely: "You look good today." "That was a good play." "Have a good day." Many children recite at meals, "God is great; God is good. Let us thank Him for our food. Amen."

That simple prayer is profound because the Bible presents "goodness" as an attribute of God (Ps. 25:7–8; 31:19). The Holy Spirit is called "good" (Neh. 9:20; Ps. 143:10). God called the created earth "good" (Gen. 1:18, 21, 31). So ingrained was this understanding of "good" in Jewish thought that when Jesus was called "Good Teacher" by a young lawyer, Jesus replied, "Why do you call Me good? No one is good but One, that is, God" (Mark 10:17–18). The young man wanted to know how to inherit eternal life. Jesus' reply showed that if the young lawyer really meant that Jesus was "good," then Jesus' answer was really God's answer and not simply another rabbinic opinion on the smorgasbord of choices.

And we know that all things work together for good to those who love God, to those who are the called according to His purpose.
—Romans 8:28

Salvation in your life is a good work that God has started and has promised to complete at the revelation of Jesus Christ. That is why Romans 8:28 makes sense in the life of a Christian. The "good" that all things are working together for is the ultimate good purposes of God. Those who "love God," "who are called according to His purpose," can face any circumstance of life with the knowledge that God's good purposes are woven into the trials, pains and joys of life.

It's really important to grasp this truth of the good work of salvation in our lives. Every Christian faces crises in life, often very serious and painful crises. Christians encounter what many people call "tragic circumstances," but we do not experience tragedy. A tragedy has no hope, no ultimate redeeming purpose. A tragedy is filled with despair and darkness. But that is not the case for a Christian. While we may not see or understand it, God's goodness is being worked through the circumstances of our lives for His ultimate will and our ultimate good. As the divine teacher, the Holy Spirit gives us grace to walk by faith regardless of life's circumstances.

THE HOLY SPIRIT GIVES A WAKE-UP CALL TO SINNERS

> God's goodness is being worked through the circumstances of our lives for His ultimate will and our ultimate good.

The Holy Spirit is busy as God's evangelist in the world. The Spirit seeks to convict sinners of sin and bring them to repentance by faith in Christ. This dimension of the Spirit's work is called *prevenient grace*. This fancy theological term refers to the grace of God that is at work in our lives prior to conversion. It is that dimension of God's grace through the Spirit whereby a sinner is brought face to face with divine truth. There are two facets of this truth we must not forget.

1. The fact that the Holy Spirit seeks sinners means that God's love is greater than His judgment.

God does not desire any to be lost. (Read Ezekiel 18:32; 33:11.) God is not sitting on a throne waiting for you to make a mistake so He can zing you with lightning bolts. The Bible informs us that God is love and desires all to be saved. A corollary to this truth is the biblical affirmation that "whoever calls on the name of the LORD shall be saved" (Acts 2:21). The Bible teaches predestination. (Read Romans 8:29–30; Ephesians 1:5, 11.) However, predestination is not presented in the Bible as God's arbitrary decision regarding human destiny in heaven or hell. Rather, predestination is the church's pastoral doctrine whereby a Christian reflects over life and recognizes the grace of God. Such reflection gives confidence for the future. One thing we must remember, the Holy Spirit seeks each lost person through the gospel.

2. It is imperative that we respond to the prompting of the Holy Spirit when He is wooing us.

In this sense, we cannot decide when we will be saved. Many people have squandered years by resisting the Holy Spirit's convicting urges. The Holy Spirit does not always strive with us, and we must respond when He does. (Read Genesis 6:3; Hebrews 3:7–13.)

CONVICTION AND CONDEMNATION

What's the difference between Holy Spirit *conviction* and *condemnation*? Does the Holy Spirit condemn us? No. The Holy Spirit convicts us of our sins. *Conviction* means that true revelation is made regarding our sin, but also true revelation is made regarding God's remedy in Jesus Christ. Conviction always leads to hope in the gospel. The Holy Spirit is not interested in making us feel bad. He is interested in leading us to Christ.

On the other hand, *condemnation* is actually a sentence of death. Outside the gospel we are condemned to eternal separation from God. Condemnation has no hope and is filled with despair. Only in Christ are we free from condemnation, as Romans 8:1 says: "There is therefore now no condemnation to those who are in Christ Jesus, who do not walk according to the flesh, but according to the Spirit."

That's why it's important how Christians relate to other people. The Holy Spirit will often use our lives as His instruments in touching a sinner's heart. It's not our place to condemn someone because of his or her attitudes or actions. We don't have to agree with the attitudes or actions of someone else, and we should speak with wise and loving boldness concerning that. However, our words should be filled with love so the person recognizes grace and not condemnation.

Phrases like "Go to hell" and "Damn you" are more than expressions of frustration or anger. They are condemning words. They do more than break the fabric of relationships—they release the spirit of condemnation.

A classic illustration is seen in the Holy Spirit's work in the life of Saul of Tarsus (the apostle Paul). Saul was present at the death of Stephen, the first Christian martyr. (Read Acts 7:58.) Saul heard the godly deacon/evangelist cry out, "Lord Jesus, receive my spirit . . . Lord, do not charge them with this sin" (Acts 7:59–60). Although Saul continued to persecute other Christians, his life was on a Holy Spirit-led journey to meet the risen Jesus. (Read Acts 9:1–9.) The Holy Spirit had already prepared Ananias, a disciple in Damascus, to meet Saul and give him a direct word of the Lord. (Read Acts 9:10–19, especially verses 15–16.)

Question: If you are a Christian, can you identify a specific instance of prevenient grace that led you to Christ?

___

___

▲▲▲▲▲▲▲

If you are not a Christian and are reading this book to learn more about the Holy Spirit, do you realize that He is trying to get your attention? Can you identify a situation, maybe to you a "coincidence," where your thoughts were turned to God?

___

___

▲▲▲▲▲▲▲

HOW THE HOLY SPIRIT COMES TO LIVE IN YOUR LIFE

A young Christian said to me, "I don't believe that James really became a Christian. He just didn't show enough remorse and cry enough over his sins." It's tempting for us to judge the spiritual experience of another by our own experience. Those converted in the emotionally driven settings of an altar call and the moving melody of "Just As I Am" struggle to understand a formal liturgy and the conversion at confirmation of an Episcopalian. The Episcopalian sometimes struggles to understand what appears to be mindless and manipulative emotionalism of many popular evangelical and Pentecostal services that seem to place the brain in neutral. The Bible does not describe one common personal experience. That's because Christian conversion is very personal and unique. The Holy Spirit knows exactly how to approach each of us to bring us to Christ.

On the other hand, the Bible does convey common truths relating to conversion that we must acknowledge and experience. The Holy Spirit takes those truths and reveals them personally to each of us so that we can grow in that grace. Let's look at some of those common truths related to how the Holy Spirit comes to live in your life.

If you confess with your mouth the Lord Jesus and believe in your heart that God has raised Him from the dead, you will be saved.

—Romans 10:9

Confession

In the Bible, to *confess* something means that you agree with a revealed truth. In other words, confession begins with hearing something that the Holy Spirit revealed to your heart as true. What you heard was you are a sinner and need forgiveness (and in your heart you knew how really true that is). Or perhaps you heard that God really loves you and that Jesus Christ rose from the grave (Rom. 10:9). For many people it was both. Through a sermon, a book, the Bible or the testimony of a friend, the Holy Spirit informed you that you are really a sinner doomed for hell, but God really loves you and has provided everlasting life. Amazingly, you believed it!

The Holy Spirit knows exactly how to approach each of us to bring us to Christ.

Forgiveness of sins

When you confess your sins, the Holy Spirit witnesses in your heart that the Lord Jesus Christ is "faithful and just to forgive" your sins and cleanse you from all unrighteousness (1 John 1:9). The Holy Spirit enables you to "confess with your mouth the Lord Jesus and believe in your heart [based on the truthful testimony of the Word of God] that God has raised Him [Jesus] from the dead" (Rom. 10:9). The reality of divine forgiveness brings forth heart humility, and the experience of the Holy Spirit is poured into your heart. (Read Psalm 51:1–3, 10–12, 17; Romans 5:5.) Divine forgiveness means restoration of fellowship with God and the joy that accompanies that restoration. (Read Luke 15:11–32.)

Repentance

Confession helps you know that you're really guilty of sin before God. This guilt is not psychologically induced but is real guilt because you are a sinner. The good news that you are forgiven leads you to repent, to turn away from the life of sin to which you willingly submitted. Repentance involves a change of your mind, a new way of thinking about God and your life and destiny. You make a conscious decision to turn away from one way of living to another way of living.

When you confess that Jesus Christ is Lord and ask forgiveness of your sins, the Holy Spirit comes to live in your spirit. The Bible sometimes calls this your *heart* or *inner person*. The Holy Spirit enabled you to hear the truth of the Word of God, and faith arose because you heard in your heart the Word (Rom. 10:17).

So then faith comes by hearing, and hearing by the word of God.

—Romans 10:17

Thus faith is not something you have to create. This is very important because faith is not something that has to be worked up psychologically or requires just the right music or other environment. This is what distinguishes faith from wishful thinking and our imagination. Faith comes by hearing the word of God (Rom. 10:17). The Holy Spirit takes the testimony of Scripture and enables you to hear it as spirit and life. (Read John 6:63.) The truth revealed through the Word creates the faith you need for salvation and everything else that God has for your life. That is why the Bible is so important in your life. The Bible is the tool the Holy Spirit uses to create faith and thus bring greater hope, peace and love in your life.

If your faith is based on good speakers, good music, your idea of the perfect church or even on the best contemporary prophets, it will not stand the test. But if your faith arises from the Word of God, you cannot be shaken.

The Bible is the tool the Holy Spirit uses to create faith and thus bring greater hope, peace and love in your life.

When you are born again, the Holy Spirit comes into your spirit and instantly makes you a "new creature in Christ" (2 Cor. 5:17). You are reconciled to God because He has taken the steps to initiate and complete the divine act of "peacemaking" (the meaning of reconciliation). While you may not be aware that you're a new creature, there are certain things you may actually experience and feel when this happens.

First, you may feel a profound sense of a burden of guilt being removed. It may be something like this incident. It was

early August 1990, and the U.S. Army Reserve unit in which I was serving as chaplain was at Fort Bragg, North Carolina, for annual training. Iraq had just invaded Kuwait, and the 82nd Airborne went on full and immediate alert. Our unit was in the field, and the company commander became very ill. He was taken to the hospital during the night and diagnosed with viral meningitis. Thankfully early diagnosis and treatment led to a complete recovery for this young captain.

I visited him a couple of days later. Through the previous months we had developed a good relationship, and I sensed the Holy Spirit was tugging at his heart. I prayed that the Spirit would give me a few minutes of uninterrupted time. In my mind I literally asked the Holy Spirit to keep any family member or medical staff from coming into the room. For a few minutes we talked about the impending war. At the right moment I changed the subject.

"You know you gave all of us and your wife a real scare the other night."

"Yeah, Chaplain, I know it. It was scary to me."

"Captain, I want to ask you a personal and important question. If you had not gotten to the hospital when you did, you probably would have died. If that had happened, do you know for certain where you would be now?"

He paused and looked out the window. Tears filled his eyes. He turned his head back to me and said, "No."

"You don't have to wonder about that any longer. We can take care of that now. I really sense the Lord Jesus is speaking to you in this situation." I shared with him Romans 10:9–10 and 13, and I led him in a sinner's prayer. It was a quiet, reflective few minutes with no interruptions.

He looked up at me, and his countenance had changed. Instead of the anxious tears of a few minutes earlier, he was beaming. He said, "I feel like a giant burden has been lifted from me." And it had. He became a new creature in Christ at that moment, and the Holy Spirit came and made alive his spirit.

This man knew that he was forgiven. He felt genuine forgiveness. However, even if he had not felt it so strongly, the forgiveness of sins was an accomplished fact because of the shed blood of Jesus. (Read Matthew 26:28; Ephesians 1:7; Colossians 1:14.)

This soldier did not comprehend that he had been "justified by faith" (Rom. 5:1). In fact, the same faith that had counted Abraham as righteous was the same kind of faith that justified this soldier. (Read Genesis 15:6; Romans 4:3, 5, 16, 20–25.) In God's sight he was declared "not guilty" because he believed that Jesus had died for his sins. This captain experienced justification as peace in his heart. But the peace was more than what he felt. It was reconciliation between him and God and enabled him to "have access by faith" into the presence of God. (Read Romans 5:2; Hebrews 10:19–23.)

The soldier was adopted as a child of God at the moment he confessed Christ (Rom. 8:15–16). When we are born again the Holy Spirit reveals God to us as our loving Father. That's why Jesus taught us to pray to God with the intimate family name of "Abba," a term of endearment that approximates our contemporary "Daddy."

For you did not receive the spirit of bondage again to fear, but you received the Spirit of adoption by whom we cry out, "Abba, Father." The Spirit Himself bears witness with our spirit that we are children of God.

—Romans 8:15–16

WHERE DOES THE HOLY SPIRIT LIVE IN YOUR LIFE?

The Holy Spirit makes your spirit alive to God and creates a place where God dwells with you on this earth. Prior to conversion, your spirit is dead to God in trespasses and sins. Your spirit is attentive to the spirit of this world and the lusts of the flesh. (Read Ephesians 2:1–3.) But after conversion your spirit is the dwelling place of the Holy Spirit. Some have thought that the Holy Spirit did not come to live in your life until you received the baptism of the Holy Spirit and spoke with other tongues. But that is not the case. The Holy Spirit comes to dwell in your spirit at the moment you confess your sins and accept Jesus as your Lord and Savior. In a later chapter we'll talk more about what it means to be "filled with the Spirit."

In reflecting on how the Holy Spirit lives in us, it helps to understand that we human beings are "spirit, soul, and body" (1 Thess. 5:23). Sometimes it's difficult to fully distinguish between our soul and spirit, but there is a difference that is clearly discerned by the Word of God (Heb. 4:12). The soul is

For the word of God is living and powerful, and sharper than any two-edged sword, piercing even to the division of soul and spirit, and of joints and marrow, and is a discerner of the thoughts and intents of the heart.

—Hebrews 4:12

the place of intellect, will and emotions. If you are conscious of being alive, your soul is the active place of that awareness.

The Holy Spirit makes your spirit alive to God and creates a place where God dwells with you on this earth.

Your spirit is reflected in intuition, the ability for self-reflection and the capacity to accurately empathize with others and to give and receive love. Your spirit is that part of your self-awareness where you feel empty after achieving all the success of the flesh, the intellect and the will. Your spirit is designed for God and will not be at peace until it finds its rest in Him. Every human being is a spiritual being. This is regardless of birth defects or damage to the body and mind through disease or accident.

The Bible refers to the human spirit in numerous ways.

- Our spirit can be "troubled" (Gen. 41:8).
- We can have "anguish of spirit" (Exod. 6:9; Job 7:11).
- We can have a "spirit of jealousy" (Num. 5:14).
- Our spirit can harbor ill will. (Read Joshua 9:23.)
- Our spirit can be "sorrowful" (1 Sam. 1:15).
- Our spirit can be "sullen" (1 Kings 21:5).
- Our spirit can be "broken" (Job 17:1; Ps. 51:17; Prov. 17:22).
- Our spirit can be "humble" (Prov. 16:19; 29:23; Isa. 57:15).
- We are to "take heed" to our spirit (Mal. 2:15).
- Our spirit can be "willing," but our flesh weak (Matt. 26:41).
- We are called to "serve [God] with our spirit" and be "fervent in spirit" (Rom. 1:9; 12:11).
- We "glorify God" in our spirit by being "holy both in body and in spirit" (1 Cor. 6:20; 7:34).
- We "pray," "sing" and "bless" with our spirit as we speak in unknown tongues (1 Cor. 14:14–16).
- Our spirit and mind work in harmony as we are "renewed in the spirit" of our mind (Eph. 4:23).

Jesus, besides being full of the Holy Spirit, also had His spirit as a human being. Jesus perceived in His spirit, sighed deeply in His spirit, groaned in His spirit and was troubled in spirit. (Read Mark 2:8; 8:12; John 11:38; 13:21.)

The Holy Spirit of God comes to establish the rule of God in our lives by coming to dwell in our spirit. He makes our spirit alive to God and thereby makes us new creatures. For the first time in our lives, we are really alive in the spirit. As new creatures in Christ, the Holy Spirit begins the lifelong process of changing us into the image of Christ. The intimate connection between the Holy Spirit and Jesus Christ cannot be ignored. The Holy Spirit will not do anything except to glorify and reveal Jesus Christ (Rom. 8:9–10). In this era of New Age spiritualism, it is imperative to discern this truth and not be fooled by counterfeit and syncretistic spirituality.

When the Holy Spirit comes into your spirit He dwells with you. The word *dwell* means that the Holy Spirit makes His home in your spirit. From this dwelling in your spirit, the Holy Spirit begins to take over your soul and body with His life (Rom. 8:11). The Holy Spirit searches all things (including the deep things of God) and reveals them to our spirit "that we might know the things that have been freely given to us by God" (1 Cor. 2:12). Through the Holy Spirit we are able to "have the mind of Christ" (1 Cor. 2:16).

The fact that the Holy Spirit dwells in us is affirmed through the lives of various figures in the Bible. Read each of the following scriptures for illustration:

- ▲ Genesis 41:38—The patriarch Joseph was "a man in whom is the Spirit of God."
- ▲ Numbers 27:18—The same phrase is used of Joshua.
- ▲ Psalm 51:11—Following his confession of adultery, King David pleaded, "Do not take Your Holy Spirit from me."
- ▲ Isaiah 63:11—There were many Israelites who wandered in the wilderness in whom was the Holy Spirit.

But you are not in the flesh but in the Spirit, if indeed the Spirit of God dwells in you. Now if anyone does not have the Spirit of Christ, he is not His. And if Christ is in you, the body is dead because of sin, but the Spirit is life because of righteousness.

—Romans 8:9–10

But if the Spirit of Him who raised Jesus from the dead dwells in you, He who raised Christ from the dead will also give life to your mortal bodies through His Spirit who dwells in you.

—Romans 8:11

- ▲ Ezekiel 2:2—The prophet Ezekiel had profound understanding of the inner work of the Holy Spirit. Ezekiel knew when the Holy Spirit entered him.
- ▲ Ezekiel 36:26–27; 37:14—Ezekiel knew that the day was coming when the Holy Spirit would come into human hearts and create a new spirit whereby we obey the Lord from heart purity and not outward obligation.
- ▲ Daniel 4:8–9, 18; 5:11, 14—Repeatedly the prophet Daniel is referred to as a man "in whom is the Spirit of the Holy God."
- ▲ John 20:22—Following the glory of His resurrection, Jesus breathed upon the disciples, and they received the Holy Spirit.

11-2-02 Complete

Question: The indwelling of the Holy Spirit within you means you can expect several things to occur. As you read the following passages, write what the Bible says happens as a result of the dwelling presence of the Holy Spirit in you.

- ▲ **Genesis 41:38–39.** Joseph is described as discerning and ________________________________.
- ▲ **Ezekiel 36:26–27.** The Holy Spirit removes your heart of ________________________ and enables you to keep the Lord's ________________________.
- ▲ **Daniel 5:14.** Daniel is described as a man in whom are found ________________________, ________________________ and ________________________.
- ▲ **John 20:19–23.** Three things happened to the disciples when Jesus breathed the Holy Spirit as new life into them. First, Jesus gave them His ____________________ in the place of their fear. Second, just as the Father sent Jesus, Jesus ____________________ the disciples with purpose. Third, the Holy Spirit enables believers to ________________ and ________________ sins.

▲ **Romans 8:11.** The same Holy Spirit who raised Jesus from the dead will also ______________________________ to our mortal bodies as the Spirit ____________________________ in us.

▲ **Romans 8:15.** The Holy Spirit enables us to call God ______________________________, a tender term for Father.

▲ **1 Corinthians 6:19.** Your body is the __________________ of the Holy Spirit.

▲ **Ephesians 3:16.** The Holy Spirit in your inner person will strengthen with ______________________________ your life.

▲ **James 4:5.** The Holy Spirit who dwells in you is ______________________________ for you.

▲ Describe how the Spirit is working in your life with some of the same characteristics you just discovered in the Bible: ____
____

▲▲▲▲▲▲▲

The Spirit's work in relation to our body is important. The human body has been made by God and is good. It is not evil, but because of its fleshly nature and fallen condition due to Adam's sin, it is vulnerable to the temptations of sin. The idea that we are redeemed in the spirit but can continue to live sinfully in the flesh is alien to the Bible. That kind of teaching, which has always been on the fringes of Christianity, is a form of Platonic Gnosticism. That is why the Bible recognizes that the body is valuable in God's sight (thus the Christian doctrine of the resurrection of the body—1 Corinthians 15—and the resurrection of Jesus).

The body houses the spirit in this life. God's desire is for our bodies to become the visible temples of His presence in the world. We become His visible presence as the Holy Spirit dwells in us (1 Cor. 3:16). The reason Christians abstain from sexual immorality is because "your body is the temple of the Holy Spirit who is in you, whom you have from God, and that you are not your own . . . you were bought with a price; therefore glorify God in your body and in your spirit, which are God's" (1 Cor. 6:19–20).

Do you not know that you are the temple of God and that the Spirit of God dwells in you?
—1 Corinthians 3:16

Taking residence in the redeemed human spirit, the Holy Spirit takes over our will, intellect and emotions. He takes over our will as we surrender our plans and purposes to His will. He takes over our intellect as we receive the mind of Christ and learn to trust His word. He takes over our emotions as the fruit of the Spirit takes over our emotional life. This is why a Christian can never say, "Well, this is just the way God made me. I'm sorry I have such a bad temper, but you'll just have to get over it." If the Holy Spirit dwells in you, He will confront that bad temper and remind you that God is at work making you a new creature without that temper controlling you. The question becomes, Are you willing for the Holy Spirit to take over every part of your life?

God's desire is for our bodies to become the visible temples of His presence in the world.

What happens to your personality when the Holy Spirit dwells in you? Do you lose your identity, your personality? Yes, and no. If you ask your friends or family if you need some changes in your personality, if they are honest they will say yes. In fact, they may be praying for the Holy Spirit to replace your anger with kindness, your fear with love, your arrogance with humility, your insensitivity with compassion. So, yes, there will be some things that you will lose, but guess what? The replacement is much better!

• Your identity will change as you become a new person in Christ. People will say, "Wow, you've changed! What happened?"

You'll probably say, "Well, I'm not sure about it all, but I can tell you that since I met Jesus, things have not been the same."

Your identity will no longer be in climbing the ladder of success (although you still may climb it).

Your identity will no longer be measured by sexual conquests (although you'll discover a freedom from compulsion and discover how to treat others with respect as persons).

Your identity no longer will be measured by comparing yourself with others and always feeling a failure. (You'll discover the joy and liberty of putting others ahead of yourself and not worrying as much about your image.)

You'll find that the talents and abilities you have will find an outlet for the purposes of God rather than for your own selfish purposes.

Yes, you'll be different, but you will still be you. It will just be you as a person controlled from the inside out by the Holy Spirit. Instead of Captain Kirk (or whatever your name is) running the *Enterprise* of your life, the Holy Spirit will be in the commander's seat calling the shots. You're going to have a great trip! There are a lot of unknown spiritual galaxies for you to explore!

WHAT HAPPENS NEXT?

OK, you've been born again. You have this new, powerful Person living inside you, and His name is the Holy Spirit. Where do you go from here? What are the implications of His dwelling inside your spirit?

You need to realize that God Himself is living inside you. That's pretty awesome stuff. The Creator of the universe is inside you. If you feel somewhat overwhelmed by that, good. You're sure not in a position to be arrogant about it. Remember, He chose you first; you didn't choose Him (1 John 4:19). You've been saved by His grace, not by any of your good works (Eph. 2:8–9). A little *fear* of the Lord (read *reverence, awe*) doesn't hurt.

You are a temple with feet. God is so powerful and loves you so much that He chooses to live inside what the apostle Paul called "earthen vessels" (2 Cor. 4:7). Sometimes you may feel more like a cracked pot than an earthen vessel. But nonetheless, the Holy Spirit lives in you.

Does this mean that everything in life is perfect overnight? Unless you just happen to die the moment you're born again, you have a lot of cleaning up and cleaning out that's going to occur. The Holy Spirit will become a pretty powerful cleanser, and He'll probably put you through the ringer. But it will be worth it. That's called *holiness*, and we'll talk more about it in the next chapter.

"Will the Holy Spirit ever decide He just doesn't want to live in me any longer? In other words, can I lose my salvation?"

We love Him because He first loved us.
—1 John 4:19

For by grace you have been saved through faith, and that not of yourselves; it is the gift of God, not of works lest anyone should boast.
—Ephesians 2:8–9

Now to Him who is able to keep you from stumbling, and to present you faultless before the presence of His glory with exceeding joy . . .

—Jude 24

That's a good question, and Christians come to different conclusions about that. The Bible seems to give us one of those *yes* and *no* answers. It's not a contradiction but more a paradox—truths that make sense to God but not always to us. But maybe a look at the Bible will help you.

Keep in mind that God does not want any person to be lost. Jesus came "to seek and to save that which was lost" (Luke 19:10). The preponderance of the Bible message is that we can live with great trust and confidence that God is faithful and is able to keep us from falling (Jude 24). You don't have to live your life worrying whether God loves you or not. So, the issue is not really from God's side. God is not going to decide one day that He doesn't love you anymore. God is love and simply cannot do that.

Although God cannot, and will not, withdraw His love from your life, you can make decisions that frustrate the grace of God in your life. First Corinthians 5 describes a Christian man living in sexual immorality. The apostle Paul commanded the church to "deliver such a one over to Satan" (excommunicate the man from active involvement in the church) so that the man would suffer the consequences of his actions in his flesh. But his spirit would then be saved by finally returning to Christ.

You are a temple with feet.

A person can also become apostate by denying Christ. (Read Hebrews 6:4–8.)

Thus while salvation is a free gift of grace, it is a costly gift and not to be taken lightly. Our disregard for God's grace is the problem—not the failure of God's grace. We are redeemed so we can grow in God's grace, enabling us to become more Christlike in heart and actions.

The same Holy Spirit who lives in you lives in every other Christian. The Spirit is building a community of people from every nation and generation as a showcase for the glory of God. The Spirit gives special gifts to demonstrate God's power and reach more people with the gospel. The Spirit calls us into the body of Christ, called the *church*, and together we eagerly await the return of Christ Himself.

LET'S TALK ABOUT IT

▲ Why is salvation called a "good work" by the apostle Paul? Who is the originator of this good work?

____

____

▲▲▲▲▲▲▲

▲ Salvation is a comprehensive term. Name some of the spiritual experiences described in the Bible that are part of the comprehensive work of salvation.

____

____

▲▲▲▲▲▲▲

▲ What is the difference between conviction by the Holy Spirit and condemnation?

____

____

▲▲▲▲▲▲▲

▲ When does the Holy Spirit come to dwell in your heart?

____

____

▲▲▲▲▲▲▲

▲ What is the Holy Spirit changing in your personality? What do you believe needs to be changed by the Holy Spirit in your life?

____

____

▲▲▲▲▲▲▲

TIME TO PLUG IN TO THE HOLY SPIRIT

Has it occurred to you that church membership is different from being born again? Attending a church no more makes you a Christian than attending a football game makes you a quarterback. There is a difference between feeling religious and the presence of the Holy Spirit in your life. The Holy Spirit enables you to confess openly that Jesus Christ is Lord

and also to believe in your heart that Jesus is alive. If you have not accepted Jesus as Savior, realize that the Holy Spirit has led you to this place in this book. Ask Jesus to forgive you of your sins and to come live in your heart. He will. You will know He is there by the love of God you will experience through the Holy Spirit. (Read Romans 5:5.)

You may have already accepted Christ as Savior and know that your sins are forgiven and that you're a son or daughter of God. But you may not have understood that the Holy Spirit already dwells in you. This is your time to ask the Holy Spirit to make His presence known in your life. If your Christian life has been unfulfilling, undisciplined and uninformed, the Holy Spirit is waiting for you to cooperate with Him. Pray the following words:

Holy Spirit, I confess that I did not realize You are alive and dwelling in me. I've tried to live a religious life instead of a Spirit-filled life. I've tried to be holy in my own strength. I've struggled to control my emotions, my mind and my body. Sometimes I really feel out of control. I love Jesus, and I need His Spirit to take over my life.

I open the door of my heart and ask You to take over my mind, my emotions and my will. Give me love for Your Word. Give me a heart of reverence. Teach me to worship You in spirit and in truth and not be so bound by my surroundings. Holy Spirit, I give You permission to change my life in any way it needs to change so that Jesus is glorified in me. Amen.

CHAPTER FOUR

The Holy Spirit and Holy People

IN THIS CHAPTER YOU WILL DISCOVER THAT . . .

- ▲ The Holy Spirit engages in a lifelong campaign to establish the full dominion of Christ over our lives.
- ▲ The Holy Spirit's fruit is a total package of transformation in your life.
- ▲ We can grieve, rebel against, quench and insult the Holy Spirit.

THE HOLY SPIRIT, WHO DWELLS IN US, CALLS US TO THE ALTAR OF CLEANSING. The apostle Paul said it like this:

> *I beseech you therefore, brethren, by the mercies of God, that you present your bodies a living sacrifice, holy, acceptable to God, which is your reasonable service. And do not be conformed to this world, but be transformed by the renewing of your mind, that you may prove what is that good and acceptable and perfect will of God.*
>
> —Romans 12:1–2

The apostle Peter wrote that we "are a chosen generation, a royal priesthood, a holy nation, His own special people, that you may proclaim the praises of Him who called you out of darkness into His marvelous light" (1 Pet. 2:9).

Holiness—it's not a very popular term in many Christian circles. For many people there is a negative image—an old-fashioned, legalistic, hard-hearted, outwardly religious emphasis from stern-looking, judgmental people. Unfortunately there have been enough instances of the negative images to reinforce the stereotype.

But there's got to be more than that. Jesus was holy and lived a holy life; yet, the Gospels present Him as dynamically engaged in life. He even drew the ire of the religious leaders because He did not do enough of the outward stuff to suit them. The Spirit that moved Jesus is the same Holy Spirit that dwells in us. So life in the Spirit does not have to be boring, legalistic or moralistic. It just has to be holy.

THERE'S FIRE IN THE AIR

Jesus came to baptize with the Holy Spirit and fire (Matt. 3:11). That means that Jesus as the Son of God had use of something that was essential to His eternal nature as God.

> I indeed baptize you with water unto repentance, but He who is coming after me is mightier than I, whose sandals I am not worthy to carry. He will baptize you with the Holy Spirit and fire.
> —Matthew 3:11

The Bible reveals that God is a consuming fire. (Read Deuteronomy 4:24; Hebrews 12:29.) Fire has several uses in the Bible—to consume sacrifices to atone for sin, as an instrument of divine judgment, as an instrument of purification and as an element signifying God's personal holiness.

Sacrificial fire

There are numerous passages in Exodus, Leviticus and Numbers that describe the use of holy fire for sacrifices. There are two important aspects of sacrificial fire. First, it is the force that produces a sweet aroma to God as the sacrifice is consumed. (Read Leviticus 1:9, 13, 17.) This aroma is the smell of an unblemished animal that was sacrificed to meet the righteous demands of God's judgment. The apostle Paul used this metaphor three times to describe aspects of the Christian life:

- ▲ Second Corinthians 2:16 mentions the "aroma" of Christian service in the world.
- ▲ Ephesians 5:2 refers to Christ who gave "Himself for us, an offering and a sacrifice to God for a sweet-smelling aroma."
- ▲ Philippians 4:18 mentions the gifts of love that the Philippian Christians sent to Paul as acts of mercy.

Holy fire

The second aspect of this fire is that it is holy and cannot be duplicated by human effort. Leviticus 10:1–3 tells of Nadab and Abihu, sons of Moses' brother, Aaron. They apparently took fire from an altar other than the altar fire that God had established and sought to use this different fire in worship of the Lord. The two sons died as the Lord sent fire in judgment. The sin of these two men was their failure to treat the Lord as holy: "By those who come near Me I must be regarded as holy; and before all the people I must be glorified" (Lev. 10:3).

Here are some important things to remember about this aspect of God's holiness:

- ▲ We cannot make ourselves holy by own efforts. We must be holy by God's methods and standards.

- God takes His holy nature seriously and expects people who go by His name to do the same.
- We cannot substitute our understanding of holiness for God's revealed holiness.

The point is this: The Holy Spirit cannot be substituted by human effort or man-made rules. This kind of "fire" is unholy and destructive. It cannot bring life. Only the Holy Spirit can bring holy life.

Judgment fire

Fire is also a symbol of God's judgment upon sin. We saw this in the judgment upon Aaron's two sons. It is a very common theme in the Old Testament. Isaiah 10:16–17 describes Assyria under divine judgment as the Lord "will kindle a burning like the burning of a fire. So the Light of Israel will be for a fire, and His Holy One a flame; it will burn and devour His thorns and briers in one day." This is part of the meaning of Matthew 3:11–12 where Jesus comes with "His winnowing fan in His hand, and He will thoroughly clean out His threshing floor and gather His wheat into the barn; but He will burn up the chaff with unquenchable fire."

Purifying fire

Fire also serves to purify. The Lord washes away spiritual filth "by the spirit of judgment and by the spirit of burning" (Isa. 4:4). The Lord's fire is a "refiner's fire" (Mal. 3:2). Our faith is purified as "it is tested by fire" (1 Pet. 1:7). Fire is used in a Christian's life as part of the Holy Spirit's making our bodies the temple of the Holy Spirit. This is particularly clear in 1 Corinthians 3:12–15. The foundation of our life is Jesus Christ, but we participate in what we build upon that foundation (1 Cor. 3:11–13). We can build with solid aspects of maturity and growth (symbolized by gold, silver and precious stones), or we can foolishly build our Christian life with worthless things (symbolized by wood, hay and straw).

At the Day of Judgment, God's holy fire will "test each one's work" (v. 13). Those who have lived wisely in the power and presence of the Spirit will discover that their work was not in vain but has spiritually endured. Those who lived foolishly will see their works consumed although they themselves

For no other foundation can anyone lay than that which is laid, which is Jesus Christ. Now if anyone builds on this foundation with gold, silver, precious stones, wood, hay, straw, each one's work will become clear; for the Day will declare it, because it will be revealed by fire; and the fire will test each one's work, of what sort it is.

—1 Corinthians 3:11–13

will be saved. (Read 1 Corinthians 3:14–15.) Therefore, since you are the temple of the Holy Spirit, you should wisely build this temple with deeds and attitudes that are of eternal worth.

Fire also symbolizes a variety of ways in which the Holy Spirit operates in our lives.

- ▲ Read Exodus 3:2; Deuteronomy 4:36—God speaks through fire.
- ▲ Read Jeremiah 20:9; Ezekiel 8:2—His word is like fire.
- ▲ Read Psalm 104:4—The Lord makes His ministers a flame of fire (perhaps a reference to angels).
- ▲ Read Exodus 13:21; 40:38—The Lord used a pillar of fire to guide Israel by night in the wilderness and to cover the temple in the wilderness.
- ▲ Read Mark 9:49—Jesus said, "Everyone will be seasoned with fire."
- ▲ Read Acts 2:3—The Holy Spirit appeared as cloven tongues of fire upon the 120 disciples in the upper room.

How does the Holy Spirit work through fire in us? We gain insight from James 4:5, "The Spirit who dwells in us yearns jealously." In the Old Testament God's jealousy is connected with fire. (Read Deuteronomy 4:24; Zephaniah 1:18; 3:8.) God's jealousy is not petty, but it is based on the fact that He is our Creator and Redeemer. The Holy Spirit in your heart is jealous that in your mind and body you do not honor other gods before Him. He is jealous that you do not listen to the lies of Satan rather than listening to His prompting. He is jealous for your love, attention and adoration rather than the ways we lust after the things of this world.

• Holy Spirit jealousy burns in our conscience. The Spirit uses the Word, other Christians and life's circumstances to get our attention. He will often allow us to experience the wages of sin so that our hearts turn back to Him. Even when we have made foolish and sinful decisions, the Spirit seeks to restore us because He is jealous for us. In order to protect the honor of Christ's name, the Spirit will first seek to draw us to repentance without public shame. But if we continually reject His overtures, the Spirit will allow our sin to become public as part of His effort to save us. This pattern is at work in Jesus' instructions on how a backslider should be brought to accountability. (Read Matthew 18:15–20.)

Since you are the temple of the Holy Spirit, you should wisely build this temple with deeds and attitudes that are of eternal worth.

It is this divine jealousy, which is actually jealousy for the honor of God's name and character, that transforms us into the character of Christ. (Read Ezekiel 39:25.) The Holy Spirit engages in a lifelong campaign to establish the full dominion of Christ over our lives. (Read Romans 6:11–14.)

Question: Are all Christians called to a holy life, or is holiness reserved for only a few?

First Corinthians 3:12–15 describes holy fire judging our lives. What is the purpose for this fire of judgment?

HOW CAN WE BE HOLY?

Earlier we saw that the comprehensive term *salvation* includes every spiritual grace needed now and in eternity. That includes *sanctification*, the process the Holy Spirit uses to declare and make us holy in Christ. This process begins the moment a person accepts Christ as Savior. We are sanctified and declared holy because Christ is our sanctification. (Read 1 Corinthians 1:30.) The "how" of sanctification is described in the New Testament as a work of the Holy Spirit (Rom. 15:16; 1 Pet. 1:2).

. . . that I might be a minister of Jesus Christ to the Gentiles, ministering the gospel of God, that the offering of the Gentiles might be acceptable, sanctified by the Holy Spirit.
—Romans 15:16

. . . elect according to the foreknowledge of God the Father, in sanctification of the Spirit . . .
—1 Peter 1:2

And you shall know the truth, and the truth shall make you free.

—John 8:32

The Holy Spirit's instruments in human transformation are:

• The truth of God's Word

Jesus said, "Sanctify them by Your truth, Your word is truth . . . And for their sakes I sanctify Myself, that they also may be sanctified by the truth" (John 17:17, 19). The first instrument the Holy Spirit uses to make us holy is the truth. Contrary to the spirit of our age, truth is not relative. The truth is the only thing that can set us free (John 8:32). Truth rejects illusions and deceptions regarding us, our adversary Satan and our Redeemer, God.

Sanctifying truth is readily found in the Bible. Just as faith comes by hearing the Word of God, truth comes alive in our lives by the Holy Spirit through the Word of God. The apostles Paul and Peter expressed the same dynamic of the Holy Spirit and sanctifying truth: "Because God from the beginning chose you for salvation through sanctification by the Spirit and belief in the truth" (2 Thess. 2:13); and, "Since you have purified your souls in obeying the truth through the Spirit in sincere love of the brethren" (1 Pet. 1:22).

Just as faith comes by hearing the Word of God, truth comes alive in our lives by the Holy Spirit through the Word of God.

• The Person of Christ

"For both He who sanctifies and those who are being sanctified are all of one, for which reason He is not ashamed to call them brethren" (Heb. 2:11). Christ is the one who sanctifies us and makes us one with Him. Sanctification brings us into spiritual unity with Christ whereby conscious and willful sin no longer stands between Him and us. This is why Christ has no shame toward us and calls us His family before the court of God. Hebrews 10:14 assures us that "by one offering He has perfected forever those who are being sanctified." That one offering was Christ's death, and His shed blood will never lose its power in our lives. The Holy Spirit sanctifies us by applying God's truth to every part of our lives and transforms us into the image of Christ. "Everyone who has this hope in

Him purifies himself, just as He is pure" (1 John 3:3).

The reign of the Spirit

In Romans 6 the apostle Paul shows the role we play in cooperating with the Holy Spirit. Most Christians are baptized in water as an outward testimony of their faith in Christ. The Spirit helps us know that going under the water in baptism is a spiritual reenactment of sharing in the death of Christ. Just as Christ died, so in Christ our selfish self died to sin. This selfish self is called the "old man" in Romans 6:6. It refers to our orientation to this world with our priorities, thoughts and passions prior to Christ.

But now that we are in Christ, we are no longer "slaves of sin" (v. 6). Because of Christ's victory over sin, we are dead to sin and alive to God in Christ (v. 11). This means that now we are conscious that sin does not the same power it had prior to our faith in Christ. Sin is still there, tempting and enticing us, but it is no longer the ruler of our lives (v. 12). We don't have to obey the lusts of sin that arise in our thoughts (v. 12). Now we can present ourselves to God as instruments in His hands (v. 13). Sin is no longer the king of our lives because we live by the grace of God (v. 14).

This liberty from the dominion of sin does not release us to do as we please; rather, it transfers us to a different dominion and king. Now our king is Jesus, and we are "slaves of righteousness" (v. 18). As Paul vividly writes in verse 22, "Now having been set free from sin, and having become slaves of God, you have your fruit to holiness, and the end, everlasting life."

Actually, it's a pretty good deal! In Christ we are delivered from an evil ruler who wants to kill, steal and destroy us and transferred to our Creator who loves us and has set us free for Himself.

Reckon yourselves to be dead indeed to sin, but alive to God in Christ Jesus our Lord. Therefore do not let sin reign in your mortal body, that you should obey it in its lusts... present yourselves to God as being alive from the dead, and your members as instruments of righteousness to God. For sin shall not have dominion over you, for you are not under law but under grace.

—Romans 6:11–14

WHEN DO WE BECOME HOLY?

We've seen some of the instruments the Holy Spirit uses to sanctify us—the truth of God's Word, the person of Jesus Christ (His shed blood) and our knowledge of change of rulers in our lives. But when does this happen?

There is therefore now no condemnation to those who are in Christ Jesus, who do not walk according to the flesh, but according to the Spirit. For the law of the Spirit of life in Christ Jesus has made me free from the law of sin and death.
—Romans 8:1–2

The spiritual reality occurred in Christ when we accepted Him as Savior. Our self-awareness usually occurs over time as we grow in the Lord. Often this includes a spiritual crisis where we discover that we can't sanctify ourselves in spite of our best efforts, and we struggle with the spiritual war between our flesh and the Holy Spirit. (Read Romans 7.) The crisis calls for a complete surrender on our part to God's power and a recognition of our inadequacy and our dependency upon God's grace.

We discover that life in the Spirit is life free from condemnation and self-defeat (Rom. 8:1). We are conscious that we are tempted and may even stumble. We are conscious that we are no longer governed by the principle of sin and death, but rather our mental, emotional and spiritual life is governed by the principle of the Spirit of life in Christ Jesus (v. 2).

There may be numerous such spiritual crises in our lives as the Holy Spirit deals with various areas of temptation and restoration of the image of Christ in us. Many Christians overcome outward sins of the flesh (drugs, sexual immorality and others) only to encounter sinister spiritual pride. The work of sanctification is a lifelong process, and none of us achieve sinless perfection in this life. Yet we can live victorious over sin as the Holy Spirit reveals more of our need and more of His provision in the different seasons of life.

Life in the Spirit is life free from condemnation and self-defeat.

SPIRITUAL PRINCIPLES OPERATING IN THE WORLD

In many respects Romans 8:1–2 are the key verses regarding spiritual victory over sin. There are two primary spiritual principles that operate in the world. The first is called *The Law* (or principle) *of Sin and Death*. You were born with this principle in your life. Theologians call this *original sin*. It's the sinful condition of all humanity since Adam and Eve blew it in the Garden of Eden. (Read Genesis 3.) There's no racial or gender discrimination here. We've all been living "east of Eden" since then.

The Law of Sin and Death includes everything we call "bad, evil." But it primarily refers to our basic orientation to life outside of Christ—we strive to save ourselves, to justify our own actions and to take care of Numero Uno. We can't help it. It's the law that operates in our sinful flesh. It is life lived according to the flesh with all its need for self-security. In the final analysis, the Law of Sin and Death is the principle by which we try to save ourselves. We think our knowledge, our money, our power, our influence and our efforts at self-improvement will save us and give us meaning in life. That's the delusion of the Law of Sin and Death.

But when you become a Christian the Holy Spirit brings a different law or principle into your life—*The Law of the Spirit of Life in Christ Jesus.* Sanctification is the process by which we realize the limits of our fleshly existence and cease depending upon the flesh to save us. Sanctification is the surrender of our existence to God's altar at the cross of Christ. This surrender leads to holiness, which is the outgrowth of the Law of the Spirit of Life in Christ Jesus. This law is the law of surrender to the life of Christ in us. It is not a negation of life but the finding of real life. In this principle, which is only present through the Holy Spirit, we leave willfulness on the altar and discover the freedom of willingness as we walk in the Spirit.

HOLINESS TRANSFORMS OUR LIVES

To this point our discussion of sanctification has focused on the issue of sin. We've seen that the Holy Spirit helps us overcome temptations and sinful desires. But there is more to sanctification than dealing with sin. There is a new person in Christ who is being formed by the Holy Spirit. This occurs as the personality of Jesus, through the fruit of the Spirit, is made alive in us. Our attitudes and actions do change, and we are different because of the new life the Holy Spirit gives us.

Question: Paul's letter to the Galatians (Christians who lived in what is now modern Turkey) provides important insights into how the Holy Spirit operates in our lives. To get the maximum impact, let's get your participation in understanding the Holy Spirit's work:

Read Galatians 2:16. How are we justified?

____

____

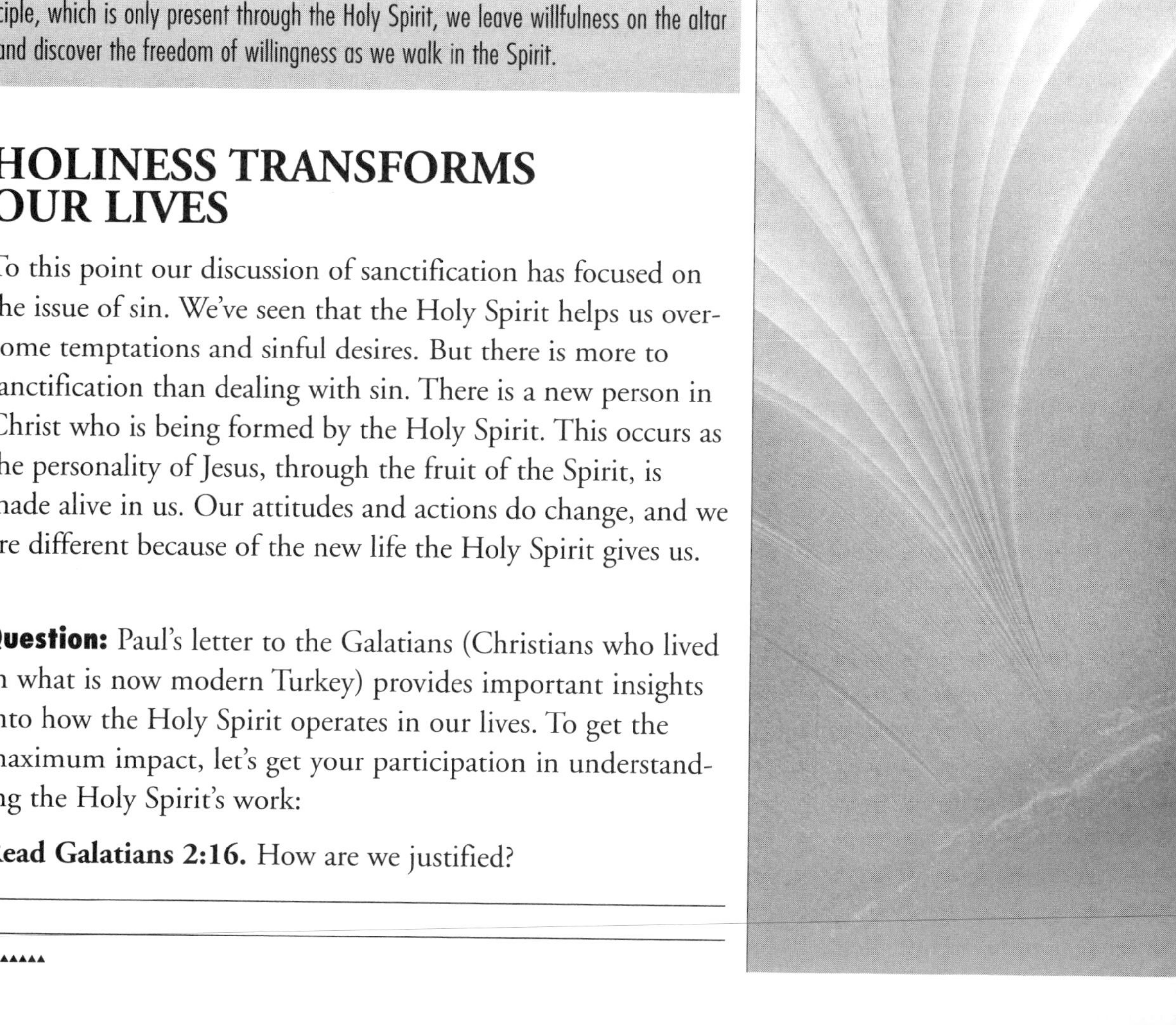

Read Galatians 2:20. How does the Holy Spirit help us to live for Christ?

______

______

▲▲▲▲▲▲▲

Read Galatians 3:2–3, 14. We do not receive the fullness of the Spirit by being perfect. How does the Spirit fill our lives?

______

______

▲▲▲▲▲▲▲

Read Galatians 4:6–7. The presence of the Holy Spirit in our lives confirms our relationship with the Father as what?

______

______

▲▲▲▲▲▲▲

Read Galatians 5:16. How are we to walk? What are we to avoid?

______

______

▲▲▲▲▲▲▲

Read Galatians 5:19–21. What are the works of the flesh?

______

______

▲▲▲▲▲▲▲

But the fruit of the Spirit is love, joy, peace, longsuffering, kindness, goodness, faithfulness, gentleness, self-control. Against such there is no law.
—Galatians 5:22–23

In contrast to the works of the flesh, the Holy Spirit is giving us His fruit (Gal. 5:22–23). Note that the "fruit" of the Spirit is singular. There are not nine fruits (plural) from which you can pick and choose. "I think I'll take a little love, joy and peace. I'll pass on the longsuffering if you don't mind" does not wash. The Holy Spirit's fruit is a total package of transformation in your life. Remember, the Spirit yearns jealously for you to be renewed in the image of Christ. You might as well surrender to the joyful journey of the Spirit-life where this fruit will become more and more evident and mature in you.

There are nine manifestations of this fruit. As we will see, every aspect of life is covered here.

Love

Since God is love, it is proper that love be the first characteristic of the Spirit to be developed in us. (Read 1 John 4:8.)

Furthermore, love is the defining relationship characteristic among Christians. (Read 1 John 3:16–23.) While faith and hope are important, the greatest Christian virtue is love. (Read 1 Corinthians 13.)

Joy

The Christian life is a joyful life. The New Testament mentions joy and rejoicing one hundred thirty-two times. Paul's letter to the Philippians is called a *book of joy.* Rejoicing and joy are characteristics of Luke's two books, the Gospel of Luke and the Acts of the Apostles. Joy is different from silliness or even emotions. Circumstances may be terrible, but joy remains. This is because Christian joy is rooted in the fundamental nature of knowing God. God's ultimate goodness for us enables us to face every trial, including death, with "joy inexpressible and full of glory" (1 Pet. 1:8).

God's ultimate goodness for us enables us to face every trial, including death, with "joy inexpressible and full of glory."

Peace

The Hebrew *shalom* stands behind the New Testament understanding of peace. But *shalom* is more than a modern greeting. *Shalom* is God's goodness realized in every sphere of life. The modern idea of peace is too limited as it tends to focus on a lack of conflict. The peace that the Holy Spirit gives us is as comprehensive as the intent of *shalom.* Every book in the New Testament contains the word *peace.* Peace includes the reality of reconciliation between hostile parties. But it is more than the cessation of conflict; it is the restoration to right relationship.

Longsuffering

Longsuffering is the Spirit-given ability to be "long tempered" (the literal meaning of the Greek word). It has to be a fruit of the Spirit, because none of us in our flesh can live with the kind of long-term patience that this word implies. It is actually used to describe God's attitude toward humanity. (Read Joel 2:13; 1 Timothy 1:12–16; 2 Peter 3:9, 15.)

In the Christian life, this kind of long-term patience with one another is not a "grit your teeth, I've got to put up with you" attitude. Instead, it is an attitude based on hope in God's purposes and the power of the Holy Spirit at work in another person or outward circumstances. We endure because

we are convinced that God's good purposes are going to be achieved. For a spouse in an abusive relationship, this does not mean staying in a home and being beaten. But it does mean that divorce will not be the first option. It means that biblically sanctioned separation is seen as an opportunity for grace to intervene in the circumstances. (Read 1 Corinthians 7:11.) Longsuffering is the Holy Spirit answer to the modern illusion of instant success and happiness.

Kindness

God is kind and manifests that kindness in nature, history, His judgments and to the afflicted. In this sense God's kindness extends to all humanity and is part of His plan to woo people to Himself. (Read Titus 3:4.) The pattern for our kindness to others is therefore God. Paul wrote that kindness is a characteristic of Christian ministry. (Read 2 Corinthians 6:4–10.) Kindness is like a spiritual coat we put on as we relate to others (Col. 3:12). The apostle Peter understood kindness as an essential element of the expression of godliness and love. (Read 2 Peter 1:5–9.)

Therefore, as the elect of God, holy and beloved, put on tender mercies, kindness, humility, meekness, longsuffering...
—Colossians 3:12

Several years ago I learned an important lesson about the power of kindness. It was just after the fall of Communism in Romania, and I was carrying a large box of medical items from north Georgia to a hospital in a small town near the large city of Oradea. I had stopped in London for a few days awaiting Austria Air transport to Vienna, and then traveling by train and car to Romania.

I had been told in the United States that the weight of the box was within limits. However, at the Austrian Air terminal at Heathrow I was told that the box was too heavy for the flight. I thought about using the assertive, tough American act, trying to intimidate the woman at the counter. There were people behind me, and I could sense their impatience as I explained to her what was in the box. I was about to raise my voice when I remembered my mother's advice, "Always treat people with kindness."

I asked her if she could speak to someone in Austrian Air who might make an exception. She left and went upstairs for about five minutes. Returning, she smiled and said, "They'll take it." I thanked her, and then she added, "They asked me how you acted when I first told you it could not go. I told them you were nice and did not raise your voice. That's when they said to put it on the plane."

In reflection I realized that the Holy Spirit took a dimension of my rearing as a child and brought it to my attention at a critical moment for a small group of people in Romania and for me. Kindness—it will take you a long way.

Goodness

In this study of the Holy Spirit we have already seen how goodness is part of God's essential nature. It is natural that this part of God's nature would become part of our nature as the Holy Spirit lives in us. Goodness implies generosity that is based on grace. A good person lives gracefully with others. We treat people with the same grace with which God has treated us. This dimension of goodness means that others do deserve kindness and love from us.

We treat people with the same grace with which God has treated us.

Faithfulness

Faith is a theological term—*faithfulness* is an ethical term. It denotes trustworthiness and reliability. It also implies stability and dependability. The Holy Spirit transforms unreliable people into people whose word can be trusted (2 Cor. 1:17–18).

Therefore, when I was planning this, did I do it lightly? Or the things I plan, do I plan according to the flesh, that with me there should be Yes, Yes, and No, No? But as God is faithful, our word to you was not Yes and No.

—2 Corinthians 1:17–18

Gentleness

Sometimes translated "meekness," this word does not imply weakness but strength. Gentleness is sometimes used in connection with lowliness and humility. (Read Ephesians 4:2; Colossians 3:12.) Gentleness is a teachable spirit.

Self-control

Self-control describes a person whose emotions, mind and body are kept in balance through the Holy Spirit. A self-controlled person in the Spirit is not a stilted, formal, aloof

person, but rather a person who lives with focused passion and intensity. Such a person is not distracted by everything but remains clear about what is important.

Paul closed his remarks about the fruit of the Spirit with the remark that "against such there is no law" (Gal. 5:23). What he meant by this statement is that these Holy Spirit self and relational qualities are not tied to human convention but to divine guidance. The formation of our character takes place not by obeying another law, whereby we have to measure ourselves, but through the life of the Holy Spirit in us. We know God loves us; we know that the Holy Spirit seeks God's good and our good; therefore, we willingly cooperate with the transformation occurring in our self.

Question: Although all nine dimensions of the Spirit are considered one fruit, you can distinguish which ones God is working on in your life. At this time, which dimension of the fruit is the Holy Spirit bringing to maturity in you?

____

____

▲▲▲▲▲▲▲

Earlier I described an episode of the fruit of the Spirit in relation to a trip to Romania. Can you describe an episode where the Holy Spirit transformed you at a particular time with one of the fruit of the Spirit?

____

____

▲▲▲▲▲▲▲

DO NOT HARDEN YOUR HEART

Although the Holy Spirit dwells with us at conversion, we can resist His work in our emotions, mind, spirit and body. We can grieve, rebel against, quench and insult the Holy Spirit. The Holy Spirit is the Spirit of truth, and He knows our hearts better than we do ourselves. Though the Spirit yearns jealously for us, He is nonetheless sensitive to our response to Him. In this section it is important that we review ways that our relationship with the Holy Spirit can be hindered and, in certain instances, actually destroyed.

Rebellion

Psalm 106:33 and Isaiah 63:10 refer to rebellion against the Holy Spirit. The psalm describes the Israelite rebellion against Moses in Numbers 20:3–13. (Read this scripture.) Moses reacted angrily to them, and his rash actions kept him from entering the Promised Land. The psalm shows that rebellion against the Holy Spirit was manifested as the people constantly complained and murmured against the Lord's anointed leader.

Isaiah 63:10 also refers to the constant complaining in the wilderness against the Lord. The remainder of verse 10 shows that the Lord Himself turns against us and fights against us when rebellion against the Holy Spirit takes over our lives.

The Hebrew word for *rebellion* has the basic meaning of bitterness. We rebel against the Holy Spirit when bitterness is rooted in our lives.

Because they rebelled against His Spirit, so that he [Moses] spoke rashly with his lips.
—Psalm 106:33

But they rebelled and grieved His Holy Spirit; so He turned Himself against them as an enemy, and He fought against them.
—Isaiah 63:10

Read Hebrews 12:15. Describe in your own words what happens when a root of bitterness springs up in us.

____

____

▲▲▲▲▲▲▲

Grief

Isaiah 63:10 and Ephesians 4:30 refer to grieving the Holy Spirit. Grief implies loss. The Holy Spirit is grieved when we rebel (the connection with Isaiah 63:10) because the Spirit knows what is being lost. Our resistance to the Spirit means lost blessings for others and us. The grief in Isaiah 63:10 is further explained in Numbers 14:11. There the Lord expresses the rejection He feels from those whom He has redeemed.

And do not grieve the Holy Spirit of God, by whom you were sealed for the day of redemption.
—Ephesians 4:30

Read Numbers 14:11. Describe other aspects of this rejection and grief.

____

____

▲▲▲▲▲▲▲

Read Ephesians 4:29–31. Verse 30 commands us to "not grieve the Holy Spirit of God, by whom you were sealed for the day of redemption." Using Ephesians 4:29–31, describe how we can grieve the Holy Spirit.

▲▲▲▲▲▲▲

Resist

Acts 7:51 and 2 Timothy 3:8 use resisting the Holy Spirit in the context of resisting the truth. (Read these scriptures.) Acts 7 records Stephen's sermon, asserting that Jesus is the Messiah and indicting the Jewish listeners for failing to believe this truth. This means that rejection of Jesus is more than an intellectual disagreement. To reject Jesus is to resist the Holy Spirit.

Question: Can you identify ways you have resisted the Holy Spirit in your life?

▲▲▲▲▲▲▲

We can smother the voice and active presence of the Holy Spirit with a life preoccupied with too many things.

Quench

The apostle Paul warns us not to quench the Spirit in our lives. *Quench* means to put out a fire or light (symbols of the Holy Spirit) by smothering. A fire is extinguished when the necessary components of air, heat and fuel are removed. We can smother the voice and active presence of the Holy Spirit with a life preoccupied with too many things.

Read 1 Thessalonians 5:11–22. Describe some things that can quench the Holy Spirit:

▲▲▲▲▲▲▲

Despise and forbid

The Holy Spirit manifests Himself in prophecy and speaking in tongues. Due to abuse or ignorance, some Christians are personally and corporately very uncomfortable with either prophecy or tongues. There were abuses of both in Paul's day. Yet, he carefully warned Christians, "Do not despise prophecies," and "Do not forbid to speak with tongues" (1 Thess. 5:20; 1 Cor. 14:39). The Bible provides guidelines for the wise and orderly manifestation of these gifts of the Spirit. (Read 1 Thessalonians 5:21; 1 Corinthians 14:1–40.)

Lying

Acts 5:1–11 describes the judgment of God against a married couple (Ananias and Sapphira) who lied to the Holy Spirit. (Read these scriptures.) The way they lied to the Holy Spirit is that they told the church one thing but did another in order to appear holy but sneak by with deception. This powerful incident reminds us that God resists our hypocrisy.

Apostasy and insult

Two passages in Hebrews describe situations where sins against the Holy Spirit can lead to eternal separation from God. A person can turn his or her back on the Lord by rejecting Jesus as the Son of God. (Read Hebrews 6:4–6; 1 John 2:22–23; 4:1–6, 12–16; 5:1–5.) The Hebrews 6 passage indicates that we can fall away from the faith by apostasy. *Apostasy* is a change of mind so that the truth of the gospel is denied and rejected. It is a mystery why those who were once "partakers of the Holy Spirit" (v. 4) would "crucify again for themselves the Son of God, and put Him to open shame" (v. 5). This is a warning to us to not take lightly the Holy Spirit who lives in us.

Hebrews 10:26–29 warns that continued willful sinning by rejecting God's truth is an insult to the Spirit of grace. (Read these scriptures.) An unrepentant heart becomes an apostate heart. It is not that God rejects this person, but that this person ultimately rejects God. An Old Testament illustration of this is when the Spirit departed from Saul after his continued spiritual rebellion. (Read 1 Samuel 16:14.) This is why David pleaded with the Lord, "Do not take Your Holy Spirit from me," when his adultery was exposed (Ps. 51:11).

It is important to remember you can trust the Lord's eternal love for you. You do not have to fear that God will stop loving you and that the Holy Spirit will arbitrarily leave you.

Question: According to the passages from Hebrews and 1 John, it is clear that *apostasy* is denying that Jesus is

____

▲▲▲▲▲▲▲

Rebellion against the Holy Spirit leads to

____

▲▲▲▲▲▲▲

Blasphemy against the Holy Spirit

Sadly, there are Christians living in continual fear that they have committed an unpardonable sin by blasphemy against the Holy Spirit. They have no peace though they cry for forgiveness. If that is your situation or if you know someone who lives in such torment, there is good news. The unpardonable sin is clearly identified by Jesus. A person who feels guilt and desires repentance has not committed such a sin and has not been abandoned by the Holy Spirit.

Mark 3:20–30 provides a clear picture. (Read these scriptures.) There were three opinions about Jesus in His early ministry: He was a godly and anointed man of God; He was out of his mind; and He was demon possessed. It was the third opinion that Jesus addressed as related to blasphemy against the Holy Spirit and the unpardonable sin. Any person who believes that Jesus' power came from Satan (Beelzebub) has already closed his or her heart to the truth of the gospel. The veil over that person's understanding is so dark and closed that he or she has no sense of needing the gospel (2 Cor. 3:14–15). That person blasphemes the Holy Spirit by calling the Spirit in Jesus a demon.

But their minds were blinded. For until this day the same veil remains unlifted in the reading of the Old Testament, because the veil is taken away in Christ. But even to this day, when Moses is read, a veil lies on their heart.
—2 Corinthians 3:14–15

What do you think about holiness now? If you're going to follow Christ, you really don't have a choice about holiness. Thinking you're a Christian but intentionally living unholy is not only foolish; it could cost you your soul.

It may be that the Holy Spirit is getting your attention with this chapter on holiness. Those little lies at the office or home are not godly. The casual flirting that you think will not affect your marriage is not godly. The Law of Sin and Death is at work.

Thinking you're a Christian but intentionally living unholy is not only foolish; it could cost you your soul.

The Law of the Spirit of Life in Christ Jesus is also at work in your life. He has your attention now. He also wants His fruit to grow and be manifested in your life. It may be that this is a divine appointment for you. Don't miss it.

LET'S TALK ABOUT IT

▲ In what three ways does the Holy Spirit work to bring about holiness in our lives?

____

____

____

▲ The two spiritual principles or laws that operate in the world are named in Romans 8:2. What are those principles, and how do they operate?

____

____

____

▲ In what way are the nine dimensions in Galatians 5:22–23 one fruit of the Spirit?

____

____

____

TIME TO PLUG IN TO THE HOLY SPIRIT

So you always thought that holiness meant you had to become part of a fundamentalist subculture or a monk in the Egyptian desert. While there's nothing wrong with either one, most of us are grateful there are more choices in the kingdom of God!

Holiness is not about dressing or acting weird, intentionally standing out in a crowd because of how we look.

Holiness is about our heart, our passion and our love for God. The real mark of holiness is how much we love God, how much we love God's people and how much we love the lost. Holiness without love is not holiness at all.

The Holy Spirit who lives in you is in a campaign to take you over with holiness. Don't fight it. Surrender. Any pain you experience as you are changed is worth it! Just ask your spouse or your close friends!

Pray the following prayer, or your own, submitting to the transformation of the Spirit in your own life:

> *Spirit of the living God, Spirit of grace, Spirit who raised Jesus from the dead, I did not realize You were so holy. I've called You "Holy" Spirit, but did not think a thing about it. I now know differently. You're the holiness of God in me. I'm sorry for the ways I've resisted You, rebelled against You, ignored You and run from You. I was afraid being holy meant being odd. Thank You for Your longsuffering with me. Through this day and through this night, transform me by Your power and grace. Amen.*

CHAPTER FIVE

The Baptism of the Holy Spirit

IN THIS CHAPTER YOU WILL DISCOVER THAT . . .

- ▲ The baptism of the Holy Spirit empowers us to witness in word and deed about Jesus.
- ▲ Simple obedience and trust in the Lord's timing are critical components of life in the Spirit.
- ▲ Using your prayer language prepares you for changes, conflicts, struggles and opportunities the Spirit will guide you into.

SO FAR WE'VE PLUGGED IN TO THESE OUTLETS OF THE HOLY SPIRIT—THE HOLY SPIRIT IS GOD, THE HOLY SPIRIT TESTIFIES OF JESUS, THE HOLY SPIRIT DWELLS IN US BY FAITH IN CHRIST JESUS, AND THE HOLY SPIRIT IS THE KEY TO HUMAN TRANSFORMATION OR HOLINESS. All these outlets are part of God's power.

But there is a further dimension of Holy Spirit power that has changed the world—the baptism of the Holy Spirit. Characterized by speaking in other tongues, miracles and a wide range of spiritual gifts, for two thousand years it has been the power surge of the church. At the beginning of this second millennium, the baptism of the Holy Spirit is the church's power for effective ministry.

THE PROMISE OF THE FATHER

God makes and keeps promises. Solomon worshiped the Lord with this certainty, "There has not failed one word of all His good promise" (1 Kings 8:56). We trust God because "He who promised is faithful" (Heb. 10:23). God has promised eternal life, and He "cannot lie" (Titus 1:2).

The Old Testament tells of God's promise to Abraham. (Read Genesis 12:1–3; 15:1–6; Psalm 105:42.) That same promise is a major theme in the New Testament. (Read Acts 7:17; Romans 4:13–20; Galatians 3:6–18, 26–29.)

God's promise to Abraham created a covenant people of His own possession, Israel. In the gospel, that promise is extended to all people who come to God through Jesus Christ. The fulfillment of this original promise and its completion through the church is expressed in Galatians 3:14: "That the blessing of Abraham might come upon the Gentiles in Christ Jesus, that we might receive the promise

Nevertheless I tell you the truth. It is to your advantage that I go away; for if I do not go away, the Helper will not come to you; but if I depart, I will send Him to you.

—John 16:7

of the Spirit through faith."

Between the Resurrection and Ascension, Jesus spent forty days teaching the disciples about the kingdom and the promises of God. Prior to His death, Jesus told the disciples that it was in our best interest that He go away (back to heaven) so that the Holy Spirit could come (John 16:7). In those final weeks of earthly ministry, the risen Lord said:

> *Behold, I send the Promise of My Father upon you; but tarry in the city of Jerusalem until you are endued with power from on high.*
>
> —LUKE 24:49

> *[Jesus] commanded them not to depart from Jerusalem, but to wait for the Promise of the Father, "which," He said, "you have heard from Me."*
>
> —ACTS 1:4

At the end of forty days Jesus met for the final time with the disciples. He reminded them of what He had said three years earlier, that He would baptize them with the Holy Spirit. (Read Luke 3:16; Acts 1:5.) But instead of asking about the Holy Spirit, they asked when Israel's kingdom would be restored. (Read Acts 1:6.) In other words, without the Holy Spirit the disciples were powerless to comprehend Jesus' mission. Jesus replied that issues related to Israel were in the Father's hands. The task for His disciples was not to know the details of the future but to "receive power when the Holy Spirit has come upon you; and you shall be witnesses to Me in Jerusalem, and in all Judea and Samaria, and to the end of the earth" (Acts 1:8).

The promised baptism of the Holy Spirit has a clear focus—to be witnesses of Jesus in an ever-widening ministry that encircles the globe. This is what the baptism of the Holy Spirit does—empowers us to witness in word and deed to the fact that Jesus is Israel's Messiah, Jesus is the Son of God and God reigns on the earth through His kingdom.

The disciples understood what the promise of the Father was about when they received the Holy Spirit. In the very first Spirit-filled Christian sermon, the apostle Peter preached that Jesus, "being exalted to the right hand of God, and having received from the Father the promise of the Holy Spirit, He poured out this which you now see and hear" (Acts 2:33). Peter prophetically announced, "For the promise is to you and to your children, and to all who are afar off, as many as the Lord our God will call" (v. 39).

THE PROMISE IN A FEAST

The promise of the Holy Spirit is foretold in the Old Testament festival of Pentecost. (Read Exodus 23:16; Leviticus 23:15–22; Numbers 28:26–31; Deuteronomy 16:9–12.)

> The promised baptism of the Holy Spirit has a clear focus—to be witnesses of Jesus in an ever-widening ministry that encircles the globe.

There are important spiritual lessons in the major Old Testament passages that describe this feast, which is also known as the Feast of Weeks or Harvest. It continues to be celebrated today in May or June by Jews and Christians.

Question: Look up each of the texts below, fill in the blanks and study the spiritual applications from these passages:

▲ **Leviticus 23:15–22**—"A ________________ grain offering shall be offered to the Lord" (v. 16). "When you reap your fields, you shall leave the corners for the ________________ and for ________________" (v. 23).

Application: The *new* grain offering describes the new work of the Holy Spirit in your life. The grain offering refers to harvest and to fruitfulness in your life through the Spirit. Pentecost is about God's power in us for the sake of others. That is why Pentecost means concern for the poor and strangers in our world.

▲ **Numbers 28:26–31**—"You shall do no ________________ ________________ work" during this feast (v. 26).

Application: The Holy Spirit is the power in us to do the work of God. In our lives, it is customary to do things

through our own strength and ability. We must put aside this natural inclination as the Holy Spirit empowers us with His gifts and anointing.

▲▲▲▲▲▲▲

▲ **Deuteronomy 16:9–12**—"You shall keep the Feast of Weeks with the tribute of a ____________________ offering" (v. 10). "You shall ____________________ before the LORD" (v. 11). "You shall remember that you were a ____________________ in Egypt" (v. 12).

Application: The Holy Spirit creates in us a generous heart. We discover that our finances are not our own, but rather we are stewards of God's gifts. Through the Spirit we discover the secret that the more we give to God's service, the more He gives us as a channel of His blessings. The Holy Spirit gives us supernatural power to rejoice in the Lord. Finally, Holy Spirit power is not a man-made "power trip." We must always remember that we are redeemed by God's grace and the power of the Holy Spirit is God's gracious gift in us.

▲▲▲▲▲▲▲

THE PROMISE PROPHESIED

Joel prophecied in 835–805 B.C. during the reign of Joash. (Read 2 Kings 11; 2 Chronicles 23.) Judah was in serious trouble with a locust plague. A plague in that day could easily destroy the nation's economy and the food resources for every family. It also meant that grain offerings and wine used in the temple would be greatly reduced. Besides the natural calamity, there was a spiritual side to a locust plague. Deuteronomy 28:38–46 warns that if God's people fail to obey His commandments, one of His judgments will be a locust plague upon the land.

Joel saw in the locust plague the judgment of the day of the Lord. (Read Joel 1:15; 2:1–3.) Many Israelites thought that the day of the Lord was God's judgment upon the heathen. But Joel warned that God's own people were not immune from His terrible and righteous judgments if they continued to rebel against His commandments.

Two trumpets were sounded in the land. The first was a

warning trumpet so farmers would start fires in their fields to kill the locust. (Read Joel 2:1; either way the fields were destroyed.) The second trumpet was a call to a fast and solemn assembly for repentance. (Read Joel 2:15.) The seriousness of repentance is described:

> *"Now therefore," says the LORD, "turn to Me with all your heart, with fasting, with weeping, and with mourning." So rend your heart... return to the LORD your God, for He is gracious and merciful, slow to anger, and of great kindness; and He relents from doing harm. Who knows if He will turn and relent, and leave a blessing behind Him?*
>
> —JOEL 2:12–14

Repentance brings God's blessings. (Read Joel 2:18–27.) In Joel's situation these blessings included grain, new wine and removal of the locust. The fields will again blossom, and rejoicing will be in the streets. The Lord promised to restore "the former rain [autumn rain at planting time], and the latter rain [spring rains just before the harvest]" (v. 23).

It is in this context that Joel had a vision of a great move of the Spirit of God among the nations. Joel saw a day when the Lord would:

> *Pour out My Spirit on all flesh;*
> *Your sons and your daughters shall prophesy,*
> *Your old men shall dream dreams,*
> *Your young men shall see visions.*
> *And also on My menservants and on My maidservants*
> *I will pour out My Spirit in those days.*
>
> —JOEL 2:28-29

It's an incredible promise. The provincial Judean prophet who came on the scene for one natural disaster (yes, an insurance company's "act of God") had a vision that encompassed the whole world. This prophet who normally would have nothing to do with Gentiles saw them included in the Spirit. There are several parts of this prophecy that demand our attention.

"I will pour out My Spirit"

The term "pour out" is used twice. An examination of other instances in the Bible will help us with this expression.

Proverbs 1:23 is strikingly similar to the context of Joel: "Turn at my rebuke; surely I will pour out my spirit on you; I will make my words known to you." Pouring out the Spirit is related to repentance in the face of judgment and the operation of prophecy ("make my words known to you").

Isaiah 32:15 promises that the Holy Spirit will be "poured upon us from on high" and blessings will come upon the land. The prior context in verses 9–14 refers to God's judgment upon complacency among His people. That complacency will not be removed "until the Spirit is poured upon us." The presence of the Spirit being poured out means there will be justice and righteousness in the land (v. 16). Righteousness will produce peace, quietness and assurance forever, and security (vv. 17–18).

Holy Spirit power means a paradigm shift, a radical break in how God deals with people and how we relate to one another.

Isaiah 44:3 promises the Holy Spirit as refreshing water: "For I will pour water on him who is thirsty, and floods on the dry ground; I will pour My Spirit on your descendents, and My blessing on your offspring." The passage is very similar to Joel's prophecy in that it points to the transgenerational work of the Spirit.

"...on all flesh"

God promised to pour out His Spirit on "all flesh." The Holy Spirit breaks into new territory with sons and daughters, old and young men, menservants and maidservants. Holy Spirit power means a paradigm shift, a radical break in how God deals with people and how we relate to one another.

A promised communication

This paradigm shift is primarily related to communication. Prophecy is promised to a new generation as the gift of a direct word of the Lord. This is the generation that believes God speaks clearly and wants to speak to us. The prophetic is better understood and accepted today than at any time in recent history.

The reference to sons and daughters implies that the parental generation has the responsibility of repentance and its accompanying reordering of life. That generation is to prepare its young to believe in and hear the Word of the Lord. One generation lives in the blessings of repentance so that a generation to come knows the goodness of the Lord.

The generation of sons and daughters lives in the dynamic of hearing God speak through His Spirit. As we have seen, God speaks in accordance with what He has revealed in the Bible. His prophetic words to a specific time will resonate with the testimony and spirit of the Bible. Thus, the generation of sons and daughters knows the Word (they've been taught it) and knows the voice of the Spirit.

Besides prophecy, two other forms of communication are promised to those filled with the Spirit. Dreams are mentioned in relation to old men. Dreams refer to those experiences where the Holy Spirit works in our subconscious thought world during sleep to create and order new perspectives. It means that the old do not have to remain locked in old paradigms. Dreams of the Spirit are that realm where past experiences are collected, shaped and focused for new experiences. There is nothing sadder than an older person desperately hanging to a familiar past that has faded into irrelevance. But there is nothing more inspiring than an older person whose knowledge and wisdom challenge others to a brighter future. Joseph, Daniel and Joseph, husband of Mary, are examples of people in whom the Spirit worked in dreams to create a new destiny. (Read Genesis 37–50; Daniel 2; 4; 7; 8; 10; Matthew 1.)

Visions are promised to young people. Visions differ from dreams in that they tend to occur in normal waking hours. For the person filled with the Spirit, the mind of Christ opens their mind to see things of the Spirit they normally would not see. Elisha was able to see in the Spirit the army of the Lord in "chariots of fire" on the mountains (2 Kings 6:15–17).

In the Book of Daniel we receive insight into how visions come to us that can be affirmed as coming from God. (Read Daniel 9:20–21.) This prophet, noted for the way the Holy Spirit worked through dreams in his life, described his spiritual activities when he received a vision. Daniel was:

- Speaking to God (personal, extemporaneous prayer)
- Praying (more formal prayers, likely recitations from the Psalms)

▲ Confessing his sin and that of Israel (agreeing with God's assessment of Israel's captivity)
▲ Presenting his supplication to the Lord (intercessory prayer)

While Daniel was in this spirit with the Holy Spirit, the Spirit sent the angel Gabriel to give another vision. While this is not a magic formula, Daniel's actions and attitude are essential for the proper spiritual posture so that the Lord can speak to us.

For the person filled with the Spirit, the mind of Christ opens their mind to see things of the Spirit they normally would not see.

This is a powerful lesson for the young to learn. God desires a new, young generation that is not preoccupied with video games, MTV or Hollywood. This generation has a heart and passion for the Spirit. This generation, like Daniel, will be supernaturally moved into key positions of influence in government, commerce and the institutions that shape cultural life. This generation understands the power of prayer as direct communication of the Holy Spirit.

The concluding portion of the Joel prophecy is related to the Holy Spirit and the New Testament. Two theological themes are combined: God's judgment upon the earth at the return of Christ and the imperative to tell the good news of the gospel. (Read Joel 2:30–32.)

Question: How old are you? There's not a magic age between old and young. It's not a question of dreams or visions, but do you experience either? In your life, what has to change for a Daniel-type relationship with God? Is it worth the price of time, energy and shifting priorities for you?

___

___

What needs to change in your life concerning your children or grandchildren? Is God getting your attention as part of a repenting generation? Are you praying for the next generation to experience the Holy Spirit more powerfully than your generation every imagined?

▲▲▲▲▲▲▲

THE DAY OF PENTECOST

Pentecost is the Greek name for the Jewish Festival of Weeks. The Greek name actually means "fiftieth" and denotes the fact that this festival was held fifty days following Passover. It was a harvest festival and is considered the birthday of the church. The three thousand converts on this day became the first fruits of the great harvest into the kingdom of God that continues to this day.

Pentecost, along with Passover and the Feast of Tabernacles, was one of the three feasts where every male in Israel was required to come to Jerusalem. The Book of Ruth became the primary Old Testament book of Pentecost because Ruth, a non-Israelite, came into the covenant family at harvest time and became a vital link in the birth of Israel's King David. Pentecost was also remembered as the day that the Lord gave the Ten Commandments to Moses at Mount Sinai.

Pentecost does not belong only to denominational groups known as Pentecostals. It is a vital part of the Christian liturgical calendar and is the longest season of the church year. Green is the color of Pentecost vestments, which implies planting, fruitfulness and harvest. Discipleship and Holy Spirit themes dominate the teaching and preaching texts of this season.

THE PROMISE HAPPENS WITH POWER

What's ten days of waiting? If your delivery date on a baby is ten days late, you're ready to be delivered. In some respects, that describes the ten days between the Ascension of Christ and the coming of the Holy Spirit at Pentecost. We've already seen that Jesus told the disciples to go to Jerusalem and wait for the promise of the Father. (Read Luke 24:49; Acts 1:8.) Simple obedience and trust in the Lord's timing are critical components of life in the Spirit.

While in Jerusalem the disciples were busy. They were in unity, prayer and supplication (Acts 1:14). They even took

These all continued with one accord in prayer and supplication, with the women and Mary the mother of Jesus, and with His brothers.

—Acts 1:14

care of church business by selecting someone to fill the place of Judas, Jesus' betrayer. (Read Acts 1:15–26). By the time the ten days ended at Pentecost, there were one hundred twenty men and women in the upper room.

The account of Pentecost in Acts 2 is riveting. The one hundred twenty knew it was a Jewish festival and were together on that day. Remember that the Jewish day began at sunset, so the reference to "fully come" refers to nine in the morning (Acts 2:15). As they continued in spiritual unity, a sound from heaven like a mighty rushing wind suddenly filled the whole house. The one hundred twenty were sitting in this room filled with the sound of wind. This was more than physical wind; this was the active presence of the Holy Spirit as the breath of God swirling in the midst.

As the sound continued, divided tongues of fire sat upon each person. These vivid symbols of the Holy Spirit—wind and fire—were physical signs of Spirit power that began to fill each person. The Holy Spirit was "poured out" upon them as though they were empty vessels filled to overflowing. Languages flowed "as the Spirit gave them utterance" (Acts 2:4).

Speaking in other languages is a characteristic of Pentecost.

As the one hundred twenty spoke in other languages, people heard "the wonderful works of God" proclaimed (v. 11). Some thought that the people in the upper room were drunk with new wine. The apostle Peter quoted Joel 2:28–32 and began to preach the gospel. As a result of the Holy Spirit's power, three thousand people were converted and baptized that day (Acts 2:41).

Then those who gladly received his word were baptized; and that day about three thousand souls were added to them.
—Acts 2:41

THE POWER OF HOLY SPIRIT LANGUAGE

Speaking in other languages is a characteristic of Pentecost. It's one of the reasons why people sometimes scoff, "Are you one of those tongue-talkers? Are you a babbler? You mean you speak in unknown tongues?" But it is a very important part of the Christian life and purpose of the Holy Spirit in the world.

INITIAL EVIDENCE

Most Pentecostal churches believe that speaking in tongues is the initial evidence that a person has received the baptism of the Holy Spirit. The reason for this position is that in nearly every instance in the Book of Acts when someone received the baptism of the Holy Spirit, tongues were evident. Let's review the biblical evidence. Read each portion of scripture as you read the text below.

Acts 2:1–4: One hundred twenty people spoke in other tongues when the Holy Spirit came in Pentecostal power. In this instance they were speaking in languages they did not previously know, but were known by the hearers. Some commentators have suggested that this is primarily a miracle of hearing. That is, the one hundred twenty spoke in their native language of Aramaic, but the other people heard in their language. This interpretation is not supported by the Bible. There the emphasis is upon the miracle of speech, not the miracle of hearing. (Read Acts 2:4, 6, 11.)

Acts 10:44–47: The Gentile Cornelius and his household received the baptism of the Holy Spirit and spoke with other tongues just as the Jews did in Acts 2:4.

Acts 19:1–6: The converts at Ephesus were Christians, but they had not received the baptism of the Holy Spirit. In fact, they told the apostle Paul they didn't even know there was a Holy Spirit. When Paul laid his hands on them, "the Holy Spirit came upon them, and they spoke with tongues and prophesied."

1 Corinthians 14: The apostle Paul presumes that most Christians speak in other tongues and encourages that it continue but with order, especially in worship services. There are three citations in Acts where the baptism of the Holy Spirit is mentioned but tongues are not described. Acts 4:31 describes Christians praying together and the house being shaken (probably by the "wind"). They were filled with the Holy Spirit "and spoke the word of God with boldness." Acts 8:14–19 is when Peter and John came to Samaria to confirm the evangelistic work of Philip. It is clear from this text that the baptism of the Holy Spirit is a separate spiritual experience from conversion (v. 12). Peter and John prayed that the new believers would receive the Holy Spirit, and they did. While the text does not say they spoke in tongues, it is clear that when Peter and John laid hands on them something happened that intrigued the sorcerer Simon. It is reasonable to assume that tongues were the initial evidence. Acts 9:17 describes the conversion of Saul (Paul) and his reception of the baptism of the Holy Spirit. While tongues are not mentioned, we know from 1 Corinthians 14:18 that Paul spoke in tongues more than the other Corinthian believers.

There are many Spirit-filled believers who disagree with the historic Pentecostal position regarding speaking in tongues as the initial evidence. Some disagree with the interpretation of the biblical data. Others have been turned off by some of the confusing ways that this view has been articulated. For instance, there are some Pentecostals who believe that you are not saved unless you speak in other tongues. That view is not biblical, and it confuses the indwelling of the Spirit in every Christian with the filling that is the baptism of the Holy Spirit. There are even some Christians who totally reject speaking in tongues for the modern era and believe it is a manifestation of the devil. But that view is as distorted as the one previously described.

One thing is certain—the Book of Acts points in the direction of speaking in tongues as a primary, if not initial, evidence of the baptism of the Holy Spirit. A Spirit-filled person will likely speak in other tongues as a personal prayer language or for some other scriptural purpose, because the Holy Spirit is active in divine/human communications.

Another thing is certain—speaking in tongues is not a badge of spiritual superiority. Christian love to one another and to the lost is what makes the lasting impact. (Read 1 Corinthians 13.)

In Joel 2 we saw the importance of communication with prophecy, dreams and visions. Through the Bible we see God communicating to us. The world was created by the "word" of God (Gen. 1:3). The living Word, Jesus Christ, "became flesh and dwelt among us . . . full of grace and truth" (John 1:14). The Bible has been given to us as the Word of God. (Read Hebrews 4:12.) Jesus said that the Holy Spirit would lead us into all truth. That truth is found in the Bible, and the Holy Spirit speaks to our spirit in languages that transcend the limitations of our natural languages.

The event in Acts 2 is the New Testament answer to the problems posed in the tower of Babel story. (Read Genesis 11.) That incident describes humanity's efforts to become like God. At that time humanity had a common language, and this fleshly unity could have meant the destruction of humanity. God confused the languages of the earth so that humanity would not be able to develop a false unity leading to its own devastation.

But there remained the need for something, a language of faith that can unite humanity under the kingdom of God. That language was first manifested in Acts 2, and its first message was the gospel of the kingdom of God ("the wonderful acts of God"). That language continues to this day in a multitude of forms and expressions affecting groups and individuals.

PURPOSES FOR SPEAKING IN TONGUES

There are four major uses of speaking in tongues in the Bible.

Initial evidence of the baptism of the Holy Spirit

As we read above, speaking in tongues is considered by many to be the initial evidence that a person has been baptized in the Holy Spirit. When you receive the baptism of the Holy Spirit, the Spirit who dwells inside you comes in a different dimension of His presence and power. He is "poured out" upon you and "fills" you. He comes to give you supernatural power as Christ's witness in the world. This is the Spirit's way of taking over your speech as you surrender your ability to speak to the Spirit. You may be aware of meaningless syllables in your conscious mind. Don't worry; you have not made that up. That is the language of the Holy Spirit, and He is speaking to Himself through your spirit. He wants you to speak those words audibly.

As you speak in tongues, you proclaim the victory of Christ in ways that change the spiritual atmosphere around you and others.

In the spiritual realm around you, spiritual darkness hears those words that are words of Holy Spirit power, love, light and victory. As you speak in tongues, you proclaim the victory of Christ in ways that change the spiritual atmosphere around you and others. It has nothing to do with how you feel about it. It has everything to do with the Spirit gaining greater dominion in your life and service for Christ. The Bible gives several examples of tongues as initial evidence of the baptism of the Spirit. (Read Acts 10:44–47; 19:1–7.)

For the purpose of evangelism

Acts 2:1–4 is the prime biblical example of tongues being used as a tool of evangelism, as the one hundred twenty spoke in thirteen different languages to convey the wonderful acts of God. There are numerous accounts of individuals who have encountered people groups whose language they did not naturally know and were supernaturally anointed to speak in that language as they witnessed of Christ. In the early days of the twentieth-century Pentecostal revival, there were hundreds of people who testified of speaking in languages they did not previously know with the fact validated by people present who did speak that language. Today, there are incidents where someone will speak in tongues, and there will be listeners in a worship service who will hear the message in their language and be convinced of the power of God.

As a message to a congregation

The use of tongues to convey a message is discussed in 1 Corinthians 14. The Corinthian church, like all New Testament churches, was a Spirit-filled church. The gifts of the Spirit operated freely, sometimes too freely. Paul addressed a situation where congregants were speaking in tongues more than in the known dialect (Greek in that church). Paul provided order so that the gospel could be preached (prophecy) in a language that the average person could understand. Paul did not prohibit speaking in tongues in the worship service; he simply provided order for the exercise of this gift (1 Cor. 14:39–40).

Therefore, brethren, desire earnestly to prophesy, and do not forbid to speak with tongues. Let all things be done decently and in order.
—1 Corinthians 14:39–40

Pursue love, and desire spiritual gifts, but especially that you may prophesy.
—1 Corinthians 14:1

Paul's guidelines remain instructive today.

1. Love is the primary motivator of any spiritual gift, and it is acceptable to desire spiritual gifts (1 Cor. 14:1). Usually the most fruitful gifts in congregational life are those that people understand. This is true of the gift of prophecy, which has a threefold purpose—edification, exhortation and comfort.

2. There is an order and authority in Christian worship services. (Read 1 Corinthians 14:26–40). Order is not contrary to the Spirit. The Spirit creates order from chaos and establishes order in the Christian community. A congregation without order is not a superspiritual church but a place of confusion where lawlessness easily asserts itself.

3. Those who speak in tongues for the congregation, usually alone and aloud, should be certain that there are people present who normally can interpret (1 Cor. 14:28). In Corinth it was common for several people to speak in tongues (meant as a message to the church) at the same time or back to back without interpretation. Paul ordered them to speak two or, at the most, three in turn, and someone should interpret (v. 27).

4. The word *interpretation* does not mean a translation of the tongue message but an interpretation of the spirit of the message. The tongue message may be two minutes in length and the interpretation one or four minutes. The reason: It is not a word-for-word translation, but the Holy Spirit gives the interpreter spiritual insight into the message.

All these guidelines should apply in a contemporary setting. Many Spirit-filled congregations discourage impromptu messages in tongues that can be emotionally driven or disruptive. Instead, people are encouraged to come to leaders in the church at a given point and share their heart. At that point the person who feels the Spirit's prompting has obeyed the Lord and submitted it to the leadership. The leadership has the responsibility to determine when and if the message should be given.

The capacity to control the message in tongues by the human will is asserted in 1 Corinthians 14:28: "If there is no interpreter, let him keep silent in church, and let him speak to himself and to God." The Holy Spirit does not violate your will and reason. The Spirit's message is transrational and His methods are not irrational. The prompting of the Spirit with a message in tongues for the congregation should cause you to assess the following:

- Is this the right time?
- Are the usual people who interpret present?
- What are the established patterns of order and authority to which I should submit?

If anyone speaks in a tongue, let there be two or at the most three, each in turn, and let one interpret. But if there is no interpreter, let him keep silent in church, and let him speak to himself and to God.
—1 Corinthians 14:27–28

For he who speaks in a tongue does not speak to men but to God, for no one understands him; however, in the spirit he speaks mysteries … For if I pray in a tongue, my spirit prays, but my understanding is unfruitful. What is the conclusion then? I will pray with the spirit, and I will also pray with the understanding. I will sing with the spirit, and I will also sing with the understanding.
—1 Corinthians 14:2, 14–15

If any of those factors cannot be determined, then you should exercise your Spirit-sanctified will and pray the message in tongues under your breath.

Singing and praying in the Spirit

Paul mentioned this important part of the Spirit-filled life in 1 Corinthians 14:2, 14–15 as well as in other portions of his letters. The human will is part of the exercise of this dimension of the Spirit. If you do not have a prayer language, you are missing a powerful avenue of spiritual blessing in your life. The release of this language in your personal life is powerful and can transform your walk with Christ.

In this prayer language you grow in your capacity to speak in the Spirit's unique language designed for you. The Spirit is praying to the Father and Son through your spirit, mind, will and body. Just as you grow in the vocabulary and syntax of known language, you should grow in the expressions and richness of the Spirit's song and prayer language. You will be conscious of meaningless syllables. Remember you have proclaimed Jesus as Lord and willingly surrendered your mind, soul and body to Him. You can trust what His Spirit is placing in your mind. He asks you to speak willingly these words and thereby release the Spirit's language as He confronts Satan's plans against you and constructs His divine purpose for your life.

When you pray in the Spirit, you are praying to God and praying spiritual mysteries (1 Cor. 14:2). Your conscious mind is not aware of these mysteries. Human language cannot comprehend them. But your spirit needs these mysteries conveyed in the depths of your being. This is where the Holy Spirit is preparing you for changes, conflicts, struggles and opportunities that He has before you.

This is what Paul meant when he wrote, "If I pray in a tongue, my spirit prays, but my understanding is unfruitful" (v. 14). Although his Greek- and Hebrew-speaking mind did not understand what the Spirit was saying in tongues, Paul knew that something powerful was happening in his inner man. That's why he concluded, "I will pray with the spirit, and I will also pray with the understanding. I will sing with the spirit, and I will also sing with the understanding" (v. 15).

Paul's insight into the Holy Spirit and the revelation of divine mysteries in us is further developed in 1 Corinthians 2:7–16. (Read this portion of Scripture.) Using Isaiah 64:4 and 65:17, Paul wrote, "Eye has not seen, nor ear heard, nor have entered into the heart of man the things which God has prepared for those who love" (1 Cor. 2:9). This meant that God's ultimate purposes for us cannot be discerned by the flesh but only through the Spirit. The things God has prepared for us are revealed to us "through His Spirit" (v. 10).

Only the Holy Spirit "knows the things of God" and brings life to our spirit (v. 11). The Holy Spirit who dwells in us at conversion seeks to bring to knowledge "the things that have been freely given to us by God" (v. 12). The Spirit does this as we speak words "which the Holy Spirit teaches" (v. 13). The natural man considers this foolishness and therefore misses what God has in store for him (v. 14). The natural man may be a Christian but a believer who operates in the realm of the rational. This believer fails to enjoy the fullness of what the Spirit of God inside of him seeks to give.

God's ultimate purposes for us cannot be discerned by the flesh but only through the Spirit.

But the natural man does not receive the things of the Spirit of God, for they are foolishness to him; nor can he know them, because they are spiritually discerned.

—1 Corinthians 2:14

HOW TO RECEIVE THE BAPTISM OF THE HOLY SPIRIT

If you have been born again, you already have the Holy Spirit dwelling in you. The Holy Spirit seeks to establish Christ's personality and life in every aspect of your life. One way the Spirit does this is to fill you with Himself through the baptism of the Holy Spirit. This baptism is different from when you were baptized in water as testimony of your faith in Christ. This baptism is the one Jesus promised—a baptism of the Holy Spirit and fire.

Like all of God's blessings, you receive the baptism of the Holy Spirit by faith. You cannot become good enough, nor can you make it happen. It is a gift of grace. But you can ask for it. That is where to start. With a humble heart, ask the Holy Spirit to fill you and empower you for greater service to Christ. The Spirit will draw to your attention any willful sins that need to be confessed and forsaken. After confession and repentance, ask the Holy Spirit to be poured out over your entire life. Begin to

praise the Father, the Son and the Holy Spirit, and offer your praise aloud. As you pray, you may find your lips stammering or have meaningless syllables in your mind. Begin to speak, because that is how the Spirit gives you the utterance.

Remember that the baptism of the Holy Spirit is to help you be a more effective witness for Christ. Speaking in tongues is the Spirit's assurance to you that He is taking over more of your life. Ask the Holy Spirit to give you a prayer language and begin to make that a daily part of your life.

LET'S TALK ABOUT IT

If you started reading this book and knew nothing of the Holy Spirit beforehand, this chapter has either intrigued you or scared you to death! Your background may have rejected the baptism of the Holy Spirit as fanatical, wild and even unscriptural. Your present interest in spiritual stuff may make this appear to be little more than one more piece of New Age mysticism.

But this is really the key to growing in your spiritual life. Go back through this chapter again and answer the following questions as you reinforce your knowledge.

▲ What are the key lessons you learned from the Feast of Weeks in the Old Testament?

____

____

▲▲▲▲▲▲▲

▲ Why is the phrase "pour out" used of the baptism of the Holy Spirit? What is the Old Testament background for this term?

____

____

▲▲▲▲▲▲▲

▲ What three aspects of communication are mentioned in Joel 2 and fulfilled in Acts 2?

____

____

▲▲▲▲▲▲▲

TIME TO PLUG IN TO THE HOLY SPIRIT

It really is time to plug in to the Holy Spirit. If you've received the baptism of the Holy Spirit and already speak in other tongues, this is a time to grow in your knowledge of what the Spirit is doing in your life in these mysteries. Jude 20 is an important verse for you: "But you, beloved, building yourselves up on your most holy faith, praying in the Holy Spirit." As you pray in tongues, the Holy Spirit edifies or builds you up in the faith. This means that Christian growth is more than Bible knowledge, accountable relationships and getting wiser. It means that something is happening in your inner self through this prayer language.

If you have not received the baptism of the Holy Spirit, there is no better time than the present. You don't have to be in church. You don't have to have the right music. You don't have to have people all around. It's just you and the Holy Spirit. He already lives in your heart. You've probably felt His presence and recognize His prompting. Now He wants to speak through you. Don't be afraid; the blood of Jesus protects you. Go ahead; jump into the river of the Spirit.

Holy Spirit, I open my life to this dimension of Your presence and power. I want to be a more effective witness for Jesus. I want the fullness of everything Father God has for me. I ask in Jesus' holy name that You will baptize me now in the Holy Spirit. Pour Your love into my heart in overflowing measure. Fill me with Your grace. Take over my speech and teach my spirit how to praise You in heavenly languages. In the name of the Father, the Son and the Holy Spirit. Amen.

CHAPTER SIX

Looking for a Plugged-in, Turned-on Church?

IN THIS CHAPTER YOU WILL DISCOVER THAT . . .

- ▲ The first generation of Christians used spiritual weapons of prayer, a profound sense of Christian community, fellowship and obedience.
- ▲ The Holy Spirit is the best organizational guru and negotiator of human conflict in the universe.
- ▲ The Holy Spirit uses people who are in a right relationship with others and faithful to the calling on their lives.

IN TWENTY-EIGHT BRIEF CHAPTERS, THE NEW TESTAMENT GIVES THE HEADLINE NEWS ACCOUNTS OF THE POWER OF THE HOLY SPIRIT AT WORK IN THE EARLY CHURCH. Known as The Acts of the Apostles, the book could be called The Acts of the Holy Spirit. There is a cast of real people, including Peter, John, Stephen and Paul. They are backed up by the likes of Priscilla, Aquila, Apollos, Barnabas and Philip. They are not isolated, "do-my-own-thing-by-the-Spirit-bless-God" Christians, but they serve with one another and local congregations.

They may be the cast, but the producer and director is the Holy Spirit. In this redemptive drama, the spotlight is on the Holy Spirit. It's really His story about how He works in the church to spread the message of Jesus Christ and the kingdom of God.

Actually, this book of the Holy Spirit is still being written. The biblical record is not a fairy tale where "they all lived happily ever after." Daily the Holy Spirit composes additional chapters. Each generation has its contemporary edition with a new cast of apostles, prophets, evangelists, pastors, teachers and a host of faithful people. Regardless of size or location, each local congregation is a laboratory of the Spirit where people are redeemed and changed by the Spirit for the glory of God.

In this chapter we're going to plug in to several local congregations described primarily in the twenty-eight chapters of the Acts of the Holy Spirit. It's going to be a great ride across two continents, multiple cultures and, in some cases, nearly sixty years of dynamic history.

Oh, you've read the Book of Acts before? Sounds like history to you? I tell you what—give this chapter at least the next five minutes. I think the Holy Spirit will help us hook you on history, at least for this chapter!

THERE'S FIRE IN JERUSALEM

Jesus promised that He would ignite a fire: "I came to send fire on the earth, and how I wish it were already kindled!" (Luke 12:49). A few verses later He shattered those illusions about being a nice guy wrapped in a mealy-mouthed, first-century version of "Why can't we all just get along?" Instead, Jesus announced, "Do you suppose that I came to give peace on earth? I tell you, not at all, but rather division" (v. 51).

Pentecost started an uncontrollable fire, which spread across Jerusalem from house to house and synagogue to synagogue. The fire started with Peter's radical preaching that if you want to be saved, you have to turn to Jesus as the Messiah. In Jerusalem, now two thousand years later, that message still goes over like a lead balloon! But there have always been people, first Jews and later Gentiles, who "were cut to the heart, and said... 'Men and brethren, what shall we do?'" (Acts 2:37). In the first weeks of the newly birthed church, thousands of people responded to the message that the same Jesus who had been crucified had been raised from the dead. They included average people, dedicated lay leaders (Pharisees), temple priests and Jews from faraway Greek-speaking cultures as well as Palestinian Jews.

Pentecost started an uncontrollable fire.

The message that Jesus is Israel's Messiah was radical (*Messiah* and *Christ* mean "anointed"). The message meant that God's promises to Abraham, David and the prophets had been fulfilled. To proclaim Jesus as Messiah meant to proclaim Him as "the way, the truth, and the life" and that "no one comes to the Father" except through Him (John 14:6).

Today that message remains controversial. Religious pluralism demands that all faiths be considered of equal value, each providing the same access to happiness and God. Modern syncretism is comfortable with that demand. It is uncomfortable when anyone claims exclusion. But that's what happens in the gospel. It is the message that faith in Jesus Christ is the only way to have peace with God.

But this exclusivism is designed to point to the right way, not to keep people out. The Holy Spirit proclaims this message so that anyone anywhere can hear this Good News. Salvation is not a mystery you discover by hard work, chance or fate. By God's grace, salvation discovers you, gives you the map home and leads the way.

The first Christians, like Jesus, were Jews. They worshiped at the temple and synagogue, memorized and loved the Torah and observed Passover. But other Jews found it hard to believe that a Galilean preacher, executed as a blasphemer, could really be the Messiah. Besides, the rumors about His resurrection were easily explained—His disciples stole the body. (Read Matthew 27:64.)

Through the Holy Spirit, the first Christians started connecting the dots of Jesus' teachings:

- If Jesus died for our sins, why do we need to sacrifice more lambs?
- If my body is the temple of the Holy Spirit, why do we need the Jerusalem temple?
- If Jesus fulfilled the demands of the Law of Moses, why do I need to worry about all these commandments?
- If Jesus died for the whole world, how do I relate to Gentiles?
- If the Holy Spirit is poured out on all flesh, what does that mean about average people as servants of God?
- If the Holy Spirit is making us priests and kings to our God, why do we need a special group of priests?

▲ If the Holy Spirit has redeemed us and poured His love into our hearts, what are the practical ways we should live with one another?

It doesn't take a brain surgeon to figure out that the institutional Jewish faith started feeling uncomfortable about this new and growing "Jesus is Messiah" movement springing up in their backyard. Arguments, legal actions, threats, beatings, expulsion and even death were used to try and extinguish this dangerous fire called Christianity. But those efforts did little more than fan sparks into dry fields, igniting a Holy Spirit firestorm.

CHRISTIANS AND JEWS

It's a shame that over the past two thousand years many Christians have been deceived by the demonically inspired spirit of anti-Semitism. This spirit has caused indescribable suffering for Jews and has discredited the cause of Christ. There is no excuse for Christians to hate Jews. The argument that the Jews are responsible for the death of Jesus is false. All of us are responsible for His death because all of us are sinners. Christians have compromised their ability to witness freely to Jews because of our intellectual foolishness and failure to understand the Bible.

The apostle Paul knew that Gentile Christians were called to live in God's blessings and in such power of the Holy Spirit that Jews would become jealous and turn to Christ. (Read Romans 9–11.) Instead, we have lived dominated by worldly political and economic agendas, which have limited the corporate witness of the church.

In recent years various Christian groups have publicly asked forgiveness of past sins against Jews (and other ethnic groups). This is an important first step in allowing the Holy Spirit to bring about an atmosphere of reconciliation. Christians can continue this spirit by rejecting anti-Semitic attitudes and actions locally and translocally.

The first generation of Christians did not respond with carnal weapons but instead turned to the Holy Spirit. Their weapons were spiritual weapons of prayer, a profound sense of Christian community and fellowship and obedience to the risen Lord. (Read Acts 2:42; 4:23–37; 5:29, 32.)

Question: Acts 2:42–47 and 4:32–35 describe how the new community of Christians lived in Jerusalem and Judea. In your opinion, what are the top three dimensions of how these Christians lived that you would like to see in the church today?

▲▲▲▲▲▲▲

Jesus' statement in John 14:6 that He is "the way, the truth, and the life. No one comes to the Father except through Me" is pretty strong. In light of the claims of other religions, how do you interpret the apparent exclusivism of Jesus' claim? Do you agree with His claim?

▲▲▲▲▲▲▲

THERE'S A FIRE IN THE HOUSE

"I want a church just like the first-century church," the young, visionary, energetic pastor exclaimed. Well, there's good news and bad news. The bad news is that two thousand years of history and cultural change make that desire all but impossible. The good news is twofold. First, the Lord wants the Holy Spirit working in the church today with the same mission and power, but in the context of our generation. Second, the young minister probably will get a church similar to the early church, but in ways he might not like. The same imperfect people of two thousand years ago, including apostles and prophets, have not changed all that much. We just dress differently, speak different languages and communicate via e-mail, cell phones and wireless. We have the same opportunities and challenges presented by Holy Spirit fire.

Sometimes fire refuses to do what we want it to. A back draft, an explosion of gases from incomplete combustion when combined with air, can occur with devastating results. In a sense, that's what happened in Acts 5:1–11 and 6:1–7 within the Christian community. (Read these scriptures.)

In spite of appearances, outside persecution was not the big problem. The big problem was inside where there were people in a willful state of "incomplete combustion." That is, they were intentionally lying to the Holy Spirit and

manipulating the people for God for their own purposes. When the "air" of the Holy Spirit through the gift of discernment came to Peter, Ananias and his wife, Sapphira, died. Years later this incident must have run through Peter's mind when he wrote, "The time has come for judgment to begin at the house of God; and if it begins with us first, what will be the end of those who do not obey the gospel of God?" (1 Pet. 4:17).

The second discovery the infant church faced was that growth has its own challenges. Just as children outgrow their shoes too quickly for a family budget and grammar school presents a new set of outside influences that Mom and Dad cannot control, so the early church faced challenges of growth and conflict.

Conflict is a given in human dynamics, and Spirit-filled believers who expect differently live disappointed and frustrated lives.

The important lesson from Acts 6 is that the Holy Spirit was prepared for these challenges. Conflict is not necessarily bad. It is one of the avenues the Holy Spirit uses to get us out of our comfort zones of power, control and complacency. This conflict had group dynamics involved, as Greek-speaking Christian widows believed that Hebrew-speaking Christian widows were getting more in the daily distribution of goods in the new community. Take this situation, change the names of the groups in the average church, add feelings of neglect and you have another Holy Spirit opportunity, such as:

- Youth ministry gets more budget than choir ministry.
- We sing more praise choruses than hymns.
- The pastor spends all his time with young adults and doesn't visit the nursing homes.

And the list goes on.

Interestingly, the Bible does not blame anyone for this conflict. Conflict is a given in human dynamics, and Spirit-filled believers who expect differently live disappointed and frustrated lives. Rather than playing the blame game, the Holy Spirit led to a solution. The solution was based on accepting God-given roles ("We will give ourselves continually to prayer and to the ministry of the word"—6:4) and recognizing that the Spirit has gifted people whom He has called and equipped to handle the problem. (Read Acts 6:3.)

The Holy Spirit is the best organizational guru and negotiator at human conflict resolution in the universe. The Spirit led to a solution where the problem-solvers had ownership and authority to act: "Seek out from among you seven men . . . " (Acts 6:3). The Spirit gave the broad parameters—these men were to be "of good reputation, full of the Holy Spirit and wisdom" (v. 3). The Spirit maintained the leadership's authority and respect: "Whom we may appoint over this business," and "They prayed and laid hands on them" (vv. 3, 6).

Situations that usually damage churches through deceit and discord are handled by the Holy Spirit at work in anointed people. While the names and situations change, the problems and solutions remain constant through the guidance of the Holy Spirit.

Question: Identify organizational and conflict-resolution principles the Holy Spirit used to guide the early church.

____

____

▲▲▲▲▲▲▲

How did Ananias and Sapphira try to deceive the Jerusalem church?

____

____

▲▲▲▲▲▲▲

Have you ever left a church because of a church split? How long did it take you to recover? Can you identify how the Holy Spirit used that situation to help you grow?

____

____

▲▲▲▲▲▲▲

LET'S GATHER AROUND THE FIRE

Looking back two thousand years creates its own problems in seeing accurately, but the Holy Spirit still gives us a good look at the church in Jerusalem. We've already seen enough to know that a Spirit-filled church is not perfect. Everyone—including leaders—makes mistakes in judgment and sometimes sins against the Lord. But there are enough evidences of genuine life that can be seen in people who are still attracted to the Lord, whom we confess and serve.

Two places in Acts give additional insight into the Jerusalem church. It is important to remember that this church, as in every city in the first century, was composed of one church that met in numerous houses or buildings. It had a larger identity across the city in terms of leaders, but in its daily life it was ordered around smaller groups of people. It was not a place where once a week you met with hundreds or thousands of people and then disappeared into the world for another six days until it was "time to go to church." That modern picture is a distortion of the Spirit's design for the body of Christ. The practice of the early church was that they met daily in the course of normal living. They probably met as a group at sunrise on Sunday mornings to celebrate the Resurrection and get to the chores of life for that day. (For Jews, Sunday was the *second day* of the week, a regular workday.) They gathered around the Spirit's fire in smaller groups of intimacy to tell the stories of faith, pray for one another and share intimately in the warmth of the Spirit's presence.

These gatherings, whether large or small, had common characteristics. They had one common faith in the apostles' doctrine. At that time Jesus' words and actions were not written in books but told person to person, group to group. They did not gather for passive Bible studies, but for dynamic "Jesus studies" as His life was poured into them. The apostles who personally saw and heard Jesus authenticated these stories. These accounts showed that Jesus was Israel's Messiah and demonstrated how He fulfilled Israel's story in the Torah, the Writings (Psalms, Proverbs) and the Prophets.

The small groups gathered for fellowship. But this was more than coffee and cake, stay an hour and go home. This was *koinonia*, a new kind of fellowship where a new community was taking shape. They knew that Jesus did not die merely to save their souls and create a private religion. Jesus died to create a new community, a new witness, of His grace and power. That's why many early Christians realized that private property rights were not as important as most of us make them. In fact, since the love of God had been poured into their hearts, the Spirit led them to genuine concern for one another. The new motto became: "As needed, what's mine is yours, and what's yours is mine." It was not a dictatorial system of communal living, but it arose from genuine love and community based on the love of Christ. No one was forced, and it appears that it was not the primary characteristic of all early Christian churches. But it remains a powerful reminder for us today as we discover afresh what it means to be Holy Spirit people.

The living word of testimony created faith, led to miracles, changed attitudes and touched the daily lives of people.

Part of their community life was experienced in "the breaking of bread." This was a fellowship meal where the poor received food. But it was not a token handout given just at Thanksgiving and Christmas. It occurred daily so that all could eat. This meal created the environment for breaking barriers of age, culture, race, language, education, power and money.

It was not a meal predicated upon man-made goals to restructure human society and redistribute wealth. It was a meal focused on the great meal of reconciliation and breaking down barriers—the Supper of the Lord. They received bread and wine in remembrance of Jesus. In this setting the Holy Spirit brought to their remembrance His words and deeds. The living word of testimony created faith, led to miracles, changed attitudes and touched the daily lives of people throughout Jerusalem. It was the point in their day when they knew that He was there with them.

THE HOLY SPIRIT AND THE LORD'S SUPPER

Jesus instituted this Eucharist (thanksgiving) meal as part of the Passover meal. He fulfilled the purpose of the Passover meal as the last meal He had with His disciples

before His crucifixion. (Read Matthew 26:26–29; Mark 14:22–25; Luke 22:14–38.) He commanded them to continue this meal "in remembrance of Me." In this meal He was present "in the breaking of bread" (Luke 24:28–35). To eat this meal is to eat His body and drink His blood. (Read John 6:53–58.)

The apostle Paul understood the spiritual implications of this meal as part of the fellowship meal. Sadly, within twenty years the fellowship meal and Lord's Supper had become a place of social and moral division. First Corinthians 11:17–34 describes how the fellowship meal had become self-centered, and people were actually getting drunk. (See verse 21.) It appears that Paul was so concerned that the spiritual vitality of the Eucharist was being ignored that he separated the two meals in order to preserve the value of both.

It would be a wonderful thing if Christians could rediscover the unity and power of the Lord's Supper and Spirit-inspired fellowship meals together as living symbols of reconciliation and hope.

Unfortunately, the Eucharist has become a point of division between Christians. Some Christians serve it only to those who belong to their church (closed communion). Christianity is divided along Catholic and Protestant lines regarding how Jesus is present in the Eucharist. How does a powerful and simple meal get so complex?

In the context of the Jesus meal and the intimacy where rich and poor were on equal footing, they learned how to pray. Their prayers included the rich liturgy of the Psalter, the prayers at the temple and new dimensions of personal and corporate prayer in the Spirit.

Earlier reference was made to the sin of Ananias and Sapphira. (Read Acts 5.) The magnitude of their sin can be seen as more than the personal sin of lying against the Holy Spirit. They lied against the Spirit's work in establishing a new community based on the death and resurrection of Jesus. Their lie was a lie against the reality of divine love shaping human lives. The lie was not a bad decision on their part. Their lie was the antithesis of the Spirit's power in their midst.

Question: How did the Holy Spirit structure the early church to meet needs?

___

___

▲▲▲▲▲▲▲

The Lord's Supper served three functions in the early church. First, the Lord was present through this meal. Second, it provided a vehicle to tell the gospel. Third, it provided a living example of reconciliation and healing. How does this compare to your experience of the Lord's Supper?

▲▲▲▲▲▲▲

Although apparently not institutionalized, the practice of the early church regarding private property is interesting. What is your gut-level response to this? Is it, "I don't like that idea; people will take advantage of you"? Or is it, "I know it's idealistic, but I wish I could experience a small piece of it"? In your own words, describe your response:

▲▲▲▲▲▲▲

ANTIOCH: NEW FRONTIERS OF THE SPIRIT

The church spread from city to city. The first major shift occurred from Jerusalem to Antioch, Syria. This city was near the Mediterranean Sea in modern southeast Turkey. In many ways it was like a modern city at the crossroads of commerce, politics and culture. The Jewish population was more influenced by Greek culture than the religious confines of Jerusalem. Greek-speaking Jews who fled Judea after the death of Stephen first established the church among other Jews in Antioch. (Read Acts 7.) It was here at Antioch that followers of Jesus were first called Christians (Acts 11:26).

The early church was characterized by two primary attributes:

Individuals had a profound sense of the grace of God.

In the first instance the person of Barnabas is a focal point. He was a Greek-speaking Jewish Christian who graciously participated in the communal aspect of the Jerusalem church. He sold land and "brought the money and laid it at the apostles' feet" (Acts 4:37). With great courage and compassion, he befriended the newly converted Paul (Acts 9:27). Barnabas

And the disciples were first called Christians in Antioch.

—Acts 11:26

But Barnabas took him and brought him to the apostles. And he declared to them how he had seen the Lord on the road, and that He had spoken to him, and how he had preached boldly at Damascus in the name of Jesus.

—Acts 9:27

remained part of the Jerusalem congregation until the revival in Antioch spread to Gentiles. The Gentiles were converted in large numbers, and new issues of the meaning of the gospel emerged: Should Christian Gentiles be circumcised and observe the worship and lifestyle patterns of the Jews?

Barnabas was sent to Antioch to check out this scene. He saw the "grace of God" in the lives of these newly converted Gentiles and in their meetings with Jewish Christians. While there he thought of Paul. As a Greek-speaking Jewish Christian and former persecutor of Christians, Paul was not overly welcomed among some Jewish Christians in Jerusalem. Realizing that Antioch was exactly where Paul needed to be, Barnabas found Paul in his hometown of Tarsus and brought him to Antioch (a hundred miles as the crow flies).

Communication gifts of the Spirit operated effectively.

The second instance is the dynamic quality of prophetic communication evidenced in Antioch. Prophets came regularly to Antioch to encourage, edify and exhort. A prophet named Agabus prophesied of a great famine, and the Antioch church of Jewish and Gentile Christians "determined to send relief to the brethren dwelling in Judea" (Acts 11:29).

The episode with Agabus reveals Christians ready to hear and obey the prophetic word of the Lord. That readiness is further revealed in an incident in Acts 13:1–4. (Read this scripture.) We will examine several aspects of this story to help you understand the environment in which the Holy Spirit seeks to work.

The Antioch church had identifiable "prophets and teachers." It's worth noting that these are two of the Ascension Gifts of Ephesians 4:11. In the contemporary church the emphasis is more upon apostles, evangelists and pastors. But the Antioch church had prophets and teachers as the primary communication devices of the Holy Spirit.

And He Himself gave some to be apostles, some prophets, some evangelists, and some pastors and teachers.
—Ephesians 4:11

PROPHETS AND TEACHERS

Prophets and teachers are two of the five primary ministries that Christ gave the church following His ascension (more about these ministries will be described in a later chapter). They are named in Ephesians 4:11 along with apostles, evangelists and pastors (some link pastors and teachers together).

What is a prophet? A *prophet* is a person who receives God's message and announces it to the intended audience. That's why the Old Testament prophets said, "Thus says the Lord." A prophet is keenly aware that it is not his or her words but the Lord's words. The contemporary prophet not only hears the Lord speak directly (always a message that conforms to Scripture), but also has "the supernatural ability to interpret the Scriptures in light of the present situation in the church."[1] Prophetic ministry builds up, encourages and exhorts people. (Read 1 Corinthians 14:3.)

What is a teacher? This particular ministry characterizes people who have a supernatural ability to understand and communicate the Word of God. This kind of teaching is more than sharing information. This gift imparts life-transformational knowledge, wisdom and understanding. The apostle Paul was appointed by the Holy Spirit to be a teacher to the Gentiles. (Read 2 Timothy 1:11.)

The Antioch church was a diverse group of Greek and Jewish converts. They came from all over the known world and included people who had been in kings' courts.

Much personal confusion over prophecy, including personal prophecies, could be avoided by the use of wisdom as seen in the Christian community of Antioch.

They were faithful in their worship of the Lord. The word *ministered* is the basis for the English word *liturgy.* It has the sense of an office of ministry wherein people were called and acted faithfully. There is a sense of regularity and normality in this expression. In other words, these prophets and teachers were doing what they normally did. This was not a special revival or period of religious excitement. They were faithfully ministering to the Lord by going about their regular duties. It is important that fasting is additionally mentioned in Acts 13:2. The early church had regular fast days inherited from its Jewish roots. But its mention here implies a time of special focus. As they went about their regular duties, but with a sense of emptying themselves for the Lord, the Holy Spirit spoke. The message was simple, direct and personal. It was a word for Barnabas and Paul (Saul). Here are several key lessons:

- The Holy Spirit spoke through one of the prophets or teachers.

- ▲ The Holy Spirit used people who were in right relationship with others and who were faithful to the calling upon their lives.
- ▲ The Holy Spirit was precise and personal. This was not a general word for everyone but a clear word for two people.
- ▲ Barnabas and Paul did not respond compulsively, but rather the entire group of prophets and teachers tested the word through time (fasting) and further confirmation (prayer).
- ▲ Once the word was confirmed to the satisfaction of the group and to Barnabas and Paul, they obeyed that word.

The principles in these three verses of Acts 13:1–3 are timeless. Much personal confusion over prophecy, including personal prophecies, could be avoided by the use of wisdom as seen in the Christian community of Antioch. The apostolic commission for Barnabas and Paul began with prophets and teachers able to discern, hear and comprehend the word of the Lord.

Question: Why do you think prophets and teachers are emphasized at Antioch rather than apostles and evangelists?

____

____

▲▲▲▲▲▲▲

What does it mean to "minister to the Lord"?

____

____

▲▲▲▲▲▲▲

In light of Acts 13:1–3 and the personal prophecy to Barnabas and Paul, do you believe that the Holy Spirit still speaks with directive personal prophecy to people?

____

____

▲▲▲▲▲▲▲

EPHESUS: FORTY YEARS OF SPIRIT-FILLED LIVING

The gospel spread across the Mediterranean world through numerous evangelists. The Holy Spirit preserved the witness of Paul and his colleagues as the primary testimony for all Christians. One church in particular is described in the New Testament in four specific time frames from about A.D. 55 to A.D. 90. Ephesus was a significant city in western Turkey, located near the modern city of Izmir. Paul first visited this city after his ministry in Corinth. (Read Acts 18–19.) The sequence is important in that it shows that Paul's Spirit-filled ministry in Corinth and the ways the Holy Spirit worked in that church were part of Paul's experience at Ephesus and when he later wrote to the Ephesians. The Holy Spirit used Paul in Ephesus for several purposes.

When Paul arrived he discovered that the disciples there knew only about repentance; they did not know about the baptism of the Holy Spirit (Acts 19:1–2). Paul's first act was to instruct them and lead them to the baptism of the Holy Spirit, where they responded with speaking in tongues (vv. 4–6).

The gospel brought deliverance to individuals and changed the surrounding culture.

Paul established a teaching ministry in the public arena of Ephesian life. The gospel was not hidden in a back alley, but the environment allowed for open discourse for any who were interested. (Read Acts 19:8–10.) Paul stayed over two years in Ephesus, laying a long-lasting foundation upon which the Holy Spirit worked for centuries.

Miracles, exorcisms and the public repudiation of the occult characterized Paul's ministry. (Read Acts 19:11–20.) The gospel brought deliverance to individuals and also penetrated and changed the surrounding culture. The Ephesians worshiped Diana, the Roman goddess of love and fertility. The gospel shattered this idolatry and brought genuine revival to the city and countryside. (Read Acts 19:24–41.)

And it happened, while Apollos was at Corinth, that Paul, having passed through the upper regions, came to Ephesus. And finding some disciples he said to them, "Did you receive the Holy Spirit when you believed?" So they said to him, "We have not so much as heard whether there is a Holy Spirit."
—Acts 19:1–2

Then Paul said, "John indeed baptized with a baptism of repentance, saying to the people that they should believe on Him who would come after him, that is, on Christ Jesus." When they heard this, they were baptized in the name of the Lord Jesus. And when Paul had laid hands on them, the Holy Spirit came upon them, and they spoke with tongues and prophesied.
—Acts 19:4–6

THE GODDESS DIANA

The Greek and Roman mythological world often overlapped with different names for the same commonly understood deities. Artemis (pronounced with accent on the first syllable) was the Greek goddess as Diana was to the Romans. In the Greek world, Zeus was her father and Apollo her twin brother. In the Roman world, Jupiter was her father and Apollo her twin brother. Zeus was king of the Greek gods, and Jupiter was king of the Roman gods. By either name, she was associated as the moon goddess. She was closely associated with the onset of female maturity and childbirth. Prior to marriage, young women prayed to her to insure fertility. She is also associated with hunting. She had a violent, unstable side to her nature and was blamed for the sudden death of women.

Ephesus was known as the temple guardian of the goddess Diana. (Read Acts 19:35.) Silver Diana idols provided a profitable living for workers. She, along with Artemis, was the Greek and Roman version of more ancient fertility cults reaching into deep antiquity. God's commandments regarding idolatry included these gods and goddesses, which often led Israel astray.

The modern environment has produced a revival of some portions of this ancient paganism. This revival is evident in the arts and in the extremes of various interest groups and in spiritual syncretism. Regardless of its version or appeal, paganism is idolatry that Christians are to avoid. This spirit of the world and the Holy Spirit cannot abide in harmony.

Paul had contact with the Ephesian congregation on three other occasions. The first of these three was a farewell visit with the Ephesian church leaders. (Read Acts 20:17–38.) In a tearful meeting, Paul warned these Spirit-filled leaders of dangers that lurked in and around the church.

The second contact was his major letter, known in the New Testament as the Letter to the Ephesians. As if to mock the worldwide appeal of Diana in her various forms, Paul wrote of the universal triumph of the Lord Jesus Christ.

As I urged you when I went into Macedonia—remain in Ephesus that you may charge some that they teach no other doctrine.
—1 Timothy 1:3

The third contact was a letter to Paul's young protégé, Timothy. Timothy was sent by Paul to Ephesus to make sure that false doctrines were not taught (1 Tim. 1:3). There are primary references to the Holy Spirit in this letter that affirm the Spirit's role:

- ▲ In the revelation of Jesus Christ (Read 1 Timothy 3:16.)

- ▲ The Spirit's express warning that in the latter days false doctrines will lead many astray (Read 1 Timothy 4:1–5.)
- ▲ A reminder to Timothy that he received a spiritual gift through prophecy and laying on of hands (Read 1 Timothy 4:14; cf. Acts 13:1–3.)

Thirty years after Paul's letter, the church at Ephesus remained a dynamic and influential congregation. It is probable that it had become the home church of the apostle John and was the leading church among at least seven others in western Turkey. Around A.D. 90 the Roman government initiated what likely was a localized but deadly serious persecution against the churches in that part of Asia Minor. John was imprisoned, and the Holy Spirit presented hope to the apostle in a mighty Revelation of Jesus Christ. Significantly, the church at Ephesus is the first to receive a personal letter from the risen Christ. (Read Revelation 2:1–7.) This church is commended because it recognizes false apostles, but it has lapsed into a formalism without the passion of first love for Christ.

THE BOOK OF REVELATION

Many Christians find this final book of the New Testament confusing and fearful. Interpretations abound trying to give meaning to this book. A popular book series takes one interpretation and wraps fictional characters around it in an effort to understand this book. Regardless of your particular interpretation, or lack thereof, if you will remember certain things, this book will become a powerful witness to Jesus Christ in your life.

1. *This is the revelation of Jesus Christ.* This book is about Jesus Christ and not about Satan, the beast, the Antichrist or anyone else. Jesus is the primary character. In this sense, we really can think of this final book of the New Testament as a fifth gospel of Jesus Christ in that it, like the other four Gospels, reveals important information about Christ and the Father's plans through Him.

2. *This book was written to Christians facing persecution from the government.* There's little doubt that the Christians who read this in Ephesus knew exactly what John meant. Perhaps only Christians who are undergoing persecution can rightfully comprehend the message and intent of this book.

3. *All the horrible things described in this book of the bowls of wrath are actually in the hands of God.* This is a book about divine judgment released against ungodliness.

4. *At the beginning and the end of the book, Jesus is the triumphal Lamb of God.* This book will encourage you when you feel that evil is everywhere and has the final word. No! God has already spoken the final word in Jesus Christ, and His kingdom shall be established in the earth!

5. *A Christian does not need to be afraid of this revelation of Jesus Christ.* However, sinners should be fearful of the consequences of rejecting the gospel.

LET'S TALK ABOUT IT

At this beginning of this chapter I asked you to stay plugged in to the history of the Book of Acts. I hope you did. I also hope you've taken time to read the entire Book of Acts. Let's take a moment to reflect on what we've learned.

▲ Considering that the Holy Spirit is still writing His story, can you identify what chapters are being written through your personal life and through the congregation of the church you regularly attend?

___

___

___

▲▲▲▲▲▲▲

▲ Of the three churches described in this chapter—Jerusalem, Antioch, Ephesus—which would you have rather been part of and why?

___

___

___

▲▲▲▲▲▲▲

▲ Which of the three churches described in this chapter is most like the church you attend now?

___

___

___

▲▲▲▲▲▲▲

TIME TO PLUG IN TO THE HOLY SPIRIT

We've looked at three different churches in three different cultures. In each one the same Holy Spirit showed His power. The Jerusalem church showed the power of Christian community. The Antioch church showed the power of prophetic and teaching ministry, calling forth apostolic ministry. The Ephesian church showed the power of the Spirit to shatter idolatrous demonic strongholds. Today the Holy Spirit, the same Holy Spirit as at Jerusalem, Antioch and Ephesus, continues to show His power regardless of culture and language.

The Acts of the Holy Spirit continues to be written. Don't forget, the Spirit is writing through your life today. Pray these words as you finish reading this chapter:

> *Heavenly Father, forgive me for dominating the pages of my life. I thought this book was about me. No wonder it has seemed so boring and powerless. But now I understand that You are using my life to show Your glory and power. So today, Holy Spirit, write Your stuff on my heart, on my mind, through my actions and words. I want You to clearly reveal Jesus through me. Here I am. Erase the mess I've made, and write the continuing acts of the Holy Spirit through me! Amen.*

CHAPTER SEVEN

God Has Ministry Gifts for You

IN THIS CHAPTER YOU WILL DISCOVER THAT . . .

- ▲ The Holy Spirit will help you to discover, develop and deploy your ministry gifts.
- ▲ The Holy Spirit is the agency through whom the Father and Son manifest divine purposes and glory in the church today.
- ▲ The Holy Spirit wants a person to serve in the body of Christ primarily through ministry gifts.

ADVENT IS THE BEGINNING OF THE CHRISTIAN CHURCH YEAR. This flies in the face of our calendar pattern of thinking about the end of a year on December 31 and the beginning of a new year on January 1. A few years ago while pastoring I decided to take advantage of the newness and opportunities reflected in Advent by preaching on the gifts of the Spirit. Each service beautifully wrapped boxes with the name of a particular spiritual gift were placed around the altar and communion table. The final Sunday of Advent we "opened our gifts" as the congregation focused on the gift of Jesus Christ and the gifts of the Spirit. It was a special time of focus on the celebration of Christmas and the discovering, development and deployment of spiritual gifts as the congregation "unwrapped" the gifts of the Spirit in their lives.

The Holy Spirit has a perfect plan for your life. In Christ, the Holy Spirit has shaped your identity as a new person. The Holy Spirit has certain spiritual gifts for you. Spiritual gifts fall into two main types: equipping and body ministry gifts, and manifestation gifts. Not everyone will be used with manifestation gifts (which will be discussed in the next chapter), but every Christian has one or more ministry gifts. God's eternal plans for you include much more than your ticket to heaven.

His plans include:

- ▲ Reshaping your personality as the fruit of the Spirit matures in you.
- ▲ Bringing other Christians into your life for mutual mentoring and influence.
- ▲ Taking your natural-born abilities and talents and using them for His glory.

- Giving you supernatural gifts of His Holy Spirit, gifts that will amaze and humble you.

The Holy Spirit has a perfect plan for your life.

Well, start thinking about your life. You really do have equipping or body ministry spiritual gifts if you're a Christian. The Holy Spirit is going to help you discover, develop and deploy these gifts. Get ready to unwrap your gifts! By the way, regardless of the season, when it comes to unwrapping the gifts of the Spirit, merry Christmas!

ARE SPIRITUAL GIFTS FOR EVERYONE?

Do you have questions or comments similar to the following?

- "I'm a Christian, but I don't have any spiritual gifts."
- "I really want to serve the Lord! When and how do I receive spiritual gifts?"
- "I want to do more for Jesus. Is it wrong for me to want more gifts?"
- "I'm not perfect. Does the Holy Spirit really use people like me?"

In this section let's take a few moments and answer each of these. It will be a serious soul-searching time for you, but you can do it.

Every Christian has spiritual gift(s).

Angela said, "I'm a Christian, but I don't have any spiritual gifts." She was a gifted, creative artist who worked for a Christian organization. Her local church had a "discover your spiritual gifts" workshop that she attended only because her husband practically made her go. She was petrified that the workshop would show that she had no spiritual gifts.

Why would a born-again Christian feel that way? One reason may be a lack of knowledge. Some people know the teachings of the Bible, but they don't understand that in Christ they are new creatures. The popular saying "What you don't know can't hurt you" is not true in the spiritual realm. What you don't know *can* frustrate God's destiny in your life. Sadly, some Christians have never been taught about spiritual gifts and are seldom encouraged to read the Bible.

When you became a Christian, the Holy Spirit came to live inside of you. He is busy transforming your life into the character of Christ. The Spirit is busy redeeming and redirecting your native talents and abilities. The Spirit is busy releasing into your life gifts that are uniquely meant for you. The failure to know this can leave you spiritually blind, never certain where you fit in the body of Christ.

Another reason that many Christians feel they don't have spiritual gifts is that they have head knowledge, but it has never penetrated their heart and identity. They often carry past failures and current wounds. If they came from a dysfunctional family, they still hear an angry parent or taunting peer, "You're no good. You're wasting your time. God can't use you. You're bad. You don't have any talents." We carry invisible baggage in and out of church, frustrated at the temporary good feelings of a worship service. We don't understand that often it takes wise counseling and prayers of deliverance.

The popular saying "What you don't know can't hurt you" is not true in the spiritual realm.

Failure to move beyond those tormenting inner voices can leave you a spiritual cripple limping in the body of Christ.

Although she was a Christian, Angela's problem was not lack of knowledge, but the taunting voices of the past. She was so convinced that she had no spiritual gifts that she actually scored a perfect zero. She was embarrassed, but not surprised. The irony is that she does have spiritual gifts, but she has such low self-esteem that she cannot recognize anything good in her, even God's goodness.

Question: Can you relate to Angela, or do you know someone like her? What would you say to Angela?

____

____

▲▲▲▲▲▲▲

If you already know about some of the gifts of the Spirit, which one(s) can you identify in your own life?

____

____

▲▲▲▲▲▲▲

"When and how do I receive spiritual gifts?"

The "when" and "how" of receiving spiritual gifts have some common elements for everyone, yet each is uniquely personal. As to the "when," Holy Spirit gifts are resident when the Holy Spirit abides in you as a Christian believer. You may not fully recognize such gifts; in many instances these gifts are similar to the talents and abilities with which you were born. As you mature in the Lord and He leads you into different situations and stages of life, other gifts of the Spirit may become evident in your life. Some gifts may be temporary, and others may be permanent in your life.

> In many instances these gifts are similar to the talents and abilities with which you were born.

As to the "how," the New Testament describes gifts as being bestowed by "prophecy with the laying on of the hands of the eldership" (1 Tim. 4:14). It is debatable whether that is a prescriptive statement. But the principles implied in "prophecy with the laying on of the hands of the eldership" are useful in helping us understand the "how."

First, prophecy does not have to mean a booming, "Thus says the Lord . . ." Rather, prophecy, which is a word of encouragement, exhortation and edification, can be exercised in a simple statement of "I see the Lord working in your life as you teach children so effectively and joyfully. You may have a spiritual gift of teaching." The person may answer, "Really? I haven't thought about it like that." But the recognition of that gift makes a person aware of what the Lord is doing through him or her.

Second, laying on of the hands of the elders acknowledges that spiritual gifts operate within the dual frameworks of authority and community. We are not given spiritual gifts for self-promotion, but for the sake of the community. Thus, laying on of hands means there is public affirmation and commissioning by people in spiritual authority.

"I want to do more for Jesus!"

Is it wrong to want more or different spiritual gifts? Most of the time, no. The apostle Paul told the Corinthian Christians that they should desire spiritual gifts (1 Cor. 14:1). The idea behind "desire" is stronger than the usual English connotation. It has the sense of "earnestly exert yourself for the spiritual gifts" (author's paraphrase). The reason Paul felt so strongly is because spiritual gifts are a manifestation of divine love. That's why Paul admonishes us to pursue the more excellent way, the way of love (1 Cor. 12:31; 14:1). Our love for Jesus should make us desire to serve Him more and more. So, in that sense, you are encouraged to ask the Holy Spirit to give you more gifts.

Actually, you will never be in a situation where the Holy Spirit will not already be prepared for what you will need. Jesus encourages us:

> *Now when they bring you to the synagogues and magistrates and authorities, do not worry about how or what you should answer, or what you should say. For the Holy Spirit will teach you in that very hour what you ought to say.*
>
> —LUKE 12:11–12

We may feel surprised by life's circumstances, but the Holy Spirit is not! (Read also Matthew 10:19–20; Mark 13:11.) If the Spirit leads us into a situation where we need the spiritual gift of administration or wisdom or interpretation of tongues, He will give it to us. When we walk in obedience and faith, then the Lord is pleased because He shows His power through us.

The real key regarding our desire for more or different gifts relates to our motives. If jealously of someone else and desire for self-recognition is our primary motivation, then the Holy Spirit will not respond to that request.

"Why would the Holy Spirit use me? I've got too much mess in my life!"

Do you have any of this mess in your life or as part of your local congregation?

But earnestly desire the best gifts. And yet I show you a more excellent way.
—1 Corinthians 12:31

Pursue love, and desire spiritual gifts, but especially that you may prophesy.
—1 Corinthians 14:1

- Division in the church over personalities and leaders
- Envy and strife in your life
- The church tolerant of sexual immorality in its midst
- Christians from the same church suing one another in public courts
- Christians confused about marriage
- Christians with a "holier than thou" attitude

If any of that relates to you or a group of Christians you know, then take heart; the Holy Spirit *still* works in people like that! Just read 1 Corinthians to find every one of those bullets—and more—described in the lives of Spirit-filled Christians.

I'll admit that's sort of a "good news/bad news" reality. The "bad news" is that it makes us uncomfortable that God does not always work in the ways that we measure godly living. The Spirit-filled leader who ministers effectively and is later exposed as violating the Ten Commandments during his or her ministry is an inconsistency that troubles us. But we only see a very small portion of the Spirit's purposes in and through that person's life. It's not an easy dilemma to reconcile, but somehow that's the nature of God's grace.

> The real key regarding our desire for more or different gifts relates to our motives.

The "good news" is that the Holy Spirit does not allow us or the church to continue living unchallenged in sinful disregard of His holiness. First Corinthians reminds us that for every carnal situation, the Holy Spirit had a call to repentance and godly thinking.

If your "mess" is that of willful sin against the Ten Commandments, then the Holy Spirit is using this moment to turn your heart to confession, repentance and restoration. You don't have to painstakingly search your soul for hidden sin. This is not an invitation to artificial guilt. This is an invitation to respond to the Holy Spirit's clear revelation through Scripture of sin and your need to turn away from that sin.

But your "mess" may not be like that. You may have some personal characteristics in your life that you don't like, and you know these characteristics hinder your life. It may be a tendency to procrastinate. Maybe you judge people too quickly. Maybe you speak before you think, and maybe you're insecure, but you hide it with pride. The Holy Spirit is still working in you bringing the fruit of the Spirit, the personality of Jesus, to maturity in you. And, good news! The Spirit shows the grace of God by using you.

After all is said and done, it's not too different from what the apostle Paul said: "We have this treasure in earthen vessels, that the excellence of the power may be of God and not of us" (2 Cor. 4:7).

Question: In your own words, write which, if any, of the four areas above you can identify as hindering your discovery of spiritual gifts.

____

____

▲▲▲▲▲▲▲

What have you discovered about the grace of God in relation to spiritual gifts?

____

____

▲▲▲▲▲▲▲

What is the lesson from 1 Corinthians about spiritual gifts and human failure?

____

____

▲▲▲▲▲▲▲

WHAT ARE SPIRITUAL GIFTS?

Interestingly, the Bible does not present the gifts in the way that most books, including this one, present them. The Bible does not list the gifts and give explanations and definitions. The Bible does not organize the gifts into convenient categories. The Bible does not present the gifts in a format of a lesson to be memorized and forgotten. Instead, the Bible presents the gifts in the context of local congregations. The gifts are living realities of the Holy Spirit, not intellectual Holy Spirit computer bytes you plug in to (no offense to the book title!). So, our efforts to categorize and define need to be taken with a little spiritual salt. This is not a lesson to pass a test; this is a lesson by which to live!

There are four major New Testament passages dealing with spiritual gifts. (Read Romans 12:6–8; 1 Corinthians 2:4–11; Ephesians 4:11; 1 Peter 4:9–11.) Some of the gifts are mentioned once, and others are mentioned several times. Some of the gifts are leadership gifts (equipping gifts), some are gifts related to native abilities, and others are unique gifts of spiritual manifestations.

THE LANGUAGE OF THE GIFTS

The apostles Paul (in Romans, 1 Corinthians and Ephesians) and Peter (in 1 Peter) used several Greek words to describe spiritual gifts. The most common term is *charisma.* (Read Romans 12:6; 1 Corinthians 12:4, 31; 1 Peter 4:10.) It is the basis for the word *charismatic*, which describes contemporary Spirit-filled Christians. It derives from the Greek word *charis*, which means grace. Thus, it describes the gifts as originating in God's grace—His desire to give us what we do not deserve. This means that any spiritual gift evident in my life is not due to my goodness but to God's goodness. My response to those gifts in me and in others is gratitude, not pride.

The usual Greek word for gifts is *dorea.* It is used throughout the New Testament. (Read Acts 2:38; 10:45; Ephesians 3:7; 4:7.)

The word *doma* is used in Ephesians 4:8, which says, "... and gave gifts to men." It refers to gifted people whom God puts in the church to equip the body of Christ. (Read Ephesians 4:11–16.)

The word *phanerosis* means "to unveil, lay bare, reveal and shine forth." Its use in 1 Corinthians 12:7–10 indicates the particular nature of those gifts.

A final word is in 1 Corinthians 12:1, where Paul used the word *spiritual (pneumatikos)* with the word *gift* being supplied in English. (Many English translations italicize words supplied by the editor of that version.) The translation is, "Now concerning spiritual [things], brethren, I do not want you to be ignorant." It is possible that Paul used *pneumatikos* to emphasize the spiritual power given in these gifts.

We are using the terms "equipping and body ministry gifts" and "manifestation gifts" in these chapters. Equipping and body ministry gifts refer to the spiritual gifts described in this chapter that primarily serve the body of Christ through the local or translocal congregation. Manifestation gifts refer to those gifts, primarily described in 1 Corinthians 12, that reveal God's supernatural power in miracles and so forth. These gifts will be discussed in the next chapter.

HOLY SPIRIT DIVERSITY AND UNITY

In three brief but immensely important verses, the apostle Paul showed the fundamental unity and diversity of the Holy Spirit in relation to spiritual gifts. The words in brackets are the Greek Paul used:

> *There are diversities* [diairesis] *of gifts* [charisma], *but the same Spirit. There are differences* [diairesis] *of ministries* [diakonia], *but the same Lord. And there are diversities* [diairesis] *of activities* [energema], *but it is the same God who works* [energeo] *all in all.*
>
> —1 CORINTHIANS 12:4–6

There are three diverse ways that the triune God is described as working. But note that the "diversities" and "differences" are the same in Greek. Whether it's the specific role of the Holy Spirit, the Son or the Father, the diversity describes the fundamental unity of God in our behalf.

- ▲ The Holy Spirit is specifically mentioned in relation to the *charisma*, the gifts of grace. Regardless of the gifts in the body of Christ, they come from the one and same Holy Spirit.
- ▲ The Lord Jesus Christ has diversity of ministries in the body, all of which reflect His glory.
- ▲ Father God has a diversity of ways that His power (the Greek denotes divine energy) is evidenced, but there is but one God.

In the church today, whether gifts, ministries or divine activity, the Holy Spirit is the agency through whom the Father and Son manifest divine purposes and glory.

And there are diversities of activities, but it is the same God who works all in all.
—1 Corinthians 12:5

And He Himself gave some to be apostles, some prophets, some evangelists, and some pastors and teachers.
—Ephesians 4:11

GIFTS OF MINISTRY

Paul understood that there are spiritual gifts that primarily serve the ministry of Jesus. First Corinthians 12:5 indicates that there are several of these gifts and their primary purpose is ministry to the church and Christ's mission to the world. Sometimes these are called the gifts of the Son.[1]

The Holy Spirit is the agency through whom the Father and Son manifest divine purposes and glory.

These ministry gifts are primarily of two kinds: equipping gifts and body ministry gifts. The equipping gifts are named in Ephesians 4:11 and are the gifts of apostles, prophets, evangelists, pastors and teachers. These are leadership gifts, and they serve to accomplish the goals of Christ described in Ephesians 4:12–16. (Read this scripture.) Not every Christian is given one of these gifts. For instance, every Christian should evangelize by sharing his or her faith, but not every Christian is given the gift of an evangelist.

The body ministry gifts named in Romans 12:7–8 and 1 Peter 4:9–10 include teacher, exhorter, ministry (service or helps), leadership (includes administration), benevolence (mercy), giving and hospitality. (Read these scriptures.) Every Christian has one or more of these gifts operating in his or her life. These body ministry gifts should be recognized and put to use in the ministries of the local church.

CHARACTERISTICS OF EQUIPPING AND BODY MINISTRY GIFTS

They are your gift-mix given you when you became a Christian. In fact, if you want to know a major part of God's will for your life, identify which of these gifts is primary in your life and begin to serve in that area. God's will is not different from the gifts He has given you. Those gifts are given to enable you to accomplish God's will in your life.

Ministry gifts are often related to natural abilities. It was not an accident of DNA or environment that caused the particular natural talents you have. God was at work in your mother's womb shaping your life and destiny. (Read Psalm 139:13–16.) God planted your musical ability, your ability to speak effectively and your creative artistic ability. Ministry gifts will often build on those natural abilities by releasing Holy Spirit power through your abilities as you surrender them to Him.

Related to the first characteristic, your ministry gift(s) is the role and position the Holy Spirit wants you to have in the body of Christ. If your primary gift is that of administration, look for a way to serve the church through your organizational, managerial and leadership gifts.

Ministry gifts often cannot be separated from the person with the gift. Ministry gifts are about gifted persons. Mark Rutland tells of speaking in a church, and following the service, a woman came to him and complained, "Our pastor thinks he is God's gift to this church." Rutland replied, "Well, madam, he is God's gift to this church." This is why we should respect and honor those who serve the body of Christ. No one is more important than another because it is the same Spirit at work in each of us. The Spirit-gifted worship leader is not more important than the Spirit-gifted janitor who willingly serves in the gift of helps.

Each Christian must discover and develop the ministry gift(s) that the Holy Spirit has given. This cannot happen in isolation, but it must occur in relationship with other Christians. This is why a Christian can never say, "I'm sick of the church. I'm going to serve the Lord in my own way." That attitude reflects bitterness and resentment, as well as poor theology. None of us serve the Lord in our own way. We serve the Lord in the way of the gifts that He has given us through the Holy Spirit.

GIFTS EQUIPPING THE CHURCH FOR MINISTRY: APOSTLES, PROPHETS, EVANGELISTS, PASTORS AND TEACHERS

Many Christians believe we are living in exciting times as equipping gift ministries of apostles, prophets, evangelists, pastors and teachers are being restored to the body of Christ. Actually, these gifts have never been absent. Sometimes (but not always) they been buried under ecclesiastical structures, and sometimes different terminology has been used to describe the same functions. While evangelists, pastors and teachers have been commonly recognized and understood in the church, the past fifteen years have produced a lot of teaching about apostles and prophets.[2]

Why did Jesus give equipping gifts to His church? Paul

answers this in Ephesians 4:12–16 with a series of penetrating insights:

- ▲ To equip the people of God for "the work of ministry" so that the body of Christ is built up (v. 12)
- ▲ To bring the body of Christ "to the unity of the faith," greater "knowledge of the Son of God," full maturity, and to fulfill the ways that Christ is going to fill the universe (v. 13)
- ▲ To keep the church from being deceived by "every wind of doctrine" (v. 14)
- ▲ To cause the church "to grow up in all things into Him" through the power of love (vv. 15–16)

That's the purpose of people whom the Spirit has called to be apostles, prophets, evangelists, pastors and teachers. In other words, that's what your local pastor is called to do: equip you to do the work of ministry the Spirit has equipped you to do. Your particular ministry is one or more of the body ministry gifts mentioned earlier.

How do these five equipping ministries function to accomplish the mission described in Ephesians 4:12–16?

Apostles are people called and sent by the Holy Spirit to spread the message of Jesus. In the ancient secular world, the word *apostle* referred to someone commissioned and sent by a higher authority to a new area with full authority to represent the claims and interest of the higher authority. When early Christians used this term, they understood apostles to be ambassadors of the coming kingdom commissioned by the King of kings and Lord of lords to spread the gospel. Today, missionaries are good examples of apostles.

But apostles are not limited to the modern concept of a missionary. There are apostolic church planters and pastors who lead large churches and influence their cities for the kingdom of God. Apostles lead groups of churches, such as denominations and ministry networks. Apostles faithfully articulate the gospel and preserve sound doctrine.

Apostles equip the body of Christ by bringing together teams to reach people who have not heard the gospel or where the gospel has been marginalized. They equip by mentoring younger generations of emerging leaders. Apostles equip by teaching sound doctrine and by believing in the power of the Holy Spirit for miracles and demonstrations of spiritual power. Apostles equip by providing leadership, vision and care to the people of God.

Prophets are people who declare the word of the Lord to edify (build up), exhort and comfort (encourage) the church (1 Cor. 14:3). The Lord first reveals His plans to prophets, who then declare that word to the appropriate persons at the appropriate time (Amos 3:7). Through their ministry prophets bring conviction of sin upon people (1 Cor. 14:24–25). Prophets lead us to true worship of God (Rev. 19:10). Prophets call forth, reveal, affirm and direct specific gifts the Holy Spirit is giving to persons within the context of eldership (1 Tim. 4:14).

THE FOUNDATION OF APOSTLES AND PROPHETS

In Ephesians Paul refers to apostles and prophets as foundational for the body of Christ: "Having been built on the foundation of the apostles and prophets, Jesus Christ Himself being the chief cornerstone" (Eph. 2:20). In Ephesians 3:5, Paul names "apostles and prophets" as the primary agents of revelation through which the Holy Spirit reveals the mystery of the gospel.

The "household of God"—a phrase used in Ephesians 2:19 for the church, the body of Christ—is built upon a solid foundation. That foundation is Jesus Christ and His testimony as revealed to and transmitted by the original New Testament apostles and prophets. (Read 1 Corinthians 3:10–12.) Contemporary apostles and prophets do not have a different revelation from Jesus Christ, but rather they declare and interpret the original revelation as it has been faithfully handed down through Scripture and the church.

The foundation of apostles and prophets means that Christians can be certain of the truth of the message, even after two thousand years of church history. Contemporary apostles and prophets are the present manifestation of this foundation as the household of God is revealed in our generation.

Evangelists are people who have the supernatural ability to communicate the gospel with conviction, thereby leading

But he who prophesies speaks edification and comfort to men.
—1 Corinthians 14:3

Surely the Lord God does nothing, unless He reveals His secret to His servants the prophets.
—Amos 3:7

But if all prophesy, and an unbeliever or an uninformed person comes in, he is convinced by all, he is convicted by all. And thus the secrets of his heart are revealed; and so, falling down on his face, he will worship God and report that God is truly among you.
—1 Corinthians 14:24–25

And I fell at his feet to worship him. But he said to me, "See that you do not do that! I am your fellow servant, and of your brethren who have the testimony of Jesus. Worship God! For the testimony of Jesus is the spirit of prophecy."
—Revelation 19:10

Do not neglect the gift that is in you, which was given to you by prophecy with the laying on of the hands of the eldership.
—1 Timothy 4:14

people to accept Christ as Savior. Every Christian is a witness of Christ, but not every Christian is called to be an evangelist. Evangelists equip the body of Christ by inspiring and enabling others to be more effective at communicating the gospel.

Pastors are people gifted to care for the flock of God. They are the shepherds of God's sheep in the local setting. Many pastors fit the traditional model of pastors as the preachers, teachers, caregivers and administrators of smaller local congregations (usually fewer than two hundred members). However, there are many people who lead cell groups, Bible studies and Sunday school classes who function in the gift of pastor within the body of Christ.

Teachers are people with a supernatural ability to teach and impart information, knowledge and wisdom to others. Sometimes this gift is linked to that of pastor. The equipping gift of teacher usually implies someone more than a local Sunday school teacher. The equipping gift teacher is someone whose ministry in speaking and writing impacts larger numbers of people. As an equipping gift teacher, this person knows how to take pieces of information, turn it into meaningful knowledge and present it in such a way as to allow life-transforming wisdom to emerge.

George Montague calls these five gifts the "builders" of unity in the body of Christ. These gifts "are primarily the offices of authority and teaching, because the unity of the body cannot be preserved without them."[3]

Question: Can you name persons in your local congregation who have equipping gift ministries?

____

____

▲▲▲▲▲▲▲

Why are apostles and prophets foundational in the life of the Christian mission?

____

____

▲▲▲▲▲▲▲

BODY MINISTRY GIFTS: EXHORTATION, TEACHING, SERVICE, HOSPITALITY, ADMINISTRATION, BENEVOLENCE AND GIVING

In this chapter we have emphasized that every Christian has one or more gifts of the Spirit. These gifts, primarily body ministry gifts, are the ways the Holy Spirit wants a person to serve in the body of Christ. As you are aware of the particular gift(s) in your life, you are conscious of the Lord's will for your life and service in His body, the church.

Persons called to minister in one of the equipping ministry gifts (apostles, prophets, evangelists, pastors and teachers) are to help other Christians discover, develop and deploy in the body ministry gift they have received from the Holy Spirit.

While there is but one body of Christ, His body has many members.

Read Romans 12:3–8 and 1 Corinthians 12:12–27. These two passages of Scripture provide the framework of how we understand these gifts in the church. While there is but one body of Christ, His body has many members (Rom. 12:4–5; 1 Cor. 12:12). Regardless of the gift, each gift comes from the same Holy Spirit (1 Cor. 12:13). God sets the gifts in the church as He pleases (Rom. 12:3; 1 Cor. 12:18). Each gift is equally important and is not an occasion for pride (Rom. 12:3; 1 Cor. 12:15–17). We need every gift of the Spirit operating in the church (1 Cor. 12:21–22). While some gifts are more prominent in human terms, each is vitally important (1 Cor. 12:22–24). Regardless of the gift, each person is to care for one another, and there should be unity of mission based on the gospel (1 Cor. 12:25–26).

Seven body ministry gifts are named in Romans 12:3–8, and if you are a Christian, the Holy Spirit has given you one or more of these gifts. Let's take a closer look at what the

Spirit has given you for service in Christ's body.

Prophecy

Having then gifts differing according to the grace that is given to us, let us use them: if prophecy, let us prophesy in proportion to our faith.

—Romans 12:6

Earlier we saw that the Spirit has given prophets to the church as equippers of the saints (Eph. 4:11). While each local church may not have a resident prophet, each local church does have someone who ministers with the body ministry gift of prophecy. First Corinthians 14 gives precise instructions on how this gift operates in the local congregation as it edifies, exhorts and encourages. In a local congregation the pastor will often be the most visible person with this gift. Thus you see a "gift-mix" with an equipping gift and body ministry gift operating together. But likely there will be others in the church who also can speak life-giving words of the Spirit.

So then faith comes by hearing, and hearing by the word of God.

—Romans 10:17

How do you use this gift? You exercise this gift in proportion to your faith. We know that faith comes by hearing the word of God (Rom. 10:17). Thus, this form of prophecy is not our own words but the Word of God, the Bible, that touches our hearts, and we speak the Word with Holy Spirit anointing and faith. It is the ability to communicate the Word so that faith arises in our hearts and in the hearts of the hearer.

Service

...or ministry, let us use it in our ministering.

—Romans 12:7

Sometimes called the gift of helps, *service* is a vital ministry in the local church. The equippers need people to come alongside who are willing to do the unseen and often unrecognized work of ministry. Without the strong hearts who can serve without public adoration, the church loses its ministry heart to the world.

Teacher

...he who teaches, in teaching.

—Romans 12:7

Similar to the equipping gift, the emphasis here is more on ministry in a local setting. It is that person who loves to prepare, pray and present the truths of God's Word.

Exhorter

. . . he who exhorts, in exhortation.

—Romans 12:8

While prophecy exhorts, an exhorter is a person who is able to stand alongside others and bring encouragement. In the Bible, Barnabas exercised this gift (Acts 4:36). The Greek word translated "exhorter" is the same word used for the Holy Spirit in John 14:16, 26—*paracletos.* An exhorter hears the Spirit call him or her to stand with another in the hour of need. An exhorter brings encouragement, hope and love to a given situation.

As a young associate pastor I experienced this gift from a group of lay leaders. Our son was born with respiratory distress syndrome and teetered on the brink of death. In the hours following his birth word spread through the church, and I vividly remember two of the deacons standing in the hall with me and saying, "Pastor, you have stood with us in our times of need. We're going to stand with you and your family." Their encouragement, prayers and active involvement were a demonstration of spiritual gifts and love as we walked through days that concluded with a healthy little boy who is now a grown man.

Giving - spiritual gift of generosity

. . . he who gives, with liberality.

—Romans 12:8

Every Christian should tithe and give love offerings to the work of the Lord. But some Christians are given a spiritual gift of generosity. In the affluent West, we tend to think of this as giving financially. But across the world it is far more than money. Whatever the "giving," the spirit behind the giving is one of generosity, liberality and joy. Those Christians with the gift of giving will not need public recognition. They usually prefer to be in the background, and they do not give in order to gain personal favor or influence. They give

And Joses, who was also named Barnabas by the apostles (which is translated Son of Encouragement). . .

—Acts 4:36

because the Spirit has given them the desire to give. The means to give has grown as they have become open and obedient channels of grace. They have discovered that the more they give, the more the Lord gives them to give.

Leadership

. . . he who leads, with diligence.

—ROMANS 12:8

A leader is someone who stands before others and gives direction and order. The verb is used in 1 Timothy 5:17, where Paul wrote of "elders who rule well." There are no shortages of leadership books in the marketplace. Christian leaders can glean much from insightful leaders and mentoring. However, there is a dimension of the leadership of the Holy Spirit that is critical to the body ministry gift of leadership. Leadership anointed by the Holy Spirit turns the secular models upside down by calling leaders foremost to be servants (Mark 9:33–35).

Then He came to Capernaum . . . and He sat down, and called the twelve and said to them, "If anyone desires to be first, he shall be last of all and servant of all."

—Mark 9:33–35

There are three ways you know if you have the body ministry gift of leadership. First, your leadership is not half-hearted but, in the language of the New King James Version, "diligent." This means that you are earnest, committed and even zealous for what the Lord has called you unto. Second, you're willing to serve anyone, anywhere and in any way as the Spirit directs. In other words, your pride and position are not as important as your servant posture. Third, your service inspires others to follow and imitate you. If you see these three signs, then you likely have the ministry gift of leadership.

Mercy

. . . he who shows mercy, with cheerfulness.

—ROMANS 12:8

Paul connects mercy with cheerfulness. In other words, the gift of mercy is not a bite-your-lip, forced act, but it flows from a heart that has itself received mercy. Mercy is our decision to not give someone the judgment he or she deserves. The Christian leader who falls into sin deserves our condemnation, ridicule, mockery and rejection. But mercy instead joyfully gives love, hope, restoration and relationship, and it holds open the door of divine opportunity. That gift is hard for many of us. That's why it's a body ministry gift desperately needed in the body of Christ.

Question: Name the three ways a person knows he or she has the body ministry gift of leadership.

____

____

____

▲▲▲▲▲▲▲

Can you identify which of the body ministry gifts operate in your life?

____

____

▲▲▲▲▲▲▲

Can you identify people in your life or congregational life who demonstrate any of these gifts?

____

____

▲▲▲▲▲▲▲

LET'S TALK ABOUT IT

Here's the key question: What is God's will for your life? What's your answer? "Duh, I don't know!" If you're a Christian, you should know. The starting point of God's will for your life is actually pretty simple:

- ▲ It is God's will that you be born again and serve Him. Describe your conversion experience:

  ____

  ____

  ____

  ▲▲▲▲▲▲▲

- ▲ It is God's will that you ask the Holy Spirit to be released in His power in your life. How has the Spirit been released in your life?

  ____

  ____

  ____

  ▲▲▲▲▲▲▲

▲ It is God's will that you recognize that the native abilities and talents you have be sanctified for His service. List your abilities and talents.

____

____

____

▲▲▲▲▲▲▲

▲ It is God's will that you discover, develop and deploy the body ministry gift(s) the Holy Spirit has in your life. What ministry gifts are you using in your life?

____

____

▲▲▲▲▲▲▲

▲ It is God's will that you be part of a group of Christians where the equipping gifts of Ephesians 4:11 can be used to help you grow in love and service. How is your church helping you to grow? Where do you need to grow more spiritually?

____

____

▲▲▲▲▲▲▲

OK, let's ask it again! What is God's will for your life? As you identify your body ministry gifts, you can joyfully and willingly answer!

TIME TO PLUG IN TO THE HOLY SPIRIT

Your spiritual gifts have been in the Father's heart from eternity. The timing of your birth, even the circumstances of your parentage, have been in Father's heart and plans for your part in fulfilling the body of Christ. While Satan cannot ultimately stop the coming fullness of Christ's kingdom, Satan can hinder our personal effectiveness in Christ's kingdom by keeping us from fulfilling our destiny through the gifts of the Spirit.

Today you can make a decision to live the remainder of your life in the Father's will. Discover, develop and deploy the spiritual gifts you have through the Holy Spirit.

Holy Spirit, thank You for giving me ministry gifts. Forgive me for not recognizing them sooner. Thank You for showing me Your purposes in my life. Thank You that I better understand how to find and live fully in Your will. Teach me to respect, love and honor every Christian regardless of his or her spiritual gift. May I not treat lightly that which You have given another. May I serve You with humility, strength, grace and peace as I serve You in the spiritual gifts You have given me. Amen.

CHAPTER EIGHT

Manifesting Spiritual Power

IN THIS CHAPTER YOU WILL DISCOVER THAT . . .

- ▲ The nine gifts of the Spirit will help you triumph over evil.
- ▲ The Spirit is free to use whomever He desires as the avenue of expressing His will.
- ▲ Messages in tongues convey the truth of the gospel and bring the listener into direct contact with the power of God.

JESUS MINISTERED IN THE POWER OF THE HOLY SPIRIT:

- ▲ Through a word of knowledge Jesus penetrated the closed heart of a Samaritan woman and she became an evangelist. (Read John 4:17–19, 39.)
- ▲ Through various means Jesus healed a multitude of diseases through the power of the Holy Spirit. (Read Mark 1:31, 34, 40–42; 2:9–11; John 9:6.)
- ▲ Jesus prophesied through the power of the Holy Spirit. (Read Luke 17:20–37.)
- ▲ Jesus discerned the spirit of those around Him. (Read Mark 2:6–8.)

But Jesus said, "Greater works than these [you] will do, because I go to My Father" (John 14:12). That is why Jesus sent the Holy Spirit. The Holy Spirit enables each generation to do the "greater works" of Jesus. Samuel Chadwick (1860–1932), pastor of Oxford Place Chapel in Leeds, England, caught the impact of what Jesus said:

> The resources of the church are in "the supply of the Spirit." The Spirit is more than the minister of consolation. He is Christ without the limitations of the flesh and the material world. He can reveal what Christ could not speak. He has resources of power greater than those Christ could use, and He makes possible greater works than His. He is the Spirit of God, the Spirit of truth, the Spirit of witness, the Spirit of conviction, the Spirit of power, the Spirit of holiness, the Spirit of light, the Spirit of adoption, the Spirit of help, the Spirit of liberty, the Spirit of wisdom, the Spirit of revelation, the Spirit of promise, the Spirit of love, the Spirit of meekness, the Spirit of sound mind, the Spirit of grace, the Spirit of glory, and the Spirit of prophecy. It is for the church to

For to one is given the word of wisdom through the Spirit, to another the word of knowledge through the same Spirit, to another faith by the same Spirit, to another gifts of healings by the same Spirit, to another the working of miracles, to another prophecy, to another discerning of spirits, to another different kinds of tongues, to another the interpretation of tongues.
—1 Corinthians 12:8–10

explore the resources of the Spirit; the resources of the world are futile.[1]

If you have been around many Pentecostal people, they will often tell you about the nine gifts of the Holy Spirit. What they are talking about are the nine gifts named by the apostle Paul in 1 Corinthians 12:8–10: word of wisdom, word of knowledge, faith, gifts of healing, miracles, prophecy, discerning of spirits, differing kinds of tongues and the interpretation of tongues. These nine are introduced by Paul as "the manifestation of the Spirit" (v. 7). When people think of the power of the Spirit, they are usually thinking of the manifestation of one of these gifts.

The Holy Spirit enables each generation to do the "greater works" of Jesus.

In the previous chapter we looked at other gifts of the Spirit as they relate to equipping and body life ministry. Those gifts are your ministry-gift mix, and they are part of your being as a believer in Christ. These nine manifestation gifts are somewhat different from the ministry-gift mix in your life. In this chapter we're going to look at these nine gifts as they manifest, or reveal, special aspects of the power of God.

HOW TO BE SPIRITUAL WITHOUT BEING STUPID

The Corinthian Christians were charismatic, and they loved spiritual manifestations and demonstrations. These demonstrations gave them weapons with which to fight against the spiritual darkness of their pagan environment. While there were plenty of spiritual demonstrations, they needed order and understanding of God's purposes for these manifestations. That's why Paul wrote this memorable phrase: "I do not want you to be ignorant" (1 Cor. 12:1). Our English word *agnostic* comes from the Greek word translated "ignorant." In other words, Paul did not want them to be agnostic, or uncertain, about the realities of the Holy Spirit in their midst. There were other demonic spirits operating in their environment, and they needed an anchor of understanding that would hold. Paul's intention is captured by Eugene Peterson's paraphrase of this verse: "What I want to talk about now is the various ways God's Spirit gets worked into our lives. This is complex and often misunderstood, but I want you to be informed and knowledgeable" (THE MESSAGE).

This is why Paul began these instructions by dealing with issues of speech and idolatry (vv. 2–3). Since many of the Corinthian Christians were Gentiles, their conversion had been from idolatry into worship of the living God. They had worshiped "dumb idols," that is, idols that did not speak. Paul's insights in verse 3 are particularly important:

> *Therefore I make known to you that no one speaking by the Spirit of God calls Jesus accursed, and no one can say that Jesus is Lord except by the Holy Spirit.*

From this verse three critical insights emerge that are important when it comes to evaluating spiritual gifts.

First, the presence of the Holy Spirit does not violate human volition and consciousness. The Christian exercise of spiritual gifts is not a descent or ascent into a loss of consciousness or self-control. The Holy Spirit will not make you speak or do anything. The Bible is the standard for recognizing whether particular manifestations are of the Spirit of God, the spirit of man or demonic spirits. The Holy Spirit will not compulsively "possess" you.

Second, the Holy Spirit will always glorify Jesus and never speak or lead you to do anything that diminishes His glory and honor.

Third, the Holy Spirit is doctrinally sound ("Jesus Christ is Lord"). He will not "inspire" you to say things that are not affirmed in Scripture. This does not mean that you may not make verbal mistakes. Rather, it means the Holy Spirit will not lead you to speak and believe false doctrine.[2]

These three together are important. The Bible must remain the ultimate source of spiritual authority regarding spiritual manifestations.

The presence of the Holy Spirit does not violate human volition and consciousness.

Manifestation gifts (the nine gifts mentioned in 1 Corinthians 12:8–10) are given to believers so that the entire body of Christ profits. The word *profit* in verse 7 means that the body of Christ is given an advantage in its battle against evil through the manifestation of the Spirit.

A WORD OF WARNING

In his book *Fresh Power*, Jim Cymbala, pastor of The Brooklyn Tabernacle, warns of abuses in the Spirit-filled community: "We have some horrendous abuses going on in the name of the Spirit of God. Many in the so-called charismatic movement have done bizarre things that are not only outside New Testament teaching but actually contradict it. When people bark like dogs, laugh like hyenas, roar like lions, and chirp like birds 'in the Spirit,' someone needs to lift a voice and say, 'Where is this found in the Bible? And how does it edify a congregation?'

"Some people, I am afraid, aren't about to submit to the authority of Scripture. They are totally consumed with the latest trendy manifestations and strange new signs that convince them 'the river is flowing.'

"Does God do things so new that they are not in the Bible? If the Scriptures are not the judge of supposed 'Holy Spirit manifestations,' where will all this end?"[3]

Question: What does the apostle Paul call the nine gifts mentioned in 1 Corinthians 12:8–10?

How do you know that the Holy Spirit will not force you to do something or cause you to act compulsively?

What do you think of Jim Cymbala's remarks?

"ADVANTAGE, CHURCH"

A few years ago I was teaching in London, England, and my son and I went to the opening round at Wimbledon. After each point the score was announced until it reached the critical point: "Advantage, Sampras." You knew that Pete Sampras was only one good serve or return away from winning the game, set and match.

The apostle Paul didn't have a tennis match in mind when he wrote that these nine gifts were for the advantage of the church. But the match he did have in mind was far more significant. These gifts are dynamic and powerful manifestations of the Holy Spirit that enable the church to triumph over evil. They are our "advantage" when demonstrated by the Spirit. At such moments we are often at the verge of great spiritual victory for Christ.

As you study these gifts you will notice a certain logic in Paul's list:

- Wisdom and knowledge are related.
- Faith, gifts of healings and working of miracles go hand in hand.
- Prophecy and discerning of spirits go together.
- Different kinds of tongues and interpretation of tongues are related.

CHARACTERISTICS OF MANIFESTATION GIFTS

Manifestation gifts are different from equipping and body ministry gifts. The following five characteristics tend to govern the nine manifestation gifts.

- ▲ They are temporary in the believer. Ministry gifts are resident in your life, but a manifestation gift is not. A ministry gift can be exercised at will. A manifestation gift can be exercised only when the Holy Spirit brings it to your life at a given circumstance.
- ▲ Manifestation gifts have no relationship to natural abilities. Your ministry gifts are part of your personality.
- ▲ Manifestation gifts usually have no relationship to your position in the body of Christ. That is, you and an apostle may be sitting in the church, and the Holy Spirit may use you instead of the apostle as the instrument of revelation, such as giving a word of wisdom.

- ▲ When manifestation gifts are exercised, the attention is on the gift and not the person.
- ▲ Because these gifts are for the advantage of the church, the church should rejoice when these gifts are exercised.[4]

SUPERNATURAL GIFTS OF INSIGHT: THE WORD OF WISDOM

For to one is given the word of wisdom *through the Spirit.*
—1 CORINTHIANS 12:8, EMPHASIS ADDED

> These gifts are dynamic and powerful manifestations of the Holy Spirit that enable the church to triumph over evil.

This is the first of two uses of "word" in verse 8. It means that whatever word we receive comes from the Holy Spirit. It is neither our word nor our interpretation of events, but a supernatural word that the Holy Spirit gives. Also, the use of the singular "word" does not mean a single word, but it refers to a total revelation that the Spirit gives. It also should be noted that these "words," while given by the Holy Spirit, are not the same as Holy Scripture. These contemporary expressions of the Spirit for our situations will always conform to the specifics and the theological whole of Scripture. Concern over this very point is reflected in the view that "word" is better translated as "teaching," so that the Holy Spirit gives a "teaching of wisdom" that is based on Scripture and thus brings Spirit-inspired scriptural illumination to a situation.[5]

The Spirit of wisdom is mentioned several times in the Old Testament. Genesis 41 describes how the Holy Spirit helped Joseph gain favor with Pharaoh by interpreting his dreams. Pharaoh said to his servants, "Can we find such a one as this, a man in whom is the Spirit of God?" (v. 38). He then said to Joseph, "Inasmuch as God has shown you all this, there is no one as discerning and wise as you" (v. 39). Isaiah 11:2 is a prophecy of Jesus and tells that "the Spirit of the LORD shall rest upon Him, the Spirit of wisdom and understanding, the Spirit of counsel and might, the Spirit of knowledge and of the fear of the LORD." The prophet Daniel was "gifted in wisdom" (Dan. 1:4). Daniel thanked the Lord that "You have given me wisdom" (Dan. 2:23). Both Daniel and Joseph reflect the emphasis in Proverbs that wisdom is related to the fear of the Lord (Prov. 9:10).

With this background in mind, the word of wisdom "usually provides an answer to a vexing problem—a solution that heals, unifies, and edifies."[6] A good biblical example is the word of wisdom James received that helped solve a problem in the early church. (Read Acts 15:13–21.)

The fear of the LORD is the beginning of wisdom.
—Proverbs 9:10

The word of wisdom is more than our natural capacity to take information and knowledge and use it wisely. The word of wisdom from the Holy Spirit brings an understanding that could not be figured out in the natural. You may be facing a myriad of problems and are overwhelmed by the complexities. You should ask the Holy Spirit to give you a word of wisdom through prayer, the Scriptures or another believer that will shed light on the situation you face.

SUPERNATURAL GIFTS OF INSIGHT: THE WORD OF KNOWLEDGE

. . . to another, the word of knowledge *through the same Spirit.*
—1 CORINTHIANS 12:8, EMPHASIS ADDED

The Holy Spirit is able to reveal specific information about someone or a situation in order to bring about redemptive purposes.

Jack Deere describes an episode of the Holy Spirit giving him a word of knowledge about a student named "Robert" at the seminary where he was an instructor. Robert was explaining to Deere why he was late on an assignment. Deere best describes what happened next:

> That's when it happened, something I had never experienced before. As I was listening to Robert, he faded away and in his place I saw the word "PORNOGRAPHY" in large, capital, block letters. *What is happening to me?* I thought. *There is no way this student is into pornography. I must be making this up.* But why would I make up something I thought to be an impossibility?
>
> I realized I was having what some believers call "a word of knowledge." It wasn't intuition; knowledge about Robert was being given to me by the Spirit of God.[7]

Deere went on to describe his awkward struggle to trust the Spirit in this situation. Finally, he caringly confronted Robert with what had happened, and Robert confessed that he had a long history battling pornography. It was the starting point of deliverance from guilt and bondage in Robert's life.

Wisdom should be used when you receive a word of knowledge concerning a person or situation. The supernatural revelation is not about your personal power over another, but it is given for the advantage of the gospel in the situation.

purpose

Question: How does the spiritual gift of a word of wisdom differ from natural wisdom?

▲▲▲▲▲▲▲

If you had been Jack Deere, how would you have handled the situation when you realized the Holy Spirit had given you supernatural knowledge?

▲▲▲▲▲▲▲

SUPERNATURAL GIFTS OF POWER: THE GIFT OF FAITH

> *... to another* faith *by the same Spirit...*
>
> —1 Corinthians 12:9, emphasis added

The Bible refers to faith in several ways. First, there is the faith that is necessary in order for any person to be saved, that is, faith in the atoning work of Jesus Christ. There is no doubt that such faith is in itself a gift from the Holy Spirit as this faith comes from hearing the Word of God and believing its testimony concerning Jesus. (Read Romans 10.)

But this is different from the gift of faith, which is a charismatic gift given to certain individuals. The Bible presents this kind of faith as operating in several ways. A woman sick for twelve years had faith to touch the hem of Jesus' garment. Jesus felt His healing power enter her body and said, "Your faith has made you well" (Mark 5:34). The apostle Paul saw that a crippled man in Lystra had faith to be healed. (Read Acts 14:9.) Jesus told the disciples that there was a kind of faith that can move mountains (Mark 11:22–24). The apostle James knew of the "prayer of faith" that could save the sick (James 5:15).

The gift of faith is related to miracles. It is the active conviction that God has revealed His will for a given situation. There are people for whom the gift of faith has become a characteristic of their walk with God. Hebrews 11 catalogs the ancients who had this kind of faith. Church history is filled with people who had the gift of faith. There are people today—some well known such as Billy Graham and Oral Roberts, and countless others who are only known locally—who walk with the gift of faith.

The gift of faith hears the voice of God for a specific situation, counts the cost and recognizes that the weight always falls on the side of what the Lord has spoken and confirmed. In this sense the gift of faith is related to vision. It is the capacity to spiritually "see" what the Lord wants to accomplish in a given situation. In the face of fear and doubt, the gift of faith enables a person to rise above the circumstances and absolutely trust in the promises of God.

The gift of faith is the active conviction that God has revealed His will for a given situation.

Acts 27 records an example of how the gift of faith was manifested in the life of Paul. For days two hundred seventy-six people were tossed on the Mediterranean Sea in a severe storm. Luke records that "all hope that we would be saved was finally given up" (v. 20). But during the night the angel of the Lord spoke to Paul, "Do not be afraid, Paul, you must be brought before Caesar; and indeed God has granted you all those who sail with you" (v. 24). Paul then encouraged everyone, "Therefore take heart, men, for I believe God that it will be just as it was told me" (v. 25). And it turned out that way. The ship was lost, but all were saved according to the word that the Lord had revealed.

So Jesus answered and said to them, "Have faith in God. For assuredly, I say to you, whoever says to this mountain, 'Be removed and be cast into the sea,' and does not doubt in his heart, but believes that those things he says will be done, he will have whatever he says. Therefore I say to you, whatever things you ask when you pray, believe that you receive them, and you will have them."
—Mark 11:22–24

SUPERNATURAL GIFTS OF POWER: GIFTS OF HEALINGS

. . . to another gifts of healings *by the same Spirit . . .*

—1 CORINTHIANS 12:9, EMPHASIS ADDED

In the Gospels and the Book of Acts, healings are often a characteristic of the gift of faith. Healings are listed after faith in this list. Notice also that this is the only gift given in the plural: There are many kinds of healings provided by the Holy Spirit.

Father Francis Martin writes movingly of the need for, and the power of, gifts of healings in the body of Christ:

> There is a great need for "gifts of healings" in our age. As we become sensitive to the unity of the human person and of the human race, we see how physical healing does more than rectify disorders of the body; it makes God present to the one healed and to all those joined to that person.
>
> To heal a poor person of the effects of malnutrition is to reverse a process created by the structures of sin of which the person may be an innocent victim. To heal a person of AIDS is to claim the victory of the Cross of Christ not only over physical disorder, but also over the very forces of death that lead to eternal ruin. To free someone from Satan's domination, gained through a life exposed to alienation and violence, is to liberate a human memory from the power of evil so that it can generate thoughts and attitudes that correspond to the truth of the gospel and become a temple in which the Father is adored in spirit and truth. In brief, healing is an essential part of the preaching of the gospel and of bearing witness to the reality and majesty of Jesus Christ.[8]

SUPERNATURAL GIFTS OF POWER: THE WORKING OF MIRACLES

. . . to another the working of miracles *. . .*

—1 CORINTHIANS 12:10, EMPHASIS ADDED

Although similar to the gifts of healings in verse 9, miracles refer to a broader range of God's power than simply healings. Jesus demonstrated power over food, the sea and the weather. (Read Mark 6:30–44, 45–51; 4:35–41).

Question: Do you know anyone who has operated in the gift of faith? Can you identify a situation in your own life when the Holy Spirit has given you special faith?

____

____

▲▲▲▲▲▲▲

What are you or someone you know facing where the gift of faith is needed?

____

____

▲▲▲▲▲▲▲

SUPERNATURAL GIFTS OF COMMUNICATION: THE GIFT OF PROPHECY

> . . . *to another* prophecy . . .
>
> —1 Corinthians 12:10, emphasis added

This is the third time we have encountered prophecy in our discussion of ministry and manifestation gifts. The first reference was in terms of the equipping gift of the prophet. The second was in relation to the body ministry gift of prophecy. In both instances the emphasis is upon the building up, encouraging and exhorting of the Christian community. In many respects the ministry-mix gift of prophecy is similar to effective gospel preaching and teaching.

The manifestation gift of prophecy is different in the sense that it may come to anyone at any time for the sake of edifying, encouraging and exhorting the body of Christ. It occurs when a group of Christians are together and someone unexpectedly, but orderly, speaks forth what the Spirit is stirring that is a clear word for those believers at that moment. It shows that the Spirit is free to use whomever He desires as the avenue of expressing His will.

As with the ministry-mix gifts of prophecy, prophetic utterances as a gift of the Spirit to the church are to be discerned (the next gift in Paul's list) and are subject to Paul's criteria established in 1 Corinthians 14. The person who gives the prophecy should willingly submit that prophecy to

the church. In that sense, the prophecy is not "mine"; it is the Lord's. That does not excuse false prophecy, but it releases us to allow the prophetic word to be tested by those God has placed in spiritual authority. Any "prophet" unwilling to submit his or her prophecies to those in authority should be avoided.

SUPERNATURAL GIFTS OF COMMUNICATION: THE GIFT OF DISCERNING OF SPIRITS

> . . . *to another* discerning of spirits . . .
>
> —1 CORINTHIANS 12:10, EMPHASIS ADDED

The New Testament use of the words translated "discern" is important. In 1 Thessalonians 5:19–21 Paul addressed three aspects of spiritual gifts: "Do not quench the Spirit" (v. 19). "Do not despise prophecies" (v. 20). "Test all things; hold fast what is good" (v. 21). The word *test* in verse 21 is a Greek word that means "to evaluate." Here the idea is that prophecies should be tested and evaluated for their legitimacy as from the Holy Spirit.

There are many spiritual realities in the world, but not all are from the Holy Spirit. John's warning in 1 John 4 evidences this: "Do not believe every spirit, but test the spirits, whether they are of God; because many false prophets have gone out into the world" (v. 1). The word *test* is the same word Paul used in 1 Thessalonians 5:21; it means that something should be evaluated for its legitimacy. Notice that this test is directly related to prophetic utterances.

> There are many spiritual realities in the world, but not all are from the Holy Spirit.

In verses 2–3 of 1 John 4, John provides the first permanent criteria regarding the origin of prophetic words:

> *By this you know the Spirit of God: Every spirit that confesses that Jesus Christ has come in the flesh is of God, and every spirit that does not confess that Jesus Christ has come in the flesh is not of God. And this is the spirit of the Antichrist.*

This is a clear reference to an early form of Gnosticism that denied that Jesus was actually incarnated (born) as a human being. This spirit ultimately denies that Jesus is the Son of God. (Read 1 John 5:5–13.) Such a denial, increasingly plausible in religious pluralism, denies that Jesus is the only begotten of the Father, denies the efficacy of His shed blood for all humanity and denies His uniqueness as Lord over all.

Anyone claiming to be the Son of God or the fulfillment of the Messiah is a false prophet. Any prophecy in the church that undermines the biblical revelation of the incarnation of Jesus as fully divine and fully human is more than theological ignorance. It is apostasy taking advantage of theological ignorance.

Interestingly Paul used a different Greek word in 1 Corinthians 12:10 and later in 1 Corinthians 14:29 when several prophets are speaking in the same service. The Greek word used here emphasizes the capacity to distinguish and give sound judgment rather than to test and evaluate. *Testing* implies use of natural components such as time. *Discernment* and *sound judgment* imply spiritual ability to discern the kind of spirit (harsh, gentle, peaceable or irritating) that is manifested in speaking forth as well as the fruit that the prophetic word may produce. Discernment implies an immediate response related to the prophetic, and testing implies waiting to see if the word is fulfilled.

Therefore, Paul's understanding of the gift of discernment is that it is the first step in determining the validity of the prophetic utterance. If theological error is present, the gift of discernment recognizes it immediately. This gift quickly determines whether the prophecy is for the entire congregation or whether it should be given privately with pastoral oversight.

Most pastoral leaders in Spirit-filled churches pray for the Holy Spirit to give them this gift as other gifts are manifested in a small group setting or larger worship service. This discernment relates to appropriate timing and form of expression of a prophecy. While no method is immune from abuse, many leaders have established groups of people who filter prophetic words that come to the congregation. Spontaneous jumping up and often disrupting the service are discouraged, and people are taught to bring their thoughts to the leaders.

Let two or three prophets speak, and let the others judge.
—1 Corinthians 14:29

The leaders then evaluate if and when the word should be spoken aloud. Experience shows that people resistant to these guidelines often have their own agenda and are not submissive to the people accountable to the Lord for that congregation. But those who are submissive discover protection and an atmosphere for spiritual maturity.

WHAT IF A PROPHET IS WRONG?

Besides the theological aspect of testing prophecy in 1 John 4:1–3, the Christian church has always had to deal with a wide range of issues relating to this gift. This gift can be powerfully uplifting, and it can be powerfully destructive.

By the end of the first century the church had established that an itinerant prophet who stayed at a home more than three days was a false prophet because he took advantage of hospitality. Obviously this should not apply when a prophet is invited to a congregation for more than three days! But it was an early warning of the manipulative power of a person who claims to speak for God. There are two specific issues regarding prophecy, whether as a ministry or manifestation gift, that are pertinent today.

First, should the phrase "Thus says the Lord" be used? There are many who argue that it should not be used because it was used by the biblical writers who had a unique anointing of the Spirit due to their words being the written Word of God. It is also difficult to disagree with the person who says, "Thus says the Lord." How do you respond to someone who says, "The Lord told me"? The speaker has put himself in a defensive position if questioned.

There is probably a lot of wisdom in saying something like, "I sense . . . " or "I believe the Lord is saying to me . . . " That's not a statement of doubt but rather humility that recognizes the Christian community has a biblical mandate to test and discern.

This leads to the second issue: What about divine judgment on false prophets? In the Old Testament a false prophet was recognized not so much by his or her words coming to pass but rather whether the prophecy conformed to God's revealed standards. First, anyone whose prophecy led to following after false gods was to be put to death. (Read Deuteronomy 13:1–18.) This specifically related to prophets who performed signs and wonders (originating from demonic spirits) and their sign came about and was used to lead people astray (vv. 2–3). The fact that their words came to pass was part of the way the Lord tested Israel's heart for Him. (Read Deuteronomy 8:2.) This is the Old Testament counterpart to 1 John 4:1–3.

Second, anyone who prophesied but their words did not come to pass was not to be feared. (Read Deuteronomy 18:22.) Contrary to popular opinion, there is not a biblical mandate to kill a prophet whose word did not come to pass. In that case, a prophet like Isaiah would have been killed earlier because many of his prophecies were not fulfilled until the birth of Christ, seven hundred years after Isaiah prophesied.

The New Testament recognizes that "prophecies . . . will fail" (1 Cor. 13:8, in reference to the fullness of Christ's kingdom when prophecy will have been fulfilled), and "we prophesy in part" (v. 9, in reference to the limitations we have of divine plans). The fact that Paul gave specific advice in 1 Corinthians 14 regarding prophecy means that he understood the limitations of this gift in the church. Yet, he also encouraged us not to despise prophecy.

In conclusion, the prophet whose words contradict Scripture should not be heeded in the Christian community. The prophet whose words have failed to come to pass should humbly submit his or her limitations to the church, and the church should minister to that person in love and wisdom. The tendency is for the leaders or people to blame the prophet as being "false" and for the prophet to blame the leaders or people for failing to pray or for being disobedient. This confusion can be avoided as leaders, prophets and people understand the priority of love as the foundation for exercising spiritual gifts. (Read 1 Corinthians 13.)

SUPERNATURAL GIFTS OF COMMUNICATION: DIFFERENT KINDS OF TONGUES

. . . *to another* different kinds of tongues . . .

—1 CORINTHIANS 12:10, EMPHASIS ADDED

Earlier we looked at different ways the Bible presents speaking in tongues: the initial evidence of the baptism of the Holy Spirit and your own personal prayer language. Here Paul has in mind tongues that are meant as messages to the body of Christ. Usually these are what are popularly called "tongues of angels"; that is, language that is not known on earth and that sounds like nonsense. When spoken with a group of believers, these tongues should be interpreted into the known language of the hearers. Occasionally a message in tongues will be given that is in a language known to a listener but not to the speaker. Such messages convey the truth of the gospel and bring the listener into direct contact with the power of God.

SUPERNATURAL GIFTS OF COMMUNICATION: INTERPRETATION OF TONGUES

> *. . . to another the* interpretation of tongues . . .
>
> —1 Corinthians 12:10, emphasis added

If you've been in a service where someone spoke in tongues for thirty seconds and someone else interpreted for ninety seconds, or vice versa, you may have wondered about the time differential. How can that be a translation?

It's not supposed to be the gift of "translation." It's the gift of *interpretation*. A translation is usually an effort for word and phrase exactness from one language to another. But the gift of interpretation is the Holy Spirit giving to an individual the essence—the application—of the tongues to a congregation. Perhaps the Spirit has desired to use you as the instrument of this manifestation. You had thoughts in your mind, but you brushed them aside because it didn't sound like a translation. The Spirit does not need you to translate. He needs you to be the willing vessel through which He can give the purpose of the message in tongues.

Messages in tongues convey the truth of the gospel and bring the listener into direct contact with the power of God.

LET'S TALK ABOUT IT

Nine manifestation gifts of the Spirit—it looks like the Holy Spirit has provided us with everything we need to accomplish the mission of the gospel for our time. Likely you've had one or more of these gifts manifested in your life and you didn't know it. You knew something happened that was beyond you. But you didn't realize it was a word of wisdom or a word of knowledge or even a gift of faith.

It doesn't have to remain a mystery to you. You can ask the Holy Spirit to use you more. Don't be surprised when He stretches you by placing you in situations where you have to depend totally upon Him. Just remember that it's not about you—it's about God's purposes.

▲ Take a few minutes and review this chapter in your own words.

____

____

▲▲▲▲▲▲▲

▲ The gifts tend to work in pairs. Match the gift on the right with the gift on the left that is its pair.

Gifts of healing	Different tongues
Interpretation	Word of knowledge
Word of wisdom	Gift of miracles
Prophecy	Discerning of spirits

▲▲▲▲▲▲▲

▲ Give examples of the gift of wisdom that are found in the New Testament.

____

____

▲▲▲▲▲▲▲

▲ Which gift is mentioned in the plural? Why?

____

____

▲▲▲▲▲▲▲

▲ How is the gift of discernment mentioned in 1 Corinthians 12:10 and 1 Corinthians 14:29 different from the discernment in 1 Thessalonians 5:21 and 1 John 4:1–3?

____

____

▲▲▲▲▲▲▲

▲ Has someone ever prophesied over your life? What has happened in regards to that prophecy?

____

____

▲▲▲▲▲▲▲

▲ Has the Holy Spirit ever used you to give a message in tongues or to interpret? If yes, how did you feel about it? If no, is that something you would like to happen, or does it frighten you?

____

____

▲▲▲▲▲▲▲

TIME TO PLUG IN TO THE HOLY SPIRIT

Although the Holy Spirit resides in you by faith in Christ and you have been filled with the Spirit through the baptism of the Holy Spirit, God's Spirit is still much larger than you can ever comprehend. He wants to you use more than you have ever imagined. Your options and possibilities are limited. The Spirit's possibilities are unlimited.

I have found myself praying that the Holy Spirit would stretch my spirit. Why don't you make that your prayer, too?

Holy Spirit, Spirit of Jesus Christ who is alive in my life, thank You for the ways You manifest Your power in the world. Thank You for miracles, for faith, for insight and knowledge, for discernment, for languages that surpass our limited intellect and for informing us of Your purposes through interpretation.

I want, no, Lord, I need more of You. Stretch my weak human spirit. Transform my will to Your will. Let my mind have the mind of Christ. Enlarge my heart through Your almighty Holy Spirit. Amen.

CHAPTER NINE

The Holy Spirit and Prayer

IN THIS CHAPTER YOU WILL DISCOVER THAT . . .

- ▲ Praying in the Spirit is a biblical mandate.
- ▲ By praying Scripture you give the Holy Spirit His own words to work into the walls and corridors of your house.
- ▲ As we pray in the language of the Spirit, we participate in the cosmic spiritual battle fought across the earth as well as in our personal world.

MISSIONARY PARENTS IN AFRICA REARED NOTED EVANGELIST AND PREACHER STEPHEN OLFORD. As a teenager he went to England, became interested in motorcycles and let his walk with the Lord become cold. One icy evening in 1935 the seventeen-year-old Olford's motorcycle spun out of control, and complications from the injuries left him with little hope for recovery. Near death, Olford received a letter from his father in Angola, a letter written three months earlier. The godly missionary, unaware of his son's condition due to extremely limited communications, three months earlier had been inspired to write these words: "My son, this is of the utmost importance: Only one life, 'twill soon be past; only what's done for Christ will last." In his weakened condition, the young Olford slipped off the hospital bed, fell to his knees and prayed, "Lord, You have won."[1]

The Holy Spirit knows how to anoint a father to write a letter and have it arrive at just the right time. As one writer put it, the Holy Spirit is the "Go-Between God," moving between heaven and earth to accomplish redemption.[2] This action by the Holy Spirit is called *intercession.* It is a form of prayer through which the Holy Spirit Himself intervenes for and through us.

Prayer is a primary characteristic of biblical faith. But at times prayer seems to be a series of sermon clichés:

- ▲ "The family that prays together stays together."
- ▲ "Revival only comes by prayer."
- ▲ "The prayer of Jabez will transform your life."

Obviously those sentences are partly true. But . . .

- ▲ Why do so many church leaders divorce their spouse?

- Why do churches struggle and dissolve in spite of prayer warriors?
- Why do some people confuse prayer with a magic mantra and lose interest in a biblical prayer?
- In spite of all the books and workshops on prayer, why do so many people pray like the woman whose morning prayer is "Whatever" and her evening prayer is "Oh, well."[3]
- In fact, why do so many workshops on prayer do everything except pray!

Jim Cymbala observes that if you want to know how popular the church is, attend Sunday morning. If you want to know how popular the pastor is, attend Sunday night. But if you want to know how popular Jesus is, attend prayer meeting![4]

Don't get me wrong. I'm not suggesting that you not read the multitude of very good books on prayer (including the one in this Journey of Faith series by Eddie and Alice Smith). While many of us know how to talk about prayer and even how to pray effectively in certain contexts, most of us do not comprehend the incredible capacity of Holy Spirit prayer. Our tendency is to institutionalize a form of prayer, whether the Book of Common Prayer or charismatic free prayer, and make it the pattern rather than recognizing the power of the Holy Spirit in prayer. Once the Holy Spirit has been recognized as the source and power of prayer, it makes little difference whether the prayer is printed or spontaneous.

In this chapter we will explore intercession from the standpoint of what it means to "pray in the Spirit." Several biblical texts will dominate our discussion. As we study what the Bible tells us about the Holy Spirit and intercession, we'll better understand Paul's heart when he wrote about prayer:

- "Now I beg you, brethren, through the Lord Jesus Christ, and through the love of the Spirit, that you strive together with me in prayers to God for me" (Rom. 15:30).
- "Praying always with all prayer and supplication in

the Spirit, being watchful to this end with all perseverance and supplication for all the saints" (Eph. 6:18).

- "Be anxious for nothing, but in everything by prayer and supplication, with thanksgiving, let your requests be known to God" (Phil. 4:6).
- "Continue earnestly in prayer, being vigilant in it with thanksgiving" (Col. 4:2).
- "Pray without ceasing" (1 Thess. 5:17).
- "I exhort first of all that supplications, prayers, intercessions, and giving of thanks be made for all men" (1 Tim. 2:1).

PRAYING IN THE SPIRIT

Praying in the Spirit is a biblical mandate, and it is the way to be built up in our faith (Jude 20).

There are two ways that the term "pray in the Spirit" is used in the Bible. First, we see in Hebrews 9:8, 14 that all prayer touching the throne room of Father God occurs through the Spirit. Such prayers are possible because of the blood of Jesus and His constant intercession for us as High Priest (Heb. 7:25; 10:19, 21).

> Praying in the Spirit is a biblical mandate and the way to be built up in our faith.

The sinner crying out for forgiveness and the mature saint interceding for others both can "draw near with a true heart in full assurance of faith" and can "hold fast the confession of our hope without wavering, for He who promised is faithful" (Heb. 10:22–23). Whether a desperate and pitiful "Help!" or a thoughtful liturgical collect, such prayers are initiated and anointed by the Holy Spirit.

Prayer in the Spirit is possible because Father God desires that we speak to Him. But we cannot gain access to Him except through the sacrifice of Jesus Christ. And we cannot

But you, beloved, building yourselves up on your most holy faith, praying in the Holy Spirit.

—Jude 20

The Holy Spirit indicating this, that the way into the Holiest of All was not yet made manifest while the first tabernacle was still standing . . . [But because of Christ's sacrifice] how much more shall the blood of Christ, who through the eternal Spirit offered Himself without spot to God, cleanse your conscience from dead works to serve the living God?

—Hebrews 9:8, 14

Therefore He is also able to save to the uttermost those who come to God through Him, since He always lives to make intercession for them.

—Hebrews 7:25

Therefore, brethren, having boldness to enter the Holiest by the blood of Jesus . . . and having a High Priest over the house of God . . .

—Hebrews 10:19, 21

gain the benefits of Christ except through the revelation of the Holy Spirit.

> Those who have discovered the joy of walking in the Spirit's presence and power know the intimacy of constant prayer in the Spirit.

But the Spirit is not playing hide-and-seek with us. As we have seen earlier, before our conversion the Spirit is on a divine search and rescue mission, seeking us out, using this and that to get our attention, longing to show us the love of Christ. The Father wants to redeem us from the dominion of spiritual darkness and bring us into the kingdom of His Son, enabling us to be sons and daughters. (Read Colossians 1:13–14.)

Those who have discovered the joy of walking in the Spirit's presence and power know the intimacy of constant prayer in the Spirit. As John Taylor puts it, "To live in prayer is to live in the Spirit, and to live in the Spirit is to live in Christ. To live in Christ is to live in prayer. Prayer is not something you do; it is a style of living."[5]

Second, prayer in the Spirit also refers to the Holy Spirit's communication through us in tongues and groanings that cannot be uttered:

> *For if I pray in a tongue, my spirit prays... I will pray with the spirit.*
>
> —1 Corinthians 14:14–15

> *Likewise the Spirit also helps in our weaknesses. For we do not know what we should pray for as we ought, but the Spirit Himself makes intercession for us with groanings which cannot be uttered.*
>
> —Romans 8:26

ARE THERE PRAYERS THAT ARE NOT IN THE HOLY SPIRIT?

Yes. Here are three examples. Prayers offered in the name(s) of god(s) who are not the God of Abraham, Isaac and Jacob and Father of Jesus Christ are not Spirit-prayers. Relativism's contention that it doesn't matter who or what you worship as long as you are sincere is a hellish illusion. In Isaiah 41:21–24 the Lord taunts idols and those who worship them by asking them to "bring forth and show us what will happen; let them show the former things, what they were . . . or declare to us things to come. Show the things that are to come hereafter, that we may know that you are gods." The taunt continues in Isaiah 44:9–20 as the Lord ridicules those who make idols and those who hold the man-made object in their hand and "prays to it and says, 'Deliver me, for you are my god!'"

This is pertinent in light of the confusion relating to Islam and Allah. Arabic-speaking Christians who refer to God as revealed in the Bible can use the name Allah. But the contention that the Allah of the Quran is the same as the God of the Bible is flatly wrong. If they are the same, which view of God is correct? If they are both correct, then God is hopelessly psychotic, and we are better off as atheists. This is not a license for disrespect for those who worship according to Islam or any other non-Judeo-Christian religion. I'm not even suggesting that they don't pray. Just the opposite is the case with Islam. However, what is clear is that these are not prayers of the Holy Spirit.

Another type of prayer that is not Spirit-prayer is where modern pluralism has confused sincerity with truth, even within the Christian community. I once visited a Spirit-filled church that had a huge banner that said, "Relationships are more important than doctrine." I knew what the pastor meant, but what came across was that "getting along" was more important than truth. What had outwardly been a thriving charismatic congregation collapsed upon itself within two years because it lost its focus on doctrinal truth. Personal sincerity is not legitimate on its own merit when it comes to genuine prayer. In fact, as in the case of the shattered congregation, personal sincerity became its own form of self-righteousness that, as always, utterly failed.

A third type of prayer that is not Spirit-prayer is prayer that asks God to condone sinful acts. The unfaithful spouse who prays that God will bless his or her adultery is not praying in the Spirit. Prayers predicated on sinful acts with the assumption that God will later forgive are prayers of presumption and not prayers of the Spirit.

Question: The box above mentions three types of prayer that are not Spirit-prayers. In your own words describe those three types of prayers. As you reflect on this, are you aware of any prayers you may have prayed that were not Spirit-prayers?

___

___

___

▲▲▲▲▲▲▲

What are the two ways that praying in the Spirit can be understood?

____

____

▲▲▲▲▲▲▲

HOW CAN I BUILD MYSELF SPIRITUALLY?

Maybe you've seen this picture: flashing lights and traffic pulled off the side of the road, power lines lifted high in the air, a huge truck cab slowly coming around the curve. Then to your amazement, there's a house coming down the middle of the road! Somebody's house is being moved!

Well, think of your life as a house being moved. Your old house has been in a run-down, desolate neighborhood of sin, selfishness and despondency. Everything seemed hopeless, and every effort to fix up, repair and sell your old house had failed. But one day a new construction engineer showed up, bought your old house with his own money and began taking you off your old foundations. He cleaned up the debris of your life, moved you to a new foundation in a new neighborhood and totally remodeled the house of your life.

The design for your new, totally remodeled house came from the heart of Father God. The construction engineer is Jesus. The mover and remodeling expert is the Holy Spirit.

That's what happened when you were born again. The new foundation of your life is Jesus Christ and His revelation handed down through the apostles and prophets. (Read 1 Corinthians 3:11; Ephesians 2:20; 1 Peter 2:6.) You cannot become a holy house for God if you insist on remaining on the old foundation. The old foundation is fatally flawed and will fail. (Read Matthew 7:24–27.)

The modern metaphor of moving a house and building it on a new foundation is applicable to Jude 20. We have a positive role in helping to build this new house on a new foundation. Yes, we're saved by grace and not by our efforts. But after we are saved, God expects us to cooperate willingly with the Holy Spirit who lives in us. Our will is not removed when we are saved. Our will is disciplined to come alongside

God's will as expressed through the Spirit. That's why Jude 20 puts emphasis upon "you, beloved, building yourselves up."

Jude encouraged us to "build yourselves up on your most holy faith." The idea of "building up" is expressed through a compound Greek word that means "to build upon something." The idea is that of addition. It means there is more that God wants to do in our lives. The phrase "God's not finished with me yet" really is true. This building up is a present and continuing reality. Jude expressed this by using a present participle to describe our action in the Holy Spirit's remodeling work in us.

But the specifics of our role in this "building up project" are not left to our imagination. As much as most of us hate it, there really are instructions that must be used in order for the house to be right. Remember that the house we're building is more than our house. It's God's house, and He calls it the temple of the Holy Spirit. (Read 1 Corinthians 3:16–17; 6:19–20.) That's why Jude reminded us that we build up this house "on your most holy faith."

Two things come to mind about "your most holy faith." First, it is not any faith but the faith that has been revealed in Scripture. In other words, this faith already has content: It is the revelation of the gospel of Jesus Christ through the Bible. Through the centuries Christians have found a way to express this "most holy faith" through The Apostles' Creed. The content of our faith has already been given to us. It does not need any other testimony of Jesus Christ. There is no secret, mysterious aspect of the gospel that you need to build yourself up in Christ.

THE APOSTLES' CREED

I believe in God, the Father Almighty, creator of heaven and earth.

I believe in Jesus Christ, His only Son, our Lord. He was conceived by the power of the Holy Spirit and born of the Virgin Mary. He suffered under Pontius Pilate, was crucified, died, and was buried. He descended to the dead. On the third day He rose again. He ascended into heaven, and is seated at the right hand of the Father. He will come again to judge the living and the dead.

I believe in the Holy Spirit, the holy catholic Church, the communion of saints, the forgiveness of sins, the resurrection of the body, and the life everlasting. Amen.

The second part of this "most holy faith" is the working of faith in your own life. That working will always be in harmony with the "content" of the gospel, but it will also be personalized for you. The Holy Spirit knows all the details of your life from the inside. He even knows the details you don't know. It requires faith for you to trust the Holy Spirit to build up your life in the exact pattern that the Father desires for you.

By praying Scripture you give the Holy Spirit His own words to work into the "walls and corridors" of your house.

That's why all of this is connected to the final portion of Jude 20, "praying in the Holy Spirit." Praying in the Spirit is God's instrument of applying His Word into every dimension of your life.

This kind of prayer may be prayer that is in your own language. Such prayer is most effective when you start by praying the Scriptures. Martin Luther called the Psalms the prayer book of Jesus Christ. By praying Scripture you allow Psalm 107:20 to become a reality in your life: "He sent His Word and healed them, and delivered them from their destructions." By praying Scripture you give the Holy Spirit His own words to work into the "walls and corridors" of your house.

BONHOEFFER ON SCRIPTURE, PRAYER AND INTERCESSION

Nearly sixty years following his martyrdom on April 9, 1945, Dietrich Bonhoeffer's resistance to the idolatry of Nazism and faithfulness to the gospel remain a powerful witness. In 1935 he shared his life as a Lutheran teacher with a small group of pastors in an underground seminary in Finkenwalde, Germany. Insights from that experience led to a little book titled *Life Together.*[6] In the chapter titled "The Day Alone," Bonhoeffer described the interaction of three Christian disciplines: meditation, prayer and intercession.

Meditation for this group of pastors was not an Eastern mysticism of chanting an unknown "Om"; it was focused entirely on the Scriptures. Referring to the three disciplines he wrote, "The period of personal meditation is to be devoted to the Scriptures, private prayer, and intercession, and it has no other purpose. There is no occasion here for spiritual experiments. But for these three things there must be time, for God Himself requires them of us."[7] Meditation of the Word is the time for us to hear what the Word of God says to us. Our tendency is to apply the Word to others while we keep a log in our own eye. (Read Matthew 7:3–5.)

To meditate on Scripture is not an easy task. It requires time, concentration and help from the Holy Spirit. Bonhoeffer warned, "It is not necessary that we should have any unexpected, extraordinary experiences in meditation."[8] To seriously examine a small portion (perhaps only a verse) of Scripture is not about our own excitement but about putting the Word deep into our hearts so that the Holy Spirit has something in our own lives with which to work.

Prayer follows meditation because Scripture, which is the Word of life, is the source of prayerful inspiration. By praying the Scripture we do not "become victims of our own emptiness. Prayer means nothing else but the readiness and willingness to receive and appropriate the Word, and, what is more, to accept it in one's personal situation, particular tasks, decisions, sins, and temptations."[9]

The combination of Scripture and prayer leads to *intercession*. Here we pray for one another and allow the Holy Spirit to rid us of our fears, envy and hatred of others—especially those near us in Christian community. "A Christian fellowship exists by the intercession of its members for one another, or it collapses. I can no longer condemn or hate a brother for whom I pray, no matter how much trouble he causes me."[10]

For if I pray in a tongue, my spirit prays, but my understanding is unfruitful. What is the conclusion then? I will pray with the spirit, and I will also pray with the understanding.
—1 Corinthians 14:14–15

But we also pray in the Spirit as we pray in unknown tongues. Paul's remarks in 1 Corinthians 14:14–15 indicate that he knew of Spirit-prayer as both prayer in his known language and prayer in an unknown language. Prayers that you pray in your own language, especially when coupled with Scripture, flow from your conscious awareness and from any insights the Spirit brings to your awareness. This is important and should not be neglected. However, there are prayers that the Spirit Himself wants to pray through you that are not primarily about your conscious awareness but are about the Spirit's plans through and in your life.

Father God has an eternal design and destiny for you. But it is impossible for you to fully comprehend that destiny in your own mind. Regardless of your native tongue, there are not words to express to your spirit what the Father has in store for and through you. But when you cooperate with the Holy Spirit in His prayer language, you enter into a different dimension of language. Words create frameworks that define and, in some instances, create reality. Words convey truth, life, hope, peace and comfort. There are dimensions of eternity that Father God wants established in your spirit that can

only be birthed through the Spirit praying through you in heavenly languages. Such prayers are the way the Spirit intercedes for you to assist in building you up, adding to the house of your life. God wants to edify you. There is nothing selfish in desiring to be built up in the Lord. It is foolish to not want to be built up.

HOW DO YOU RECEIVE A PRAYER LANGUAGE IN THE SPIRIT?

A prayer language is not something you make up or create. It is not something learned in a natural sense. It is not rote repetition of sounds you have heard others say. A prayer language is the Holy Spirit's unique vocabulary through your own spirit, mind and voice. Every Christian has the capacity to pray in this fashion as the will is open to the Holy Spirit. There is a sense in which a prayer language grows as you trust the Lord and exercise the Holy Spirit's ministry in this way. As Paul wrote in 1 Corinthians 14:14–15, your human will is intimately involved in praying in the Spirit: "I will pray with the Spirit." It is a conscious decision on your part to allow words that you do not understand to flow through your mouth. You may speak aloud or under your breath, but you willingly cooperate with the Holy Spirit's desire to speak His words through you. In a real sense when you pray in the Spirit, it is God speaking to Himself through you to accomplish His purposes. If you have never prayed like this, you can begin today.

There is nothing selfish in desiring to be built up in the Lord.

First, if you are not a Christian, you need to confess your sins and accept Jesus Christ as your Savior and Lord. Satan can imitate speaking in other tongues, and outside of the blood of Christ your spirit is vulnerable to Satan's efforts to bring confusion and establish demonic strongholds in your life. Speaking in other tongues is not a distinctive Christian phenomenon, and it requires faith in Christ for the Holy

Spirit to be the one praying through you.

Second, as a Christian, you should pray that the blood of Jesus continues to cover your mind, soul, spirit and body. Any conscious sins should be confessed, and repentance should be genuine. You should pray that the mind of Christ be established in your mind as you pray.

Third, ask the Holy Spirit to pray through you. This conscious act of giving permission is important because it means you are willing to step outside the bounds of controlling your life through your own understanding and move into a realm of spiritual life where your understanding is given over to the Holy Spirit. It is not an escape from reason, but rather it is a step into the supernatural dimension of God's love and provision in divine-human communications.

Fourth, rather than being out of control, you will likely be aware of nonsense syllables in your mind. The Holy Spirit will work through your mind and tongue in order to speak. The sounds in your mind will seem nonsensical to you, but they will be the Spirit's words that He desires for you to express.

Fifth, usually this kind of prayer does not need interpretation since it is not a message for the Christian community. However, it may be appropriate to ask the Holy Spirit to reveal to your conscious mind what He is saying through you.

Sixth, the Holy Spirit will guide you as you speak. Remember, you are edifying and building up your faith as you pray in the Holy Spirit. The Holy Spirit is doing something in the spiritual realm that at the right time will become conscious awareness for you.

√CAN I PRAY IN THE SPIRIT WHENEVER I WISH?

As a born-again, Spirit-filled Christian, you can pray in the Spirit whenever you desire. This kind of prayer is not dependent on a particular song or place. Remember, your will is intimately involved in this kind of prayer. The Holy Spirit lives inside of you. Your body, wherever you are and whatever you are facing, is His temple, and He has something to say about everything in your life.

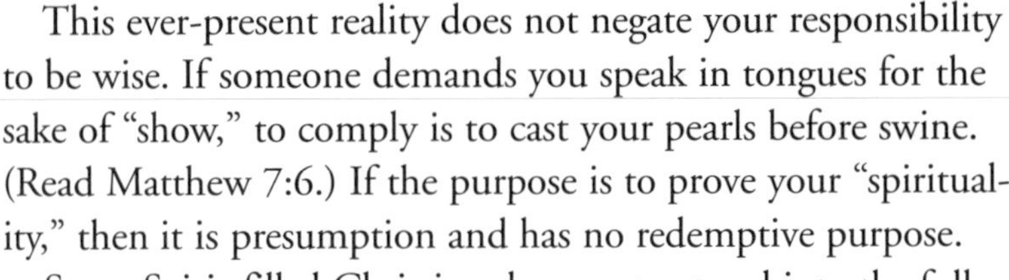

This ever-present reality does not negate your responsibility to be wise. If someone demands you speak in tongues for the sake of "show," to comply is to cast your pearls before swine. (Read Matthew 7:6.) If the purpose is to prove your "spirituality," then it is presumption and has no redemptive purpose.

Some Spirit-filled Christians have not entered into the fullness of this dimension of the Holy Spirit because they were afraid they would be "in the flesh." To be in the flesh in a carnal sense is to use tongues to prove one's own spirituality. It is to live a segmented life where you pray in tongues before others, but your personal life is in willful rebellion and disarray.

As a born-again, Spirit-filled Christian, you can pray in the Spirit whenever you desire.

But some Christians have confused *perfection* with *obedience.* We are all aware of our need to grow in Christ and that we have areas of life where the Spirit is still doing "house cleaning." But a person who is consciously, to the best of his or her awareness, seeking to serve Christ does not have to live in constant fear of not being good enough for God. Everything the Spirit does in us is a manifestation of God's love and grace to us. Praying in tongues makes none of us more holy than anyone else. It simply means we have recognized and released another dimension of God's grace at work in these earthen vessels.

Question: What's wrong with this statement: "Only people who are absolutely spiritually perfect can pray in tongues." Why is that statement not true?

____

____

How is the Holy Spirit moving your life from a foundation of sin to the foundation that is Christ? As you reflect on the various "rooms" of your heart, are you aware of some areas where the Spirit is asking you to allow Him in?

____

____

Review in your own words the six steps involved in praying in the Spirit in tongues.

___

___

___

▲▲▲▲▲▲▲

HOW DOES THE HOLY SPIRIT HELP US IN OUR WEAKNESSES?

As we saw at the beginning of this chapter, the apostle Paul had a profound and rich personal experience with the Holy Spirit. Paul did not write theological theory but from real experience based on the life of the Spirit in him. Read Romans 8:1–28, and let's discover what the Holy Spirit showed Paul.

First, in verses 1–11 Paul reminds us that we don't have to be perfect in ourselves for the Spirit of God to dwell in us. Our perfection is "in Christ," and we live with "no condemnation" for the frailties of human existence (Paul is not thinking here of continual willful disobedience or apostasy). This is because we walk "according to the Spirit" and have our minds (conscious awareness) set on the things of the Spirit, which are revealed in Scripture (vv. 1, 5). One way we know we are living in the Spirit is that there is a profound spiritual sense of life and peace in us, not condemnation (v. 6). Paul reminds us that spiritual life is not life attuned to any spiritual reality but life lived through and by Jesus Christ (vv. 9–10). As Christ lives in us by the Holy Spirit, then Christ's life flows from our spirit into every aspect of our physical life through the Holy Spirit. This is because the same Spirit who raised Jesus from the dead is living inside of us (v. 11)!

Stop right here! Read that last sentence again: The same Spirit who raised Jesus from the dead is living inside of us. Jesus did not raise Himself from the dead, but He was raised by the Spirit of holiness (Rom. 1:4). That same Holy Spirit is alive inside you. Once you really, really believe that Jesus Christ has been raised from the dead and know that the same Spirit is alive inside you, then your Christian life becomes a life of indescribable joy and love (Rom. 10:9).

And declared to be the Son of God with power according to the Spirit of holiness, by the resurrection from the dead.

—Romans 1:4

That if you confess with your mouth the Lord Jesus and believe in your heart that God has raised Him from the dead, you will be saved.

—Romans 10:9

Based on the fact that the Holy Spirit lived inside him, the apostle Paul knew that he was adopted as a son of God (Rom. 8:12–17). Through the Spirit Paul knew that he could call Father God the same name that Jesus called Him, "Abba." This is an intimate term of loving relationship. This is not a term of disrespect but a term of endearment.

But this intimacy with Christ is not a lottery ticket designed to give you a life of riches and pleasure. The blessings of Christ are not a version of an eternal game show with prizes to the lucky winners. The gods of mammon in Western consumerism have co-opted the blessings of Christ among some Christians and made Christianity look like a giant get-rich scheme. Paul knew better: "If [we are] children [of God], then heirs—heirs of God and joint heirs with Christ, if indeed we suffer with Him, that we may also be glorified together" (v. 17). Our life on this side of heaven, regardless of our physical blessings or lack thereof, is "not worthy to be compared with the glory which shall be revealed in us" (v. 18).

The same Spirit who raised Jesus from the dead is living inside of us.

In verses 19–22 Paul connects our personal lives with God's redemptive purposes for His entire creation. Just as the Holy Spirit lives within every Christian, the Holy Spirit is alive and working across the created order for the fullness of redemption to be revealed. The created order of this earth continues to suffer from the consequences of Adam's sin manifested in humanity's disregard for God's purposes for the earth (vv. 20–21). This is why the creation "waits for the revealing of the sons of God" (v. 19). We are the sons of God who are called in our generation to be people who understand the comprehensive redemptive purposes of God. Because of this, Christians are called to be:

- "Peacemakers" (Matt. 5:9)
- Ministers "of reconciliation" (2 Cor. 5:18)
- "Ambassadors for Christ" (2 Cor. 5:20)

This threefold call is how we demonstrate Spirit-filled living to the world.

- ▲ That's why it's appropriate for Christians to care more about peace than hating our enemies.
- ▲ That's why Christians aggressively, compassionately and truthfully seek for reconciliation based on justice and truth.
- ▲ That's why Christians must remember that our citizenship in the kingdom of God takes priority over the nationalism that easily divides us.

Some philosophers and scientists look at the created universe as a dying entity. They tell us that the sun will burn out in x-number of billions years. In other words, the second law of thermodynamics, the law of entropy, is the dominant law operating in the universe. But Paul saw a different law operating in the universe. He saw the universe not dying, but in labor pains for the birthing of the new heavens and earth that will be revealed in the return of Christ and the revelation of the sons and daughters of God. (Read Romans 8:22; 2 Peter 3:10–13; Revelation 21:1–22:5.)

Spirit-filled Christians have a role to play in this redemptive drama. The Holy Spirit groans in us as a spiritual prayer for the fullness of redemption to arrive. The Spirit and the bride cry to the Lord, "Come!" (Rev. 22:17). The Spirit prays through us prayers of hope, faith and love that are greater than the sin-stained world in which we live.

In the previous chapter we looked at various manifestations of the Holy Spirit, including miracles, faith and healings. These are more than manifestations to make us feel better in the church. These are ways that the Spirit reveals the ultimate redemptive will of the Creator. We cannot see this in the "fog" of spiritual war in which we live. Only the Holy Spirit enables us to see clearly (revelation).

That is why the "Spirit also helps in our weaknesses. For we do not know what we should pray for as we ought, but the Spirit Himself makes intercession for us with groanings with cannot be uttered" (Rom. 8:26). In our weakness we

struggle personally against sin, but we also struggle as peacemakers, ministers of reconciliation and ambassadors for Christ against the principalities and powers in the spiritual realm that are manifested in the world structures and systems of thought, economics, entertainment and government.

We don't know how to pray and even how to relate in this arena. But the Holy Spirit does. As we pray in the language of the Spirit, we participate in the cosmic spiritual battle fought across the earth as well as in our own personal world.

The Spirit "searches the hearts" and "knows what the mind of the Spirit is" (Rom. 8:27). That's why praying in tongues is so critical. Our capacity to pray with full understanding is severely limited. But the Spirit can pray through us and thereby make "intercession for the saints according to the will of God" (v. 27). That's why prayer in the Spirit is always prayer according to God's will. If you want to be certain that you are praying God's will, then pray in the language of the Spirit.

Your confidence to pray in this fashion is based on the same hope of the created order: The Creator is good, and His goodness will be manifested in the earth. In our own understanding we don't see the goodness of God in the death of a friend, a parent, a child, the terrorism of September 11, 2001. But in the Spirit God's goodness is prayed in such a way that we can "know that all things work together for good to those who love God, to those who are the called according to His purpose" (v. 28).

LET'S TALK ABOUT IT

▲ Based on insights from Romans 8 about the Holy Spirit, is a Christian a born-again pessimist or a born-again optimist? Explain your answer.

____

____

▲▲▲▲▲▲▲

▲ Explain the roles in which the Holy Spirit seeks to use us in the world and how we can fulfill our work in those roles.

____

____

▲▲▲▲▲▲▲

▲ How can we know for certain that we are praying God's will?

___

___

▲▲▲▲▲▲▲

TIME TO PLUG IN TO THE HOLY SPIRIT

This chapter has introduced you to the Holy Spirit as intercessor. We have seen that the Spirit's power in prayer is a manifestation of divine grace. It is also a manifestation of the Holy Spirit's power in our lives capable of producing more faith and fruit in us than we have ever imagined.

Do you have a prayer language in the Holy Spirit? If not, refer back to the six important areas discussed earlier in this chapter. As a Christian, why not begin to ask the Holy Spirit to give you this wonderful part of His life in you? Jesus said that we can ask, seek and knock, and we will receive, find and discover open doors. (Read Luke 11:9–10.) Our heavenly Father, the One to whom the Spirit enables us to say, "Abba," wants to give the Holy Spirit to you. (Read Luke 11:13.)

If you already pray in the language of the Spirit, hopefully this study of Romans 8 has given you a broader perspective of the Spirit's purposes through your life. Remember, the Holy Spirit is doing a redemptive work through you whether you realize it or not.

If you are have not begun to pray in the Spirit, read and settle in your heart if you want to seriously pray this prayer:

Holy Spirit, I confess that this is hard for me. I want to understand everything, and I'm afraid of being out of control. I don't want to look or be foolish, and above all I don't want to presume upon You.

So please help me. I've read Your Word, and I know that You have this gift for me. Give me grace to trust Your Word and Your work in me. I confess with my mouth that Jesus is Lord, and I believe in my heart that Jesus has been raised from the dead by You. So be released in my life, my mind and my tongue for Your glory. Amen.

CHAPTER TEN

Take a Power Walk!

IN THIS CHAPTER YOU WILL DISCOVER THAT . . .

- ▲ Walking in the Spirit means to obey the words of Jesus and the promptings of the Holy Spirit.
- ▲ Life in the Spirit is about Jesus' life in and through us.
- ▲ Walking in the Spirit is not always fun.

AT A CRITICAL POINT IN THE MOVIE *THE MATRIX,* MORPHEUS SPEAKS TO TRINITY ABOUT NEO. "There is a difference between knowing the path and walking the path."

Many of us have "knowing the path" knowledge of God. There's something to be said for that. It is important to know the truth intellectually. God is not anti-intellectual. God just wants us to get it right in terms of His wisdom and truth and stop this idolatrous charade that human wisdom has all the answers when half the time we don't even have the right questions!

But many of us don't have "walking the path" knowledge. It's like studying a map and marking the right roads, but never taking the trip. Theology in the Bible is always a "doing" theology. The Holy Spirit is in the business of getting us attuned to the right map (the Bible) and then getting us on the road!

A LITTLE TRAVELING MUSIC, PLEASE

Read this sampling of how the Bible describes a godly life:

> *When Abram was ninety-nine years old, the LORD appeared to Abram and said to him, "I am Almighty God;* walk *before Me and be blameless."*
>
> —GENESIS 17:1, EMPHASIS ADDED

> *You shall* walk *in all the ways which the LORD your God has commanded you.*
>
> —DEUTERONOMY 5:33, EMPHASIS ADDED

> *Blessed is the man who* walks *not in the counsel of the ungodly.*
>
> —PSALM 1:1, EMPHASIS ADDED

He has shown you, O man, what is good; and what does the LORD *require of you but to do justly, to love mercy, and to* walk *humbly with your God?*

—MICAH 6:8, EMPHASIS ADDED

Therefore we were buried with Him through baptism into death, that just as Christ was raised from the dead by the glory of the Father, even so we also should walk *in newness of life.*

—ROMANS 6:4, EMPHASIS ADDED

Let us walk *properly, as in the day, not in revelry and drunkenness, not in lewdness and lust, not in strife and envy.*

—ROMANS 13:13, EMPHASIS ADDED

We walk *by faith, not by sight.*

—2 CORINTHIANS 5:7, EMPHASIS ADDED

Walk *in the Spirit, and you shall not fulfill the lust of the flesh.*

—GALATIANS 5:16, EMPHASIS ADDED

For we are His worksmanship, created in Christ Jesus for good works, which God prepared beforehand that we should walk *in them.*

—EPHESIANS 2:10, EMPHASIS ADDED

Walk *in love... For you were once darkness, but now you are light in the Lord.* Walk *as children of light... See then that you* walk *circumspectly, not as fools but as wise.*

—EPHESIANS 5:2, 8, 15, EMPHASIS ADDED

Walk *worthy of the Lord, fully pleasing Him, being fruitful in every good work and increasing in the knowledge of God.*

—COLOSSIANS 1:10, EMPHASIS ADDED

As you therefore have received Christ Jesus the Lord, so walk *in Him.*

—COLOSSIANS 2:6, EMPHASIS ADDED

He who says he abides in Him [Christ] ought himself also to walk *just as He walked.*

—1 JOHN 2:6, EMPHASIS ADDED

In Ephesians 6:15 Paul said that our feet have been shod "with the preparation of the gospel of peace," so in Christ, in the words of an old secular song, "these boots are made for walking" in the Spirit.

Let's take a moment and review what the Bible tells us

about our walk with God. Abraham was called to walk before the Lord and live a blameless life. Psalm 1:1 tells us that the person who does not walk after the ungodly receives a blessing. Micah reminds us to walk humbly before the Lord, and Paul reminds us that we walk by faith and not by sight. First John 2:6 tells us that our walk is to be patterned after the way that Jesus walked.

This "traveling music" from the Bible is a great reminder that we are on a journey with the Holy Spirit. We are to stand firm in the faith, but not get our spiritual feet stuck in the ruts of legalism and false piety. The biblical metaphors reveal the paradox of the Christian life: *You can only walk in the Spirit by standing firm in the Lord, and you can only stand firm in the Lord by walking in the Spirit.*

WALK AND OBEY, FOR THERE'S NO OTHER WAY

If you are familiar with the old hymns of the church, you may realize that the title of this section is a play on the words of the hymn "Trust and Obey": "Trust and obey, for there's no other way to be happy in Jesus, but to trust and obey."[1] Walking in the Spirit means to obey the words of Jesus and the promptings of the Holy Spirit. But what does it mean to obey? How can we learn to more fully obey?

UNDERSTANDING OBEDIENCE

The main word used in the Old Testament for *obey* is the Hebrew verb *shama,* which means, "hear." It actually has the sense of to hear intelligently. The focus is upon something that is understood and capable of being done by the hearer. Read Exodus 24:7; Deuteronomy 11:27–28; 21:18, 20. In these passages you can find examples of the use of *shama.* One of the meanings of the Hebrew word *marah* in the Old Testament is "disobey," as in 1 Kings 13:26. *Marah* is also means, "bitter, rebel."

The Old Testament understood that failure to obey was never excused by ignorance. God's law had been revealed, and the prophets made sure that people heard that law. That's why Samuel told Saul, "To obey is better than sacrifice" (1 Sam. 15:22). Obedience means that God has spoken and that the listener has heard and taken God seriously. It denotes genuine fear of the Lord.

Failure to obey means intentional rebellion and stubbornness. Again, Samuel did not hesitate to draw the logical conclusions of Saul's disobedience: "For rebellion is as the sin of witchcraft, and stubbornness is as iniquity and idolatry" (v. 23).

In the New Testament the primary words for obedience and disobedience are from the verb meaning "to hear." However, the word *peitho,* which means *obedience* on the basis of persuasion, is used in Romans 2:8; Galatians 5:7; Hebrews 13:17; and James 3:3. The word *pisteuo* means to "trust" and is used in Hebrews 3:18–19.

The Hebrew verb translated "obey" in the Old Testament is *shama.* It literally means, "hear." The same is true in the Greek of the New Testament but primarily with the compound verb *hupakouo.* The Latin word *obaudire,* which is the root of our English word *obey,* also means "to hear" (you can literally hear it in the main verb *audire,* as in *auditory*). Compounds are important in Greek and Latin. In Greek the word *obey* is composed of the preposition *upo,* which means "under," and the word *akouo,* which means, "I hear." Thus, to obey in the New Testament is to come under the authority of what is said by another. Obedience is an issue of three things:

- Recognizing Christ's lordship over us
- Learning how to discern Christ's voice
- Willingly submitting to and coming under the guidance and authority of what Christ has spoken

If obedience means to come under the authority of what is spoken and heard, then what is disobedience? In Greek the prepositional compound changes to *para,* which means "beside." The verb is the same "I hear" that we saw earlier: *akouo.* Thus, "to disobey" means that I hear what the Lord says to me, but rather than coming "under" the authority of His Word I choose to stand "beside" what I hear. I'm no longer "under" the Word but removed from it. The Word becomes an object of my consideration whether or not it applies to me. Rather than the Word controlling my life, I control what if any of the Word I will submit to. In other words, I choose to stand alone with my own thoughts and plans rather than God's thoughts and plans.

Think of God's Word as coming to you from above through an umbrella. As long as you are "under" the umbrella, you are positioned to "hear" and do what the Lord says. While "under" the umbrella you are kept in the goodness of God's gracious blessings. But once you step out from under the umbrella, even though you can still hear His voice, you have chosen to no longer be under His authority. Such actions mean that you have stepped outside of His gracious blessings and entered into the realm of self-will, disobedience and, if you harden your heart, into the realm of severed relationship with Christ.

The umbrella analogy is interesting because it contrasts what it means to listen to God's voice from "above" and listening to the multitude of voices from "below." The late Dutch priest Henri Nouwen gave a good personal example of this. In the midst of many personal struggles, Nouwen met Mother Teresa and decided to use that time to ask her advice. He wrote, "I started explaining all my problems and difficulties—trying to convince her of how complicated it all was!" After about ten minutes he stopped to hear her advice. "Mother Teresa looked at me quietly and said, 'Well, when you spend one hour a day adoring your Lord and never do anything which you know is wrong . . . you will be fine!'"

The simplicity of Mother Teresa's answer broke through the fog that had enveloped Nouwen's life. He later wrote, "I realize that I had raised a question from below and that she had given an answer from above. At first, her answer didn't seem to fit my question, but then I began to see that her answer came from God's place and not from the place of my complaints."[2]

We can allow the issues of life and the complicated questions to arise from below. When that happens we become like Nicodemas, whose spiritual senses were dulled because he lived, thought and believed from below, that is, from the sphere of human understanding and wisdom (John 3:4, 9). When we are preoccupied with the "below" problems and solutions, then we stand alongside the voice of the Spirit rather than simply standing under His voice. We reject the

Nicodemus said to Him, "How can a man be born when he is old? Can he enter a second time into his mother's womb and be born?. . . How can these things be?"

—John 3:4, 9

simplicity of His Word from above because we are afraid, arrogant and too self-sufficient to really trust Him.

But the Holy Spirit who lives in us constantly calls us back under the umbrella. Under the umbrella of the Word we discover the sound of His voice, the intimacy of His fellowship and the joy of walking step by step with Him. We discover the joy of life from above!

Question: List the three issues of obedience.

____

____

____

▲▲▲▲▲▲▲

Using the umbrella analogy of obedience and disobedience, describe a time when you stayed under the umbrella and when you stepped alongside the umbrella.

____

____

▲▲▲▲▲▲▲

What do you think of the simplicity of Mother Teresa's response to Father Nouwen?

____

____

▲▲▲▲▲▲▲

RECOGNIZING CHRIST'S LORDSHIP OVER US

Walking in the Spirit is living as Christ would have us live. Life in the Spirit is about Jesus' life in and through us. Although emphasized earlier in this book, it bears repeating:

- ▲ The Holy Spirit testifies about Jesus Christ. (Read John 15:26; Revelation 19:10.)
- ▲ The Holy Spirit helps us remember Jesus' words. (Read John 14:26.)
- ▲ The Holy Spirit always leads us into truth. (Read John 14:17; 16:13.)
- ▲ The Holy Spirit will teach us all things we need to

know about our inheritance in Jesus Christ. (Read John 14:26; 16:13.)

- ▲ The Holy Spirit will glorify Jesus Christ. (John 16:14.)

These biblical insights are worth repeating because they warn us against distorted spiritual enthusiasm. A carnal excitement about spiritual things can arise when we lose contact with the ultimate purpose of the Holy Spirit. We can pursue spiritual experiences and gifts and confuse personal feelings of happiness and contentment with life in the Spirit. We can compete with one another regarding gifts and the "spiritual level" of local congregations. Madison Avenue spiritual advertising and gimmicks bombard us. Many Christians are so controlled by their emotions that they fall prey to anything that looks spiritual even when it is not even Christian.

Walking in the Spirit is living as Christ would have us live.

But when we are anchored in Jesus Christ as revealed in the Bible, we are able to more effectively discern and comprehend the work of the Holy Spirit in our lives. The Holy Spirit reveals Jesus as the Savior of the world and Messiah of Israel. We must be careful to not be confused by the spirit of our age that seeks to lower all religions to one common denominator of love and peace. The Holy Spirit will not lead us in that direction. The Holy Spirit will enable us to stand in the face of ridicule, marginalization and even persecution when we confess that Jesus Christ is Lord and there is no other.

Those who walk in the Spirit will live with that testimony on their lips and Christ's gracious and sacrificial love in their actions.

At the beginning of this chapter there are several passages from Ephesians, Colossians and 1 John that showed the connection of walking in the Spirit and the priority of Jesus Christ. Let's look specifically at Colossians 2:6 and see where

it leads us as we discover what the Holy Spirit is doing in establishing the lordship of Jesus Christ in us.

Colossians 2:6 encourages us, "As you therefore have received Christ Jesus the Lord, so walk in Him." Paul intentionally designated Christ Jesus as "the Lord." This was a life-and-death issue for early Christians because it was an act of political treason to call someone else other than the Roman emperor "Lord." To publicly confess that Jesus of Nazareth was "Lord" was to deny the deity of the Roman emperor and deny the empire's claim to world dominion. This confession flew in the face of all worldly political, economic and military wisdom, and it required faith that Jesus Christ had truly been raised from the dead and is the living King of kings and Lord of lords.

Paul did not leave it to the Colossians' imagination as to what it meant to "walk" in Christ. You walk in the Spirit in Christ Jesus the Lord as you are "rooted and built up in Him and established in the faith, as you have been taught, abounding in it with thanksgiving" (Col. 2:7). "Rooted" indicates strength, stability and constancy; it means that you are fully grounded in Christ Jesus. This grounding includes intellectual knowledge, thought and understanding through the Bible as well as the emotive elements of a personal relationship with Jesus Christ.

The same idea of "rooted" is found in Ephesians 3:17. However, to fully comprehend what it means to be "rooted in Christ" and the role of the Holy Spirit in this, we need to look at Ephesians 3:14–21.

> *For this reason I bow my knees to the Father of our Lord Jesus Christ, from whom the whole family in heaven and earth is named, that He would grant you, according to the riches of His glory, to be strengthened with might through His Spirit in the inner man, that Christ may dwell in your hearts through faith: that you, being rooted and grounded in love, may be able to comprehend with all the saints what is the width and length and depth and height—to know the love of Christ which passes knowledge; that you may be filled with all the fullness of God. Now to Him who is able to do exceedingly abundantly above all that we ask or think, according to the power that works in us, to*

Him be glory in the church by Christ Jesus to all generations, forever and ever. Amen.

As we study this passage of Scripture we see that Paul was keenly aware of the Holy Spirit in his life. His "for this reason" in verse 14 actually picked up on the thought started in Ephesians 3:1. Paul dictated his letters, and the flow of arguments and ideas reflects that kind of verbal/thinking process.[3] The "reason" that Paul bowed his knees was because he understood that Christ had accomplished two major things in His death and resurrection. First, Christ had reconciled both Jew and Gentile to God and "by one Spirit" made it possible for all humanity to come to the Father (Eph. 2:14–18). Second, Christ had created a new humanity, a new household of God, that "grows into a holy temple in the Lord" and has become "a dwelling place of God in the Spirit" (Eph. 2:21–22). This new humanity and new dwelling place is the body of Christ established in His universal church.

It was "for this reason" that Paul humbled himself in worship to God, the Father of our Lord Jesus Christ (Eph. 3:14). The reality of this household of God is reflected in the fact that all who are redeemed in Christ are part of a new "family in heaven and earth" (v. 15). God is our Father, and through Christ we are adopted into this family as sons of daughters who pray to God as "Abba."

Paul's reference to bowing his knees primarily denoted humility before the sovereign Lord. His petitions are those of a citizen who has come before his sovereign asking something for every other citizen. Each petition is critical to our understanding of what it means to "walk in the Spirit."

Paul first petitioned the Father to grant us "to be strengthened with might through His Spirit in the inner man" (v. 16). He appealed to the Father's "riches of His glory" as the source for this spiritual might in the Spirit (v. 16). These riches are found in Jesus Christ (2 Cor. 8:9). The Father has granted to us that we be "strengthened with might." The word *strengthened* (*krataioo*) has the sense of strength manifested. Think of a poster of Arnold Schwarzenegger bulging in muscles. Now think of a movie where he manifested and revealed the

For you know the grace of our Lord Jesus Christ, that though He was rich, yet for your sakes He became poor, that you through His poverty might become rich.
—2 Corinthians 8:9

strength in those muscles. It's that second thought of manifested strength that lies behind Paul's petition.

This "manifested muscle" is seen in the "might" that Paul prayed would be given to all of us. The word *might* means ability and capability to perform. The Greek word *dunamis*, which is the basis for our English word *dynamite*, does not imply an explosion of power as much as it implies the capability of power.[4]

Thus, Paul prayed that the Father would enable us to have manifested strength, the spiritual muscles if you please, that would allow us to make use of the spiritual capabilities we have through the Holy Spirit in us. The English text reflects the emphasis in the Greek that it is through the Holy Spirit we are strengthened with might, not through our own inner man. This emphasis is critical because it sets the stage for the purpose of our being strengthened in might through the Holy Spirit.

The purpose of this manifested might is "that Christ may dwell in your hearts through faith" (Eph. 3:17). The Holy Spirit creates the dwelling place of the throne of Christ in our hearts. This does not happen naturally by human efforts to be good or to achieve more success, but it happens by faith. It is through faith that Christ is enthroned in our hearts as Lord. God created our hearts as His dwelling place. Only by faith in Christ can the Holy Spirit establish His rightful throne in our hearts.

When Christ reigns as Lord in our hearts through the incredible manifested might of the Holy Spirit, then we are "rooted and grounded in love" (v. 17). This "being rooted" is the same word (*rhizoo*) we saw in Colossians 2:7 that sent us on this journey into Ephesians 3:14–21. The verb "grounded" (*themelioo*) is used in Colossians 1:23, and the noun (*themelios*) is used in Ephesians 2:20 in reference to the "foundation of the apostles and prophets, Jesus Christ Himself being the chief cornerstone." It denotes that another has put something in place. We are "rooted and grounded in love" as the Holy Spirit establishes the life of Christ in us. This is consistent with Romans 5:5 where "the love of God has been poured out into our hearts by the Holy Spirit who was given to us."

. . . rooted and built up in Him and established in the faith, as you have been taught, abounding in it with thanksgiving.
—Colossians 2:7

If indeed you continue in the faith, grounded and steadfast, and are not moved away from the hope of the gospel which you have heard, which was preached to every creature under heaven, of which I, Paul, became a minister.
—Colossians 1:23

So far we have seen Paul use two words for power and strength (Eph. 3:16). In verse 18 Paul added a third word that is translated "may be able" in English. However, the Greek is much stronger than the English meaning. *Exischuo* means to be in full strength and "is the strongest word available to indicate strength or ability."[5]

In three verses Paul shows us the power of the Holy Spirit that is working in us. This power is God's ability seeking to be manifested and revealed through us. It establishes the reign of Christ in our hearts and firmly establishes us in love. By being thoroughly rooted and grounded in love we have the greatest spiritual power imaginable to comprehend God's redemptive purposes. Thus, the Spirit leads us to a fuller reality of God's love, which is the basis for our understanding the great mysteries of life.

In your Bible read 1 Corinthians 13 and Romans 8:31–39. In these passages of Scripture Paul emphasizes that love is the key to comprehending God's purposes. Love is the greatest of all spiritual gifts and realities, and the love of God in Christ Jesus our Lord is able to sustain us regardless of what comes against us.

As you walk in the Spirit, you are being given manifested might and an incredible ability to comprehend and know the "love of Christ which passes knowledge" (Eph. 3:19). This work of the Spirit will also fill you "with all the fullness of God" (v. 19).

The Spirit leads us to a fuller reality of God's love, which is the basis for our understanding the great mysteries of life.

The phrase "piling on" is used in football to describe too many defensive players hitting a downed ball carrier. While this incurs a penalty in football, there is no penalty in what Paul understood happens in us through the Holy Spirit. Paul "piled on" the phrases of "manifest might" and incredible ability in Ephesians 3:16, 18. But just when you thought he ran out of words, Paul piled on some more in verse 20 to describe what the Holy Spirit is doing in us: The Spirit is able

to do "exceedingly abundantly above all that we ask or think, according to the power that works in us." The English language has to use two words, "exceedingly abundantly," to translate the single Greek verb *perissos*, which by itself means "more than enough, abundance." This Greek word is used by Jesus Himself in John 10:10 to describe the abundant life we have in Him. But Paul piles on two Greek prefixes—*huper*, which means "over," and *ek*, which means "from"—to create a word describing the incredible, beyond description of words or even imagination, power of the Holy Spirit at work in us. With that in mind, here is my paraphrase of Ephesians 3:20: "The Holy Spirit is able to do abundantly more than you have ever asked or even thought to ask, and when you have walked in His presence to where you have never even asked, the Spirit will do even more, and when you have walked with Him there, He will from there do even more than you have ever asked or thought."

But all this divine power is conditioned by the work of the Holy Spirit in us. Paul concluded this "power discourse" with "according to the power [*dunamis*; divine capability] that works in us." God is looking for people of faith who will allow the Holy Spirit to be released in their lives. God's "exceedingly abundantly" can only manifest itself in participation of our faith in His holy presence who dwells within us.

The Holy Spirit will do all of this because Jesus is Lord over your life, the church and the entire universe. Now are you ready to start walking in the Spirit!

Question: Name some of the ways that Paul "piled on" how the Holy Spirit works His power in us.

____

____

▲▲▲▲▲▲▲

Read Romans 8:31–39; 1 Corinthians 13; Ephesians 3:17. Describe why love is so important in the Christian life.

____

____

▲▲▲▲▲▲▲

LEARNING HOW TO HEAR THE VOICE OF GOD

Once at our office staff Christmas party I read the traditional story of Christ's birth from Matthew 2 and Luke 2. Rather than giving my mundane devotional thoughts to people who were already comfortably sitting stuffed from eating a wonderful meal, I asked them to tell us who or what in the story meant the most to them. It was interesting to hear their observations about Mary, Joseph, the shepherds and the wise men. If you boiled down their observations to a common denominator, it would be that they marveled that each of these people heard God speak. The fiancé of an office secretary, a young man who would graduate a week later with an engineering degree and begin work with a major petroleum company, said, "It seems that it was so easy for them to hear God speak. The shepherds saw and heard angels. Mary saw and heard an angel. Joseph and the wise men had unambiguous dreams. Why can't God make it simple for me today?"

You have probably felt that way at times. I remember the time I was facing a major decision regarding a possible change in ministry location and function about fifteen years ago. I struggled to hear the voice of God in the midst of a fruitful pastorate and another opportunity. One Sunday afternoon I sat in the yard, looked into the sky and prayed that God would write His will in the clouds. Suddenly a perfect cross formed before me. My heart leapt. *Follow the cross,* I thought. But in a few moments the vapor trail cross of two jetliners turned into parallel tracks in the jet stream. I decided that trying to read jet vapor trails was pretty close to reading tea leaves!

> The problem is not that God speaks. The problem is that I find it difficult to hear and then listen.

When you walk in the Spirit, you discover two things. First, you discover that God really does speak. Second, you discover that He speaks in ways that are both easy and difficult. Usually the problem is not that God speaks. Usually the problem is that I find it difficult to hear and then listen.

There is a difference between hearing and listening. Just ask any wife. She can tell you when her husband is only hearing or when he is really listening. Most of the time God speaks pretty loudly through His megaphone called the Bible.

I don't have much trouble hearing what He says. I do have trouble really listening to what He says, though, especially when His voice challenges my presuppositions, agendas and attitudes. Sometimes God has to break into our routine, even our routine Christian life, to get us to listen to Him.

Henri Nouwen tells of how God got his attention and changed the direction of his ministry. At that time Nouwen was on the faculty at Yale Divinity School. He had been praying, "Lord, show me where You want me to go, and I will follow You." One day he was preparing to leave his apartment to go to class when he heard the doorbell. He answered, and standing there was a young woman who said, "I am Jan Risse and have come to bring you greetings from Jean Vanier."

Jean Vanier was a Frenchman who was known for his work with mentally handicapped people at L'Arche community. Nouwen had heard of Vanier but had never had any contact with him. "Well, thank you. What can I do for you?" he replied.

Risse said, "Oh, nothing. I just came to bring you the greetings of Jean Vanier."

This awkward exchange continued for a few moments as Nouwen thought she was there to invite him to lecture at L'Arche. Finally Risse asked, "Can I come in?" Nouwen let her in and soon left for his appointments at Yale Divinity School.

When he returned, he found his kitchen table set with linen, nice plates, flowers, a burning candle, a bottle of wine and a nice meal. "Where did you find all of this?" the surprised priest asked.

"In your own kitchen and cupboards. You obviously don't use them too often!" she replied.

Nouwen wrote, "A stranger had walked into my home and, without asking me for anything, was showing me my own house." When the woman left she reminded him, "Jean Vanier sends his greetings to you."

Sometime later Jean Vanier came to America, called Henri Nouwen and invited him to Chicago for a prayer retreat. Out of that simple experience with Jan Risse bringing greetings and asking nothing in return, Nouwen began to listen to the voice of the Holy Spirit leading him from academia at Yale and later Harvard to the mentally handicapped at L'Arche and finally to Daybreak, Vanier's ministry in Toronto. There Nouwen ministered until his death in September 1996.[6]

Nouwen's discovery is a vivid reminder for us to listen to the little surprises that each day brings. We may hear the voice of God in those little moments that add up to significant change.

Through this study of the Holy Spirit we have observed numerous ways that God speaks: a powerful sermon, an influential book, a word of wisdom, knowledge or prophecy, dreams, visions, a message in other tongues—just to name a few. Regardless of the particular way that God speaks and we listen, the key is found in walking in the Spirit. This is the intimate life of communication between Creator and creature.

All hearing must be grounded in the biblical revelation of Jesus Christ.

In 1929 Karl Barth, one of the most significant theologians of the twentieth century, gave a series of lectures that were published in 1938 in the small book *The Holy Ghost and the Christian Life*. Barth remarked, "It is purely and simply the office of the Holy Ghost to be continually opening our ears to enable us to receive the Creator's word." He also warned against our tendency to associate our "external and internal urges" with the Word of God.[7] Both insights are essential elements of hearing the Holy Spirit. We are certain that He speaks to us. We are also certain that Satan will seek to substitute another word for God's Word. That is why all hearing must be grounded in the biblical revelation of Jesus Christ. To use the imagery from the first part of this chapter, we must stand under the umbrella so that our hearing is obeying.

I WILL WALK IN THE SPIRIT

It's not only two-year-olds who have problems with their "will." You may be born again, sanctified and filled with the Spirit, but you recognize that sometimes your will and God's

will are not the same. There is really no compromise in this issue. We cannot do God's will by our own will. Abram heard the promise of God concerning a son. Instead of waiting for God's will to be accomplished through him, Abram and Sarah took matters into their own hands. Their plan seemed the right thing. Their plan was an honest attempt to "help" God. But their plan birthed an Ishmael.

As a Christian you have the will of the Spirit and your own will operating in your consciousness. Your will is your capacity for decision making. Your will is your real self because the actions of your will reflect what you really are.

In an especially insightful section of *The Spiritual Man*, Chinese Christian Watchman Nee wrote about the will. Salvation included a "cutting off" and a "uniting with." Those things in our lives that are not in the Father's will, those things not birthed by the Holy Spirit, are to be cut off from us. This separation is the same as sanctification, which was described earlier in this book. Our old self-will, our willfulness, fights hard to preserve itself. It will even use religion as a guise so that we fool even ourselves. Whenever we use religion, even in its best sense, to make ourselves appealing to God, we actually become filthy rags in His eyes (Isa. 64:6; Phil. 3:7–8). In Colossians 2:23 Paul wrote of man-made efforts at religion that that "indeed have an appearance of wisdom in self-imposed religion, false humility." The words translated "self-imposed religion" literally mean "will-religion." Our will substitutes our version of obedience for what the Holy Spirit wills. When we do this, we step outside the umbrella of listening and walk in our own path. This "willfulness" must decrease, cease and ultimately die if we are to walk in the fullness of the Spirit. Nee wrote, "Real greatness rests not on how much we have but on how much we have lost. Authentic life can be seen only in the abandonment of self."[8]

But we are like an unclean thing, and all our righteousnesses are like filthy rags.
—Isaiah 64:6

But what things were gain to me, these I have counted loss for Christ. Yet indeed I also count all things loss for the excellence of the knowledge of Christ Jesus my Lord, for whom I have suffered the loss of all things, and count them as rubbish, that I may gain Christ.
—Philippians 3:7–8

The "uniting with" is the same as "in Christ," Paul's frequent expression of the Christian life. To be "in Christ" is to walk according to His will through the Holy Spirit. Nee points out that our "union" with Christ has two steps: "...the union of life and the union of will. We are united with Him in life at the time we are regenerated (born again) and receive His life."[9] The second step is the uniting of our will with His will.

To be united with Christ in will means first that God "subdues the activities of our will," and second, it means that God "conquers the life of our will." Nee expressed these "measures" by referring to the first as having an "obedient will" and the second as a "harmonious will."[10] Let's phrase what Nee said in more contemporary terms: As a Christian I choose to obey the leading of the Holy Spirit (obedient will), and I also know and appreciate the heart of God in the matter (harmonious will). You can serve God with an obedient will but a heart that is not in harmony. You can identify that person, maybe yourself, by resentment, hardness of heart and legalism. But to walk in obedient will and harmonious will is "the zenith of anyone's spiritual walk."[11]

Walking in the Spirit is the way of real life. It's the life of paradox:

- The only way to conquer is to surrender.
- The only way to live is to die.
- The only way to have more of God is to have less of yourself.

But it's worth it!

LET'S TALK ABOUT IT

We've covered a lot of ground in this chapter. You may be tired from all this walking! Walking in the Spirit is not always fun. Watchman Nee spent the last twenty years of his life under the oppression of Communism. Dietrich Bonhoeffer was martyred days before the end of World War II. Mother Teresa gave her life to lepers, and Henri Nouwen followed the Spirit-walk away from Yale and Harvard to a life with those on the margins of society.

- Watchman Nee offers interesting insights into the nuances of walking in the Spirit. Can you identify a time in your

life where you obeyed the "letter of the law" but your heart was not in it? How did you feel?

____

____

▲▲▲▲▲▲▲

▲ What is the Holy Spirit saying to you about how He wants you outward obedience and your heart's understanding and affection for Him?

____

____

▲▲▲▲▲▲▲

▲ In the space provided draw a stick figure of yourself. Now draw an umbrella. Ask the Holy Spirit to show you where to put the umbrella in relation to yourself.

____

▲▲▲▲▲▲▲

▲ Is the umbrella lying unopened on the ground? Is the umbrella opened in your hand? Is the umbrella opened but on the ground or to your side? Or, is the opened umbrella over your head where you come under what God says with your will united with Him?

____

____

▲▲▲▲▲▲▲

TIME TO PLUG IN TO THE HOLY SPIRIT

We've seen a lot as we've walked through this chapter: umbrellas, obedient and harmonious wills, manifest might and the reality of Christ's lordship in us. But we have also seen the fact that God loves us and pours His love into us through the Holy Spirit. While we've seen a lot about obedience, walking in the Spirit is obedience based on the reality and power of divine love. The King of kings loves you!

In the fall of 2001 my wife, Susan, had been studying about God's love and His dominion over our lives. One night she came to me with this simple poem that expresses much of what we have seen as we've walked through this chapter.

Did You Ever See a King?

Did you ever see a King
Dancing with glee
Laughing and skipping
And slapping His knee?

Did you ever hear a King
Calling your name
Saying He loves you
He's so glad that you came?

How can this happen?
How can it be?
It happens each time
You bend your knee.[12]

Holy Spirit, thank You for showing me the King of glory who loves me. Thank You that You have empowered me to walk after You. Thank You that You have not abandoned me even when I've walked without the umbrella. Thank You that You are touching my heart now and washing away the stuff that has cluttered my heart. Thank You that You speak to me through Your Word. Give me ears to hear as You speak through the circumstances and people who will touch me today. In the holy name of Jesus, amen.

CHAPTER ELEVEN

The Holy Spirit and the Big *Es*

IN THIS CHAPTER YOU WILL DISCOVER . . .

- The three big *Es* of the Spirit.
- A powerful set of keys to lock and unlock the purposes of God in the world.
- What would happen today if local congregations began to think of themselves as "vanguard" movements in their communities and cities.

THIS CHAPTER REMINDS ME OF TAKING A TRIP. Come with me, and we'll catch a flight to Phoenix, rent a car and drive up I-17 to Flagstaff. In a couple of hours we'll climb seven thousand feet from dry desert to lush green Alpine. We'll stop at Sedona and view the red rock formations. I can't wait for you to marvel at the twelve-thousand-six-hundred-feet high San Francisco Peaks, which dominate Flagstaff. After lunch we'll drive north on US 89 about an hour to the Painted Desert. You'll love these wonderful sights, and you'll think it can't get any better. Until . . .

Until we turn west and arrive at the Grand Canyon. All of a sudden everything else fades in comparison. There's nothing like this majestic hole in the ground. The rock formations, the colors and the sheer drop into what looks like a bottomless abyss will take your breath away.

If you think the Grand Canyon is something, the journey of faith with the Holy Spirit makes it look like a rut in your backyard. Life in the Spirit is filled with glimpses of eternal joy and life. We have wonderful experiences of and with the Spirit in worship, personal devotion, hearing the Word, ministering in the gifts and walking in obedience. We think we've seen it all. Until . . .

Until we see the three big *Es* of the Spirit. The three *Es* demand our attention. They refuse to be stuck on the back burner of our personal priorities. The Holy Spirit cries out for us to see and hear the three *Es:*

- Ecclesiology
- Evangelism
- Eschatology

As you reflect back over what you have read, we have talked about each of these. But in this chapter we want to focus a little more clearly on what the Holy Spirit is doing in these *Es*.

ECCLESIOLOGY

Do you remember the opening scenes in *Saving Private Ryan?* GIs hit the Normandy beaches with great sacrifice and courage to establish a beachhead in Europe. At Pentecost the Holy Spirit established a second beachhead on the earth with the church. (Read Acts 2.) (The first beachhead was established with the faith of Abraham and the formation of Israel.)

Hans Küng calls the church the vanguard on Planet Earth anticipating the returning King.[1] But our vanguard assaults are not with power designed to maim and kill. Our power is love, truth, righteousness, life and justice in the power of the Holy Spirit.

The study of this vanguard movement is called ecclesiology. That's a theological mouthful meaning the study of the church. It derives from the Greek word for "church," *ekklesia*, meaning, "called out." The church is people who are called out of the world by the gospel, formed into a new community with new citizenship and making an impact upon the world in the powerful name of her King and Lord, Jesus Christ (Phil. 3:20).

For our citizenship is in heaven, from which we also eagerly wait for the Savior, the Lord Jesus Christ.
—Philippians 3:20

EARTHLY AND HEAVENLY CITIZENSHIP

The word *citizenship* in Philippians 3:20 is from the Greek word *politeuma*. You can easily see the English *politics* in this word and, from high school history, recognize the Greek *polis,* or city-state. Like the apostle Paul we have dual citizenship in this world. Paul was a Roman citizen and enjoyed all associated rights. (Read Acts 16:35–39.) But he understood that Roman citizenship was temporary. His eternal citizenship was in heaven with Christ as Lord. When the two conflicted, there was no question which citizenship took priority.

Paul recognized this dual side of human existence in Romans 13:1–7, the classic New Testament passage regarding a Christian and worldly government. (Read 1 Peter 2:11–17.) Jesus recognized the legitimacy of the Roman Empire and instructed His followers to pay taxes. (Read Matthew 17:24–27.) Both Jesus and Paul knew that the Roman Empire was not a godly empire. It was idolatrous, power hungry and arrogant. Yet, God ordained it.

The New Testament teaching reflects the biblical witness found in the Old Testament that the nations are but a drop in the bucket to God. (Read Isaiah 40:15, 17.) The Lord God is sovereign over all nations regardless of politics, human power or culture. This affirmation allowed Paul, as it does us, to recognize that civil government is part of God's order in the world. Isaiah showed that God used the pagan ruler Cyrus as an instrument of deliverance for Judah. (Read Isaiah 41:2, 25; 45:1–7, 13.)

The Bible provides a framework for several Christian approaches to how we live in relationship with government.[2] Christians can be proactive when government acts contrary to God's moral standards. But Christians are not commanded to establish a "Christian state." Such efforts have usually reflected worldly political agendas rather than kingdom values. There is a middle ground for Christians personally and corporately so that God's agenda of mercy, truth and justice is made appealing to the world. The church is a living laboratory where God's power is demonstrated publicly. When this happens the world cannot help but notice.This living laboratory is described in the New Testament. There we discover that the apostles and evangelists did not focus primarily on reforming or changing the Roman Empire. They focused on proclaiming the kingdom of God and living as citizens of that kingdom as a visible demonstration of the kingdom that is indestructible and eternal.

The fact that Jesus will return as "King and Lord" means that the church is not about our ideas and agendas.

The fact that Jesus will return as "King and Lord" means that the church is not about our ideas and agendas. Since Jesus is the head, and we're the body, the church is about His ideas and plans. This means we do what the Head tells us to do. Jesus does not make suggestions or offer referendums for us to vote upon to decide whether or not we want to do them. Jesus gives commands and expects us to obey. Let's look at some of His commands:

- Matthew 28:19–20—"Go therefore and make disciples of all the nations, baptizing them in the name of the Father and of the Son and of the Holy Spirit, teaching them to observe all things that I have commanded you."
- John 13:34—"A new commandment I give to you, that you love one another; as I have loved you, that you also love one another." (Read also John 15:12, 17.)
- John 15:8—"By this My Father is glorified, that you bear much fruit; so you will be My disciples."

- John 15:14—"You are My friends if you do whatever I command you."

Question: The Ten Commandments is another passage where God has clearly indicated how His people are to live in the world. Read Exodus 20:1–17, and name five of the commandments that you think are most pertinent to how Christians should live today:

____

____

____

____

____

▲▲▲▲▲▲▲

JESUS TALKS ABOUT HIS BODY

Jesus spoke directly about His body, the church, in two places. The first instance is:

> *And I also say to you that you are Peter, and on this rock I will build My church, and the gates of Hades shall not prevail against it. And I will give you the keys of the kingdom of heaven, and whatever you bind on earth will be bound in heaven, and whatever you loose on earth will be loosed in heaven.*
>
> —Matthew 16:18–19

Jesus spoke these words to Peter and the other disciples while they were with Him in Caesarea Philippi. He asked, "Who do men say that I, the Son of Man, am?" They responded with several answers, and then Jesus turned the question directly to them, "Who do you say that I am?" Simon Peter replied that Jesus was "the Christ [Israel's Messiah], the Son of the living God." Jesus responded to Peter that this confession, that Jesus is the Messiah and the Son of God, could only have come by revelation from heaven (Matt. 16:13–17).

The first "Rocky" was not a cartoon character (Rocky and Bullwinkle), a heavyweight champion (Rocky Marciano) or a fictional Philadelphia street fighter (Sylvester Stallone). Early in His ministry Jesus identified Simon as the first "Rocky" (John 1:42). Jesus called Simon "Cephas," which in Aramaic means, "stone" (in Greek it is *Petros*, hence the English Simon Peter). That background is important because Jesus reinforced that name at Caesarea Philippi and said to Simon, "You are Petros (which was a smaller stone), and on this rock (Greek *petra*, a mass of rock distinct from the smaller stone) I will build My church."

Roman Catholics believe that Jesus designated Peter as the rock and that Peter's call and authority continues today through the papal office.[3]

Historically, Protestants have held that the "rock" refers to Peter's confession that Jesus is the Messiah and Son of God.[4] In recent years both Catholic and Protestant scholars have taken a middle position whereby Jesus meant that Peter himself was "the rock but functioning in this capacity in an unrepeatable way."[5]

Regardless of your theological heritage, it is clear that Peter was given divine revelation to recognize who Jesus really is—Israel's Messiah and the Son of God. It is that same recognition that the Holy Spirit gives the church today as we worship the living Lord Jesus Christ. The Holy Spirit sustains the church by revealing the truth of Jesus Christ to people in every generation.

Jesus said that He would build His church. That means that Jesus' church is composed of men and women of all colors, languages, cultures and generations. Jesus' church arises anywhere God's active reign on earth (the kingdom of God) is manifested by the Holy Spirit. Our response to the fact that Jesus builds His church is not passivity but bold obedience in the knowledge that we are participating in Jesus' work in the world.

The Holy Spirit sustains the church by revealing the truth of Jesus Christ to people in every generation.

The "gates of Hades" cannot prevail against Jesus' church. Some have thought that this word picture portrays Hades attacking while the church "circles the wagons" to defend itself. But the word picture is just the opposite. Jesus' church

is on the offensive, and the "gates of Hades" are not strong enough to withstand the onslaught of truth, righteousness and love in the gospel.

The church has a powerful set of keys to lock and unlock the purposes of God in the world. "Binding" and "loosing" describe the ways that rabbis interpreted permissible and not permissible behaviors in terms of God's will. As used by Jesus, the term probably has this use as well as the power of the gospel to release people held by the "gates of Hades" and to restrain the power of evil through intercessory prayer and righteousness. Whatever else you think about the "keys," it is certain that most of us have not comprehended the power of the Spirit that is implied in what Christ has given the church.

Question: As you read Matthew 16:16–18, what is more important to you: Peter as the rock, or the confession that Peter made concerning Jesus as the rock? Why?

▲▲▲▲▲▲▲

Do you believe that you have use of the "keys of the kingdom" as you intercede?

▲▲▲▲▲▲▲

Jesus mentioned the church a second time in Matthew 18:17: "And if he refuses to hear them, tell it to the church. But if he refuses even to hear the church, let him be to you like a heathen and a tax collector."

Why would Jesus talk about the church in such personal terms? (Read Matthew 18:15–20.) Why does "binding and loosing" appear a second time in relation to the church (v. 18). The setting is profoundly practical—how do Christians relate to other Christians when sin is revealed? We know the sick feeling when the secular and religious media report on moral failures of religious leaders. *Saturday Night Live* mocks the church for its apparent hypocrisy. Sometimes the church

Assuredly, I say to you, whatever you bind on earth will be bound in heaven, and whatever you loose on earth will be loosed in heaven.
—Matthew 18:18

embarrassingly throws its wounded into that large pile of abandoned and wasted ministries.

From the beginning Jesus knew that His followers would be tempted by sin, and many would fail. In His circle of twelve disciples, Jesus had two whose failures are reported in the Bible: Peter denied Him, and Judas betrayed Him. (Read Matthew 26:69–75, 47–50.)

RESTORING A FALLEN CHRISTIAN

Jesus teaches us that church is the Spirit's framework for redemptive and restorative grace in the life of a disciple who falls into sin (Matt. 18:15–20). Have you ever wondered why some people's sins become public and others apparently do not? This passage helps us understand the quiet ways that the Spirit seeks to restore us to the Father.

1. The Holy Spirit does not want to publicly embarrass any one.

Public sins defame the name of the Lord and harden sinner's hearts to the gospel. Obviously the Holy Spirit does not want us to enter into sin in the first place. But when we fall, the Holy Spirit tries to get our attention while the sin remains "hidden" and to bring us to confession and repentance. That's why it's important to be established in a congregation where we regularly hear the Word of God and where the Holy Spirit can speak to us through His Word.

2. Confront privately first.

Jesus said, "If your brother sins against you, go and tell him his fault between you and him alone. If he hears you, you have gained your brother" (v. 15). That means that if he or she repents, then the matter is settled and should never be repeated. There's no place for prayer requests that serve as a front to tell people what we know and provide a cover for gossip.

3. Confront with one or two "witnesses."

But what if the Christian continues in his or her sinful activity or attitudes? Jesus instructs us to "take with you one

Whoever is deserving of death shall be put to death on the testimony of two or three witnesses; he shall not be put to death on the testimony of one witness.

—Deuteronomy 17:6

or two more" and lovingly confront and seek reconciliation (v. 16). The fact that with this instruction Jesus appealed to Old Testament law as stated in Deuteronomy 17:6 shows that God looks upon these issues in the context of His justice and righteousness. Eternal purposes are at stake. God takes sin seriously and expects us to act righteously in regard to the unrepentant person.

4. If the person continues in sin then "tell it to the church" (Matt. 18:17).

Does Jesus mean that you stand up on Sunday morning and announce to a couple of hundred people that Brother So-and-So is a recalcitrant sinner? Or does Jesus mean that the established elders in the church should be told so that they may enforce any aspects of church discipline and order?

God takes sin seriously.

One way to answer this question is to look at how the early church dealt with it. We've already seen in Acts 5:1–11 the confrontation was very public. In 1 Corinthians 5:1–5, Paul rebuked the Corinthian believers for tolerating known sexual immorality within the church. (Read this scripture.) He told them, "When you are gathered together . . . deliver such a one to Satan for the destruction of the flesh, that his spirit may be saved in the day of the Lord Jesus" (vv. 4–5). Paul taught that elders who sin should be rebuked "in the presence of all" (1 Tim. 5:20).

These passages point toward public rebuke or excommunication of those who blatantly continue in sin. But whether the action of the church is public or private, the ultimate intent is not punitive—it is salvation. It means that the spirit of the action is one of humility, grace and openness to the future that redemption may bring. Read each of the following Scriptures, which demonstrate this openness to grace: 2 Corinthians 2:4–11 (possibly in reference to the man mentioned in 1 Corinthians 5:1–5); Galatians 6:1 (the "spirit of gentleness"); James 5:19–20; and 1 John 5:16–17. These passages remind us that church discipline is exercised within the context of truth, love, wisdom and restorative grace.

Jesus taught that the church has profound relational and redemptive power. The power of judgment, redemption and restoration is connected to the power of binding and loosing, to agreement by the body of Christ and to the power that two or three disciples have in Jesus' name. The statement about "two or three gathered in My name" is not about small attendance at church! It's an indication of the spiritual power to bind and loose that is available to small groups of intercessors and leaders who have a heart for sinners and grace.

Question: Name the three steps that Jesus said should be followed in the church regarding a Christian who has fallen into sin.

____

____

▲▲▲▲▲▲▲

If a Christian has confessed according to Matthew 18:15–16, what should you do if someone begins to gossip or talk about the situation?

____

____

▲▲▲▲▲▲▲

EVANGELISM

In the early 1930s, Dr. Harold Ockenga was preaching in Poland when rival religious groups, instigated by the communists, disrupted the service. Returning to his hotel room, Ockenga found two soldiers with questions about the gospel. In spite of the disruption, they had heard the gospel and wanted to know more. Ockenga led these men to Christ, and one soldier said, "In Poland it's a race between Christianity and Communism. Whichever makes its message a flame of fire will win."[6] Sixty years later, Christianity's flame of fire was still burning in Poland as atheistic ideology crumbled around Pope John Paul II and Lech Walensa.

Whether in first-century Roman Empire or twentieth-century communist Poland, the Holy Spirit has ignited evangelistic and revival fires that have withstood the test of time. Many of these fires have been intimate, personal one-to-one moments when someone was led to Christ. Other fires have impacted entire cities and nations through mass evangelism, as illustrated through Billy Graham's simple gospel sermons, Reinhard Bonnke's miracles in Africa and Carlos Annacondia's power confrontations in Argentina.

Each generation of Christians faces the challenges of sharing the gospel in its own generation. Outside of the power of the Holy Spirit, the church is only one generation removed from extinction. America enters the twenty-first century with generational challenges—Builders (born before 1946), Boomers (1946–1964), Busters (1965–1976), and Bridgers (1977–1994). Each of these generations has significant distinguishing characteristics and a significant difference in church attendance. The following percentages showing people who attend church each weekend demonstrate the need for effective evangelism: Builders—51 percent; Boomers—41 percent; Busters—34 percent; Bridgers—29 percent.[7]

Each generation of Christians faces the challenges of sharing the gospel in its own generation.

What is the Holy Spirit doing in our time to draw people to Christ? Some Christians are examining the ancient ways the early church used to engage and change predominately pagan societies. One such way is the impact of Celtic Christianity upon Ireland, England and the European continent in the fourth and fifth centuries. Popularized in Thomas Cahill's *How the Irish Saved Civilization*, and described in George Hunter III's *The Celtic Way of Evangelism*, the Celtic understanding of evangelism shows the power of Spirit-filled people who really believe the gospel.[8]

Celt missionaries, beginning with St. Patrick, spread the gospel by establishing monastic communities in pagan lands. They evangelized by understanding their new neighbors and communicating the gospel in ways that connected with the people they were seeking to reach. In other words, these Christians were not afraid to learn and interact with the culture of their non-Christian neighbors. They were not afraid of the world. Their communities existed as vanguards of good news—not as holy hideaways.

What would happen today if local congregations began to think of themselves as "vanguard" movements in their community or city? What if instead of thinking of the church as a place for Christians to get away from the pressures of the world, they began to think of themselves as "beachheads" of grace for sinners? What would the church look like?

ADAPT FROM EARLIER EXAMPLES

Two examples from the New Testament illustrate some Holy Spirit principles about reaching people. Study these examples, and consider their adaptation to your church today.

Jesus, the Holy Spirit and a really thirsty woman

Read John 4:4–26, and note the key principles from this case study of Jesus, the Holy Spirit and a really thirsty woman.

- ▲ Jesus did not avoid controversial places, but He needed to go through Samaria (vv. 4–5). Devout Jews considered Samaritans as not pure and theologically heretical; they avoided even entering territory where Samaritans lived (v. 9).
- ▲ Jesus recognized a Holy Spirit moment when a woman came for water, alone and at the heat of the day at noon (vv. 6–7).
- ▲ Jesus was not offended by her presence or question (vv. 9–10).
- ▲ Jesus was not distracted by her arguments, but He remained focused on the main issue (vv. 11–15, 20–24).
- ▲ The Holy Spirit gift of knowledge was exercised to touch her heart (vv. 16–19).
- ▲ The reality of Jesus as the saving Messiah was revealed (vv. 25–26).

The ministry of Philip

Now read Acts 8:26–40, and note the principles behind the ministry of Philip. Remember that first-century

Christians did not divide people into clergy and laity. All of them were what today we would call laity. They understood that every Christian had the responsibility to share the gospel when the Holy Spirit opened a door into someone's life.

- ▲ Philip willingly left the excitement of a revival in order to fully obey the Holy Spirit (vv. 12–13, 26–27).
- ▲ Philip was not intimidated by a man of political prestige (v. 27).
- ▲ Philip obeyed the exact directions of the Holy Spirit in how to approach the Ethiopian (v. 29).
- ▲ Philip knew the Bible and was able to explain it in terms that touched the Ethiopians heart (vv. 30–35).
- ▲ Philip recognized the power of grace and led the Ethiopian to Christ (vv. 36–38).

Did you notice that Jesus met a woman at a well and talked about the very stuff they wanted to taste—water? He used a cup of water to tell His story and to rewrite the ending of her story. Philip realized that a political eunuch personalized the story of someone whose experience seemed like his own—"as a lamb before its shearer is silent, so He opened not His mouth. In His humiliation His justice was taken away, and who will declare His generation?" (Acts 8:32–33; cf. Isaiah 53:7–8). Philip linked the life-giving story of Jesus to a man who until that day had no future at all.

It's that story–the story of Jesus–that is at the heart of Spirit-led evangelism.

Leonard Sweet writes, "Every kid in the world knows these four words: '*Erzahl mir eine Geshicte*' (German); '*Raconte-moi une histoire*' (French); '*Nanika hanashite*' (Japanese); '*Gao su wo i ge gushi*' (Chinese). Or, in English, '*Tell me a story.*'"[9] In the words of a hymn, it's the "old, old story of Jesus and His love" that the Holy Spirit wants us to tell.[10] It's that story—the story of Jesus—that is at the heart of Spirit-led evangelism.

Question: Why do you think that fewer Busters and Bridgers attend church than their parents and grandparents?

▲▲▲▲▲▲▲

We learned that Celtic evangelism was effective because it was not afraid to engage a new culture. In your perspective, how is the church you attend afraid of the influence of the world? How does your church show that it wants to engage the world?

▲▲▲▲▲▲▲

As you read John 4 and Acts 8, what principles impressed you as effective for communicating the gospel?

▲▲▲▲▲▲▲

ESCHATOLOGY

Eschatology is from a Greek word meaning "the study of last things." But if you're expecting this section on eschatology to include the typical timelines, charts and all that stuff, you're going to be disappointed. The Holy Spirit is up to something entirely different, which we shall see as we reflect on the fact that Jesus Christ is coming again. I want to help you connect the dots of ecclesiology, evangelism and eschatology.

These three *Es* are all connected because they are part of a story that is going somewhere. This section is more like, "Let's make sense of church; go tell it on the mountain; and guess Who's coming to supper." The wind of the Spirit is blowing the church (ecclesiology) and her mission (evangelism) in a particular direction (eschatology). Although it may sometimes feel like it, we are not going in circles. We are moving forward through history, and Someone is coming to meet us. Early Christians used the Aramaic confession, *Marantha*, to express their hope: "O Lord, come!" (1 Cor. 16:22). This cry of praise and hope from early Christians was tied to the Holy Spirit, and to the church's anticipation of the Lord's return (Rev. 22:17).

And the Spirit and the bride say, "Come!" And let him who hears say, "Come!" And let him who thirsts come. Whoever desires, let him take of the water of life freely.
—Revelation 22:17

...who is the guarantee of our inheritance until the redemption of the purchased possession.

—Ephesians 1:14

How do we live in this eschatological spirit without it becoming an escape into isolation that denies the very mission of the church? One way is to remember that the Spirit has birthed the church as the vanguard, the advance party, of the coming King and the fullness of His kingdom. As the vanguard, Christians have authority, but not absolute authority, in Christ's name. As the vanguard, Christians have the Spirit as the guarantee of something more that is coming (Eph. 1:14). Vanguard Christians live in the dynamics of overcoming and being overcome, of being holy but struggling with sin, of having faith and having questions. It's not unlike Paul's recognition of reality in 2 Corinthians 4:7–18. (Read this scripture.)

We can live in this tension because we know the King is really coming. We know He is really coming because He has been raised from the dead. We know our "labor is not in vain" because of His resurrection (1 Cor. 15:58). We know that the church and her mission will not fail because the Word of the Lord does not fail. We know that the Holy Spirit is striving in us to grasp more of what His kingdom will be and bring more of it to reality in our daily lives. We know that His coming will be another demonstration of grace and not the result of our work. We know all of this because He is alive in us through the Holy Spirit.

The church and her mission will not fail because the Word of the Lord does not fail.

This is why Paul so often used political language to describe the coming kingdom. We are "ambassadors for Christ" and have been given "the ministry of reconciliation" (2 Cor. 5:20, 18). As ambassadors we represent another king and kingdom to the kingdoms of this world. We operate from the spiritual building known as "the ministry of reconciliation." This means we are peacemakers in the world, and Christ has given a special blessing to the peacemakers: "They shall be called sons of God" (Matt. 5:9). But this peacemaking is not for softies and wimps. Immediately after this blessing, Jesus said, "Blessed are those who are persecuted for righteousness' sake, for theirs is the kingdom of heaven" (v. 10). Christian peacemaking is not based on human-constructed ideologies. This is not about Democrats, Republicans, social Democrats, Libertarians, conservatives, liberals or any other human expression of social structure. Christian peacemaking is about what the King, the Lord Jesus Christ, has accomplished in His death and resurrection and what He is going to do when He returns. It is the radical announcement to this world that its presidents, emperors, congresses, economies, universities and social movements do not have the final word. The final word comes from the One who is Alpha and Omega. Jesus Christ is the final word.

Spirit-filled people understand the interconnections between the Big *Es*. When those connections are understood, Spirit-filled people will no longer think of themselves in religious terms. We have bought the lie of compartmentalizing our lives into "religious" spheres where godliness and the power of the Spirit are marginalized. Instead, we will begin to think in terms of "ambassadors" and "ministry of reconciliation." We will see the church as the vanguard of the coming kingdom. The mission of this vanguard is to tell the story of this kingdom and to live as if that kingdom is already among us.

This chapter began with observations about the "politics" of the kingdom. We conclude with the "politics" of the kingdom, where the connections of the Big *Es* are nowhere more evident than in the compelling witness of Helmuth James, Count von Moltke, in January 1945.

Von Moltke was thirty-eight when martyred by the Nazis. He opposed Hitler's National Socialism and was arrested in January 1944. On January 23, 1945, he was executed by the Third Reich. His January 1945 letters to his wife testify to the power of the Holy Spirit to tell us what to say in the hour of trial. (Read Matthew 10:19–20.) Standing before the People's Court headed by Herr Freisler, von Moltke listened to Friesler's cynical statement, "We (National Socialism) and Christianity resemble each other in only one respect: We

claim the whole man! From whom do you take your orders? From the world beyond or from Adolf Hilter? To whom do you owe loyalty and faith?"

> The mission of this vanguard is to tell the story of this kingdom and to live as if that kingdom is already among us.

Von Moltke's faith did not falter in the hour of death. He wrote to his wife of his love for Christ and how the Bible continued to speak to him. (Read Joshua 19–21; Job 10–12; Ezekiel 34–36; Mark 13–15.) He closed his letter of January 11 with these lines from 2 Corinthians 13:14, "The grace of the Lord Jesus Christ, and the love of God, and the communion of the Holy Spirit be with you all. Amen."[11]

LET'S TALK ABOUT IT

- Think about yourself as an ambassador for the kingdom of God. What kind of authority do you have? Do you speak on your own authority, or has the Lord given you something to say and do for Him?

- What did you think of Herr Freisler's remark that the worldly system he represented "claim[s] the whole man"? Is that true of the worldviews in which you live? Does our culture "claim the whole man"? Does Christ "claim the whole man"?

- Discuss the interrelationship of the Big *Es*.

▲ If you think of the Holy Spirit as building a place on earth among Christians called "The Ministry of Reconciliation," what are the kinds of things you would find there to equip you to be a peacemaker?

____

____

____

▲▲▲▲▲▲▲

TIME TO PLUG IN TO THE HOLY SPIRIT

The Big *Es* are *ecclesiology, evangelism, eschatology.* The mission of the Vanguard Movement is the coming kingdom.

Many Christians have an individualized, privatized way of living in the Spirit. Maybe this chapter has helped you rethink that outdated and unbiblical way of living. The Holy Spirit calls us to something beyond our own agendas, limited vision and cultural phobias. The Holy Spirit calls us to see the world as Christ sees it—the place He died to redeem, claimed as His own and is coming back to take. The Holy Spirit calls us to the Big *Es.* Don't you think it's time we got to it?

Holy Spirit, it is so easy for me to marginalize You. I like keeping You in the "religious and spiritual" part of my life. It makes it less awkward to live with my friends that way.

But it also makes my life so boring, so meaningless, so empty. I'm beginning to understand that You've called me to something else. You've called me to Christian community, Christian mission and Christian hope for this world. Holy Spirit, teach me how to think Your thoughts and have the mind of Christ. Give me courage to be a peacemaker in anticipation of the coming Prince of Peace. Amen.

CHAPTER TWELVE

The Wind Is Blowing in the Trees

IN THIS CHAPTER YOU WILL DISCOVER THAT . . .

- ▲ The Holy Spirit has moved through the lives of men and women through the ages.
- ▲ The power of the Holy Spirit is greater than any deception Satan tries to bring.
- ▲ The light of the Spirit has shone through the ages, filling believers with His presence.

THE HOLY SPIRIT ANOINTED JESUS "TO PREACH GOOD TIDINGS TO THE POOR." In doing so, the Spirit made Jesus heaven's apostle "to heal the brokenhearted, to proclaim liberty to the captives, and the opening of the prison to those who are bound; to proclaim the acceptable year of the LORD, and the day of vengeance of our God; to comfort all who mourn, to console those who mourn in Zion, to give them beauty for ashes, the oil of joy for mourning, the garment of praise for the spirit of heaviness; that they may be called trees of righteousness, the planting of the LORD, that He may be glorified" (Isa. 61:1–3).

People redeemed by Christ are destined to become "trees of righteousness." This metaphor of strength (the meaning of the Hebrew word used here) is reinforced by a similar use in Psalm 1:3. "He [the "blessed" person of verse 1] shall be like a tree planted by rivers of water, that brings forth its fruit in its season, whose leaf also shall not wither; and whatever he does shall prosper." In this psalm the tree is that person who is firmly established in the Torah (the will) of the Lord because "his delight is in the law [will] of the Lord" and "he meditates day and night" upon the Lord's revealed will (v. 2).

This final chapter concerning the power of the Holy Spirit is about the Holy Spirit blowing through the trees—that is, how the Holy Spirit has moved through the lives of countless men and women through the ages. There is a great heritage of righteous trees who have been incredibly fruitful and whose leaves have not withered as the Holy Spirit has empowered them.

Using the tree metaphor, we're going to look at three stands of forests through which the Spirit has blown since Pentecost. The first great forest is through Spirit-filled people from church history to the beginning of the twentieth century.

Many of these ancient trees are shrouded in the mist of history, and we only catch a glimpse of what they experienced of the Holy Spirit.

The second forest is more recent, and we have much more information about it. It is the forest of righteous trees who began the great Pentecostal revival at the beginning of the twentieth century.

The third forest is younger still and reflects the past forty years of the Charismatic Movement.

Don't worry about getting lost in these forests. The trails are clearly marked, there are majestic views in the clearings, and at the end you will see that there is growth in a new forest of righteous trees. Guess what, you may be a tree in this new forest where the Spirit is blowing![1]

ANCIENT FOREST OF HOLY SPIRIT RIGHTEOUSNESS

Some Spirit-filled Christians have a limited perspective of church history. They think that after the first and second generation of Christians died, the power of the Holy Spirit disappeared from the face of the earth. In this view, the church replaced the power of the Spirit with organizations, church councils and formal worship. While it is true that all three things occurred, it does not mean that the Holy Spirit disappeared until the twentieth century.

Actually, organizational structure, church councils and a consistent form of worship were part of the work of the Spirit as the church adjusted to new times and different cultures. Were all these adjustments perfect? Of course not. Were there times when carnal desires were more evident than spiritual life? Of course. Was the Holy Spirit at work in the midst of this? Absolutely yes. Did charismatic gifts of the Spirit cease? Absolutely not.

In some respects, it was the operation of spiritual gifts without reference to church authority that caused some of the problems that second- and third-century Christians faced. Stanley M. Burgess observed that the diminishing of prophetic ministry and other gifts "resulted from the inability of prophets and priests to find common goals for the church, from prophetic excess and abuse, and from an institutionalization process in which Spirit *charismata* came to be localized in the office of the bishop."[2] While church leaders did sometimes overreact in their response to these early charismatics, it is also true that these early charismatics gave plenty of reason for the reaction. The historical situation of eighteen hundred years ago is pertinent to how our situation can better resolve the inherent tensions between individual spiritual enthusiasm and church leadership concerns for truth and order.

Organizational structure, church councils and a consistent form of worship were part of the work of the Spirit as the church adjusted to new times and different cultures.

Second- and third-century writings reveal that regular Christians continued to exercise charismatic gifts, especially the gift of prophecy. This gift was exercised so freely that the church had to develop guidelines to help discern between false and genuine prophets. At the same time these writings reflect the growing importance of local bishops as discerners of genuine and false prophets and teachers.[3]

As noted earlier, one of the reasons the church had to establish more control over the "gifts" was because of excesses and abuses. As the church moved further from its original Jewish and Palestinian roots, it encountered a far more diverse and theologically hostile world. Three major threats were faced in the first centuries.

GNOSTICISM

While there were numerous Gnostic religions, the usual common characteristics included radical dualism (the belief that good and evil are equally powerful entities). Dualism included the view that the human spirit was divine and the body was evil. The only way the spirit could be set free was by special knowledge of revelation. The word *Gnostic* is from the Greek word for knowledge, *gnosis.* According to the Gnostics, salvation was not a free gift by virtue of the atoning

death of Jesus Christ. Salvation came as a result of the Holy Spirit giving special knowledge. Redemption was not moral transformation but intellectual transformation. The church rightfully rejected Gnosticism because it is ultimately an unbiblical view of God, humanity and redemption.

In our contemporary setting there is an appropriate place for knowledge that the Holy Spirit gives. However, that "revelation" always conforms to Scripture and is not the basis for salvation. Any person—whether claiming to be a prophet, apostle or teacher—who teaches a "new revelation" that is connected to salvation or deliverance needs to submit willingly to established church leaders in order to protect him (or her) and the flock of God from modern forms of Gnosticism.

"Revelation" always conforms to Scripture and is not the basis for salvation.

And in case any of you actually wonder about who is more powerful, there is no question that power belongs to God (Ps. 62:11). Satan's power is limited by the sovereign will of God. The power of the Holy Spirit in your life is greater than any power that Satan can bring against you.

God has spoken once, twice I have heard this: That power belongs to God.
—Psalm 62:11

MONTANISM

Many Pentecostal historians appeal to Montanism to prove that charismatic gifts, especially speaking in tongues, operated in the second and third centuries. That appeal, while correct, also shows why the church moved toward an institutional control of the gifts. Montanism began in A.D. 156 through the preaching of a converted pagan priest named Montanus. His prophecies came while he was in a frenzied state, apparently out of control of body or will. Two women left their husbands, followed Montanus and began prophesying. Montanus and his followers claimed that their prophecies were of greater authority than the Bible and that the established church authorities were not legitimate. They also required a very strict lifestyle for their followers.

The church reacted strongly against Montanism, but it was

not able to successfully defeat it until after the church was given state sanction by Constantine in the early 300s. The church affirmed the authority of Scripture, but in doing so it became fearful of prophetic messages.

The history of Montanism is a warning to contemporary prophets and the contemporary church that:

- Respect for the Scriptures has to go hand in hand with respect for the work of the Spirit through an individual.
- Respect for the ways the Spirit works in individuals must go hand in hand with respect for the various ways the church structures itself for mission in a given time and place.
- The moral quality of Christian living must be in accord with Scripture and cannot be modified to fit a particular situation because that person "feels led by the Spirit."

MARCIONISM

In the middle 100s an Asia Minor ship owner named Marcion was excommunicated from the church. A radical dualist, Marcion rejected the Old Testament, God as revealed in the Old Testament (he considered God to be the creator of evil) and the incarnation of Christ. Although he focused his false teachings on his distorted view of the apostle Paul, Marcion ignored the Holy Spirit. Partly because of this, the church developed more fully the deity of the Holy Spirit in response to Marcion's teachings. Marcion's rejection of the Old Testament has reappeared at times in history when the church has forgotten her roots with Abraham, Isaac and Jacob. This has had terrible results in the sinful anti-Semitism the church has occasionally wrongly sanctioned.

While Gnosticism and Montanism were serious threats to the second- and third-century church, it was Marcionism that most seriously threatened the doctrinal truth of the gospel. All three movements, among other things, had distorted views of the person and work of the Holy Spirit. As

we look into this ancient forest, we can hear the Holy Spirit moving through giant oaks reminding us to know and understand the Scriptures, acknowledge the Spirit's work in church authority and respect the Spirit's work through individual believers.

CESSATIONISM

This is the name given to Christians (normally self-described fundamentalists) who believe that many of the charismatic gifts, specifically miracles and speaking in tongues, came to end at the close of the second century. While there were some in the Roman Catholic tradition who held to cessationism, the church at Rome has historically recognized that these gifts have been manifested at times and can continue to be manifested. It was really the Protestant Reformers who laid the foundation for modern cessationism. In the words of Jack Deere, "The Reformers argued that the primary purpose of New Testament miracles was to authenticate the apostles as trustworthy authors of Holy Scripture." By this logic, now that we have the Bible written by the apostles, it is no longer necessary for miracles to exist to prove the gospel.[4] The Reformers rejected the miracles claimed by many Roman Catholics, and because the Reformers did not have the experience of miracles in their own ministry, they were convinced that real miracles had ceased. The modern version of this teaching was popularized by Benjamin F. Warfield, and it is in this form that those who hold this teaching continue.

Modern cessationists argue that speaking in tongues is no longer necessary because people can hear the gospel in their own language. In fact, many cessationists hold that speaking in tongues is demonic. Needless to say, that is not the position of this book!

What is our response to the cessationists' argument? First, our response is one of love. We are still fellow Christians with those who hold such views. We still hold to the authority of Scripture, the incarnation of Jesus Christ, His atoning death and bodily resurrection. Second, our response should be knowledgeable and not argumentative.

As the church moved into the fourth and fifth centuries, there are numerous accounts of Spirit-filled priests, monks and devout believers who allowed the Holy Spirit to work in their lives in accordance to the revelation of Scripture. The Middle Ages were not nearly as "dark" as we think. The light of the Spirit was shining, and many believers were filled with

His presence. There were miracles, healings, dancing and praise in worship, and heartfelt preachers who walked in the power of the Holy Spirit.[5]

As noted above, the Protestant Reformers, Luther and Calvin, were more concerned with establishing the principle of the authority of the Scriptures alone against the dual authorities of church tradition and Scripture in the Catholic tradition. But even in their time (sixteenth century) and afterwards, there were outpourings of the Holy Spirit where people prophesied, spoke in other tongues and manifested other charismatic gifts.

As you move through the younger growth of this first forest, there are righteous trees in the eighteenth and nineteenth centuries who were filled with the Holy Spirit and power and did mighty exploits for God. It is those people who helped prepare the way for the second great forest that emerged at the beginning of the twentieth century.

An illustration of the Holy Spirit's charismatic workings during this period is the Scottish Presbyterian pastor Edward Irving. One writer calls Irving "the forgotten giant" whose passion for Christ opened the doors of spiritual renewal in London, England.[6] In the early 1830s Irving pastored the National Scotch Church in Regent Square. Throughout London the Spirit was speaking through prayer meetings about Acts 2 and the restoration of apostolic gifts. By April 1831 people in prayer meetings were speaking in tongues and singing in the Spirit. Irving received the baptism of the Holy Spirit, and his writings and teachings illustrate that there were many in the English church of that day who were open to the gifts of the Spirit as in the days of the apostles. By October 1831 charismatic gifts were openly present in regular church services.[7]

Question: Name the three primary threats against Christianity in the first two centuries. Which of the three do you think is most dangerous to the faith? Why?

___

___

___

How should Spirit-filled Christians respond to Christians who believe that charismatic gifts ended at the close of the apostolic age?

▲▲▲▲▲▲▲

A TREE GROWS IN LOS ANGELES

The twentieth century began on January 1, 1901 with a young woman named Agnes Ozman in Topeka, Kansas praying in other tongues.[8] Her experience was the culmination of the search of Charles Parham's students in December to ascertain the evidence of the baptism of the Holy Spirit. Ozman desired to be a missionary, and she believed that if she spoke in tongues it would confirm and equip her for this call. Her experience soon spread to others in the school.

Parham began to preach that speaking in tongues was the initial evidence of the baptism of the Holy Spirit, and for a few years he was instrumental in bringing Pentecostal revival to several areas. By 1906 Parham had moved to Houston, Texas, and started another school. It was in Houston that a young black preacher named William Seymour heard Parham's message and then went to Los Angeles in the early spring of 1906.

Los Angeles in 1906 was very different from today's glittering movie image. In the early 1900s there were powerful prayer meetings and revivals throughout the city. Frank Bartleman, whose first person accounts of the Azusa Street revival still stir your soul, wrote in 1905, "We are crying, 'Pasadena for God!'"[9] Reports of the great Welsh revival with Evan Roberts at the beginning of the new century inspired many in the Los Angeles area. The spiritual atmosphere was right for the Holy Spirit fire that fell in April 1906.

Seymour began preaching in the black community at a house at 214 Bonnie Brae Street, not far from downtown Los Angeles. Quickly the crowds outgrew the little house, and the services moved across town to a building on streetcar-accessible Azusa Street.[10]

THE AZUSA STREET REVIVAL

W. E. B. DuBois, the first African American to receive a doctorate from Harvard University (1895) wrote, "The problem of the twentieth century is the problem of the color-line." Many believe that the solution to the unique "color-line" in the United States was evidenced at Azusa Street as whites and blacks from across the country humbled themselves in spiritual unity in the 40- by 60-foot mission. White Christians from the southern United States came and allowed the thirty-six-year-old Louisiana-born African American William Seymour to lay his hands upon them as they received the baptism of the Holy Spirit.

Seymour's core beliefs at Azusa Street included justification by faith, sanctification as a second work of grace, the baptism of the Holy Spirit evidenced by speaking in other tongues, divine healing, world evangelism and the Second Coming of Jesus Christ.[11] He founded the Pacific Apostolic Faith Movement and the *Apostolic Faith*, a magazine that chronicled the great revival and spread the story literally around the world.

The building at 312 Azusa Street had an interesting history: an African Methodist Episcopal church, a stable and a warehouse. Frank Bartleman wrote that the worshipers had cleaned the place enough to "lay some planks on top of empty nail kegs, with seats enough for possibly thirty people. These were arranged in a square, facing one another."[12] The humble Seymour prayed behind a small pillar of two empty shoeboxes, and the services were left to the direction of the Holy Spirit. People came to the revival from around the world. Although speaking in tongues was noticed by the Los Angeles press, tremendous emphasis was placed upon spiritual cleansing by the blood of Christ and holy living. Bartleman was so moved by his experiences there that he wrote, "I would rather live six months at that time (Azusa Street) than fifty years of ordinary life."[13]

The revival began to wane in 1908 as leadership issues emerged. As someone has observed, divisions in the body of Christ do not happen among the people of God as much as they do among those who feel called to be leaders. Although the revival at Azusa Street never reached the peak it had in 1906 and 1907, the fire that God started there spread throughout the world. Most of the historic Pentecostal movements of our time trace their roots to Azusa Street. By 1914 and World War I, the spiritual tide of the nation had turned. Seymour continued to preach until his death in 1922. He is buried in a simple grave at Evergreen Cemetery in Los Angeles.

The revival, briefly described above, made an immediate impact in the United States and the world. The emphasis upon the baptism of the Holy Spirit began to transform several groups that already existed as nineteenth-century holiness

churches. Those churches with Wesleyan holiness roots that became Pentecostal after 1906 included the International Pentecostal Holiness Church (Oklahoma City, Oklahoma; www.iphc.org) and the Church of God (Cleveland, Tennessee; www.churchofgod.cc/). Meanwhile, there were many other congregations and fellowships that were impacted by the turn-of-the-century Pentecostal revival. Coming from diverse backgrounds, many of these leaders met in Hot Springs, Arkansas in 1914 and formed the Assemblies of God (Springfield, Missouri; www.ag.org). Charles H. Mason received the baptism of the Holy Spirit at Azusa Street and returned to Memphis, Tennessee to form the largest African American Pentecostal group in the United States, the Church of God in Christ (www.cogic.org). Through the 1920s a variety of other movements and denominations were formed, including the International Church of the Foursquare Gospel (Los Angeles, California; www.foursquare.org). In time, the 1906 revival spread across the nation primarily through the subculture of thousands of Pentecostal churches and believers. In the eyes of the established mainline Protestant churches, these Pentecostal churches were "on the other side of the tracks" and composed of "holy rollers."

"We are crying, 'Pasadena for God!'"

You may wonder, "Why didn't all these Pentecostal groups become one large denomination?" The reasons are found in slightly differing theologies (with a few exceptions), different cultural settings and different leadership gifts. Besides, that kind of organizational unity is not what the Holy Spirit was, and is, up to. The Spirit's unity is in message and mission and the loving spirit of God's people regardless of their denominational or movement "tribal group" (to use an analogy from Israel's tribes). However, most of the historic Pentecostal denominations cooperate through the Pentecostal and Charismatic Churches of North America. In 1996 the white and African American Pentecostal churches met in the historic "Memphis Miracle," where a serious effort began at bridging the "color-line" that had started at Azusa Street, was shattered by the cultural power of Jim Crow institutional racism, and was at the heart of the Holy Spirit at the close of the twentieth century.

The various trees in this post-Azusa Street Pentecostal forest have their own stories to tell. But each have in common an emphasis upon winning people to Jesus, holy living, the baptism of the Holy Spirit with speaking in tongues, joyful worship services, belief in the power of prayer for miracles and healings, aggressive and courageous world missions and a lively hope of the soon return of Jesus Christ.

In the late 1940s and into the 1950s the American Pentecostal subculture began to make an impact upon the larger culture through healing evangelists who effectively used radio and television to enter directly into American homes. The most widely known was the Oklahoma-born Oral Roberts. Originally an evangelist in the International Pentecostal Holiness Church, Roberts's ministry was a bridge into the next growth forest of the 1960s, the Charismatic Movement. This is evidenced by the 1951 formation of the interdenominational lay movement called the Full Gospel Businessmen's Fellowship International by Demos Shakarian in Los Angeles with Roberts as the first speaker.

By the end of the decade Henry Van Dusen, president of the liberal Union Theological Seminary in New York, wrote in the June 9, 1958 issue of *Life* magazine that Pentecostalism was a "third force in Christendom" along with the Roman Catholic and Protestant churches. In fifty-two years Pentecostalism in the United States had moved from a small warehouse in Los Angeles to public recognition in a national magazine.

The Pentecostal Movement rooted in the Azusa Street revival remains strong today around the world. Many of the organizations named earlier in this section have adjusted to differing cultural shifts and organizational paradigm shifts related to growth, yet they have maintained the powerful impact of the presence of the Holy Spirit. These churches have formed outstanding colleges, universities, Bible schools and seminaries. The Pentecostal tradition has also preserved its history through denominational archives and the Society for Pentecostal Studies (founded 1970; www.sps-usa.org).

While many Pentecostals in the Azusa Street tradition were theologically very conservative and suspicious of mainline Protestantism and the Roman Catholic Church, there were some Pentecostals who saw the value of dialogue with other Christians in the world. David J. Du Plessis was the leading Pentecostal figure to march to the beat of a different drum in this regard. Born in South Africa, Du Plessis was a leader in the Apostolic Faith Mission and later a member of the Assemblies of God. In 1947 he became head of the Pentecostal World Conference (a biennial meeting of denominations born from the Azusa Street revival). Du Plessis was used by the Holy Spirit in the 1950s, 1960s and 1970s as a bridge to the churches of the World Council of Churches. He lectured on Pentecostalism at Princeton, Yale and Union, and he met several popes, including the significant John XXIII. His tireless efforts at communication and faithfully sharing the Holy Spirit led to the popular title, "Mr. Pentecost."[14]

The Spirit's unity is in message and mission and the loving spirit of God's people regardless of their denominational or movement "tribal group."

Question: What were the main theological themes of the Azusa Street revival? What were the main social themes of the revival?

____

____

What is the basis of unity in the body of Christ?

____

____

Discuss the historical significance of Oral Roberts and David Du Plessis.

____

____

THE THIRD STAND OF FOREST

We have seen that the shadows of the Azusa Street forests reached into the mainstream of American social life in the late 1950s. People in mainstream Protestant churches were speaking in other tongues, being healed, casting out demons and being empowered for ministry. While some left to join Pentecostal churches, many of these Episcopalians, Lutherans, Presbyterians, Methodists and Roman Catholics (to name a few) did not want to leave their church heritage. It took the spiritual experience of an Episcopal priest in Van Nuys, California to initiate what is now known as the "Charismatic Movement." Dennis Bennett, rector of St. Mark's Episcopal Church, received the baptism of the Holy Spirit in November 1959. In 1960 he moved to St. Luke's Episcopal Church in Seattle, Washington, where his ministry became the catalyst of Holy Spirit revival among Episcopalians. His book, *Nine O'clock in the Morning,* reflected the hour in Acts 2 and the hour when he received the baptism of the Holy Spirit. People around the world read Bennett's book and books written by another Episcopalian, John Sherrill, including *They Speak With Other Tongues* (1964) and Sherrill's account of David Wilkerson's ministry in New York City, *The Cross and the Switchblade* (1963). As they read these books, they were inspired by the power of the Holy Spirit at the beginning of the modern Charismatic Movement. The charismatic work of the Holy Spirit among Episcopalians continues and can be reviewed through Acts 29 Ministries (www.a29.com).

Through the 1960s the Charismatic Movement among Protestants and Catholics continued to grow as Spirit-filled individuals began to meet in enclaves at their various denominational gatherings.

The Roman Catholic charismatic renewal began at Duquesne University in February 1967 and quickly spread to Notre Dame University and Michigan State University. The background for this move of the Spirit among Catholic laity and priests included the Second Vatican Council, which met from 1962 to 1965. Commonly called Vatican II, this church council brought significant change in worldwide Roman Catholicism and opened the church of Rome to ecumenical dialogue. It also helped with the recognition that the "charismatic gifts, whether they be the most outstanding or the more simple and widely diffused, are to be received with thanksgiving and consolation, for they are exceedingly suitable and useful for the needs of the church."[15] In many ways

the renewal was the answer to Pope John XXIII's prayer, "O Holy Spirit, pour forth the fullness of Your gifts . . . Renew Your wonders in this our day as by a new Pentecost." (John XXIII died in 1963.)

Annual meetings of Catholic charismatics were held at Notre Dame. First numbering in the few hundreds, by 1973 the meeting was moved to the football stadium to accommodate the more than twenty thousand participants. By 1976 over thirty thousand were attending the meeting at Notre Dame. Although the large crowds forced the leaders to change to regional meetings, the Catholic Charismatic Renewal continues as a worldwide force in prayer, social engagement and spirituality that crosses denominational lines. The movement has an office in Rome at the International Catholic Charismatic Renewal Office (www.iccrs.org), and the United States is served by the National Service Committee of the Catholic Charismatic Renewal (www.nsc-chariscenter.org).

The move of the Spirit through Protestant churches is described in Vinson Synan's *The Century of the Holy Spirit: 100 Years of Pentecostal and Charismatic Renewal* 1901–2001 (Nashville, TN: Thomas Nelson Publishers, 2001). For more information on the Lutheran renewal, you can visit their website at www.lutheranrenewal.org. For more information on the Methodist renewal, visit www.aldersgaterenewal.org. For more information on the Presbyterian renewal, visit www.prrmi.org. You can contact your pastor or denominational offices for more information about Holy Spirit renewal in your church tradition if it is not mentioned here.

While the Holy Spirit was working among Roman Catholics and Protestants in the 1960s and 1970s, the Spirit was also creating a wide river of Spirit-filled people and movements that seemingly touched every part of culture. Among the more notable parts of this river are the following:

- ▲ Publications. The Renewal Movement produced magazines such as *Acts 29* (Episcopal), *Logos Journal, New Wine, New Covenant* and the popular *Charisma* magazine. Significant publishers and writers included Jamie Buckingham, Don Basham, Derek Prince, Bob Mumford, Vinson Synan, Jack Hayford and Stephen Strang. A wide range of books from various renewal and charismatic publishers and authors is available at almost any Christian and often secular bookstores.

- ▲ The "Jesus Movement" arose in California as young people from the post-Vietnam and hippie era accepted Christ. Many were baptized in the Pacific Ocean, and new forms of congregational life emerged in groups such as Calvary Chapel.
- ▲ There were large gatherings of Spirit-filled Christians that caught national attention. The first was in Kansas City in 1977, where thousands filled Arrowhead Stadium to praise the Lord. From this was formed the North American Renewal Service Committee (NARSC), which provided leadership and a vehicle to organize other such events, including the 1986 and 1987 North American Congress on the Holy Spirit and World Evangelism held at the New Orleans Superdome. The 1987 event had over forty thousand in attendance. In 1990 the World Congress on the Holy Spirit and World Evangelism was held in Indianapolis with over twenty-five thousand attendees.
- ▲ A major shift in music styles emerged in the 1970s as traditional, hymn-based church music was replaced with contemporary praise and worship music that reflected the chords and rhythms of popular culture. Significant contributors included Maranatha Music, Hosanna! Integrity and music from major revival renewals including Vineyard, Australia's HillSongs and Brownsville.
- ▲ While revival has been a major theme of the historic Pentecostal churches and the new movements that have emerged in the wake of the Charismatic Movement, until the 1990s such revivals tended to be local or at the most regional. But in 1994 the

Holy Spirit broke forth in the first of several revivals that had worldwide impact. The first was in at the Toronto, Canada, Airport Vineyard. People from around the world flocked to Toronto. The spiritual manifestations at Toronto spread to such places as the Anglican Holy Trinity Brompton in a fashionable area of London. From Holy Trinity Brompton came the effective evangelistic tool Alpha, which has reached thousands of people in informal supper gatherings where the gospel is presented. The second occurred in 1995 with another worldwide revival as thousands were converted at Brownsville Assemblies of God in Pensacola, Florida. In the latter 1990s revivals from Australia and Argentina impacted the United States and spread around the world. From Australia it was primarily revival music, and from Argentina it was powerful deliverance ministry through leaders such as Carlos Annacondia and Claudio Friedzon.

- International prayer ministry became a focus through the Holy Spirit working in the historic Pentecostal churches and the various groups in the Charismatic Renewal. Many Pentecostal denominations established full-time prayer ministries in their headquarters. The various prayer leaders have bridged gaps among the numerous groups and have forged relationships that have brought spiritual unity in the body of Christ.

LET'S TALK ABOUT IT

- What was important about Pope John XXIII's prayer in the early 1960s? How was Vatican II used by the Holy Spirit to bring renewal to the Roman Catholic Church?

____

____

▲▲▲▲▲▲▲

- Have you ever read any of the magazines of the

Charismatic Renewal? How have they helped you better understand the work of the Holy Spirit?

▲▲▲▲▲▲▲

▲ Have you been impacted by the changes in Christian music over the past twenty years? Has it caused tensions in established churches? How does Spirit-filled music help you worship the Lord?

▲▲▲▲▲▲▲

▲ Did you attend any of the services at the major revivals that occurred in the 1990s? Have you found your heart hungering for more of God because of what you have experienced or heard about these revivals?

▲▲▲▲▲▲▲

TIME TO PLUG IN TO THE HOLY SPIRIT

This chapter has been a small sampling of the mighty waves of the Holy Spirit that are evident in this great forest at the turn of the millennium. There are countless others, including emerging apostolic networks, renewed emphasis on apostles, prophets, evangelists, pastors and teachers, powerful national revivals in Africa and Eastern Europe, the amazing house church movement in China, powerful international youth ministries such as Youth With A Mission and signs of renewal in Western Europe.

At the beginning of the twenty-first century we are living at a time when spiritual forces of competing world religions are taking center stage in a spiritual, and sometimes physical, battle for the souls of millions. This has been recognized by those with profound spiritual insight (George Otis, Jr.'s insightful *The Last of the Giants,* Chosen Books) and those with profound secular analysis (Samuel P. Huntington, *The Clash of Civilizations and the Remaking of World Order,* Simon

& Schuster, 1997). We have moved into a time when following Jesus is critically important not just for the Christian witness but for the world.[16] We have moved into a time when powerful revivals, strong churches, compelling music and best-selling Christian books must by the Spirit lead us into the loving force of people with incredible passion for Jesus. It is this passion for Jesus, fueled by the Holy Spirit that will:

- Enable us to live with and understand the poor.
- Raise up a generation of missionaries to the Islamic world.
- Cause us to move past our petty personal kingdoms and learn how to love one another in Christ.
- Free us from the bondage of besetting sins and liberate us into true holiness.
- Give us grace to accomplish what God has planted in our hearts by faith.

In closing, my prayer for you begins with Pope John XXIII's prayer:

O Holy Spirit, pour forth the fullness of Your gifts... Renew Your wonders in this our day as by a new Pentecost. Through Your Word and by the power of Your Holy Spirit, transform our lives so that Christ is seen in all we do, say and think.

Empower us by humbling us before the cross of Christ.
Empower us by teaching us how to think with Your wisdom.
Empower us by the power of Your grace.
Empower us with the spirit of gratitude.
Empower us with the fire of the Holy Spirit.
Empower us with Your love. In the name of the Father, the Son and the Holy Spirit. Amen.

Notes

Introduction

1. J. R. R. Tolkien, *The Hobbit* (New York: Ballentine Books, 1978), 18.

Chapter One
Who Is the Holy Spirit?

1. George Barna, *The Second Coming of the Church* (Nashville, TN: Word Publishing, 1998), 22.
2. St. Patrick, "The Breastplate of St. Patrick." Also known as "The Deer's Cry" and "The Lorica." This prayer is reported to have been composed by Saint Patrick in the year 433. This version of this prayer is quoted in Thomas Cahill, *How the Irish Saved Civilization: The Untold Story of Ireland's Heroic Role From the Fall of Rome to the Rise of Medieval Europe* (New York: Doubleday, 1995), 16.
3. Francis Schaeffer, *The God Who Is There* (Downers Grove, IL: Intervarsity Press, 1998); Francis Schaeffer, *Genesis in Time and Space* (Downers Grove, IL: Intervarsity Press, 1972).
4. Martin Luther, *Luther's Works, Lectures on Genesis,* Volume 1 (St. Louis, MO: Concordia Publishing House, 1958), 84.
5. John Wesley, *Sermons on Several Occasions* (London: The Epworth Press, n.d.).

Chapter Two
The Holy Spirit, From Someone Who Knows Him Best

1. Raymond Brown, *The Gospel According to John* (Garden City, NJ: Doubleday & Company, Inc., 1966), 327.

Chapter Three
How the Holy Spirit Makes New Creatures

1. C. S. Lewis, *The Last Battle*, Book 7 of The Chronicles of Narnia (New York: HarperCollins, 1994).

Chapter Six
Looking for a Plugged-In, Turned-On Church?

1. B. E. Underwood, *Spiritual Gifts: Ministries and Manifestations* (Franklin Springs, GA: LifeSprings Resources, 1984), 21.

Chapter Seven
God Has Ministry Gifts for You

1. The categories of gifts used here, particularly between ministry and manifestation gifts, are drawn from B. E. Underwood in *Spiritual Gifts: Ministries and Manifestations.*
2. See resources at the close of the book.
3. George T. Montague, *Holy Spirit: Growth of a Biblical Tradition* (Peabody, MA: Hendrickson Publishers, Inc., 1976), 226.

Chapter Eight
Manifesting Spiritual Power

1. Samuel Chadwick, *The Way to Pentecost*, reprint (Dixon, MO: Rare Christian Books, n.d.), 19; quoted in Jim Cymbala, *Fresh Power* (Grand Rapids, MI: Zondervan Publishing House, 2001), 18–19.
2. These three insights are developed from the commentary in *The Spirit-Filled Life Bible*, New King James Version, Jack W. Hayford, general editor (Nashville, TN: Thomas Nelson Publishers), 1736.
3. Cymbala, *Fresh Power,* 28–29.
4. Underwood, *Spiritual Gifts: Ministries and Manifestations*, 15–16.
5. This view is mentioned by C. M. Robeck, Jr. in "Wisdom, Word of," article in *Dictionary of Pentecostal and Charismatic Movements*, edited by Stanley M.

Burgess, Gary B. McGee and Patrick H. Alexander (Grand Rapids, MI: Zondervan Publishing House, 1988), 890–892.

6. Underwood, *Spiritual Gifts: Ministries and Manifestations,* 65.
7. Jack Deere, *Surprised by the Voice of God* (Grand Rapids, MI: Zondervan Publishing House, 1996), 13–17.
8. Francis Martin, "Healing, Gift of," *Dictionary of Pentecostal and Charismatic Movements*, 350–353.

Chapter Nine
The Holy Spirit and Prayer

1. John Phillips, *Only One Life: The Biography of Stephen F. Olford* (Neptune, NJ: Loizeaux, 1995), 33.
2. John V. Taylor, *The Go-Between God* (Philadelphia: Fortress Press, 1973).
3 Anne Lamott, *Traveling Mercies* (New York: Anchor Books, 1999), 82.
4. Jim Cymbala, *Fresh Wind, Fresh Fire* (Grand Rapids, MI: Zondervan Publishing House, 1997), 28.
5. Taylor, *The Go-Between God,* 226–227.
6. Dietrich Bonhoeffer (translated by John W. Doberstein), *Life Together* (San Francisco: Harper & Row, 1954).
7. Ibid., 81.
8. Ibid., 83.
9. Ibid., 84.
10. Ibid., 86.

Chapter Ten
Take a Power Walk

1. "Trust and Obey," words by John H. Sammis, music by Daniel B. Towner. Public domain.
2. Henri Nouwen, *Here and Now: Living in the Spirit* (London: Darton, Longman and Todd, Ltd., 1994), 75.
3. We see this in Romans 16:22, where Tertius is identified

as the writer when Paul dictated, and in 1 Corinthians 16:21 where Paul usually signed the closing in his own hand to authenticate a letter.

4. Greek word meanings are from Walter Bauer, William F. Arndt, and F. Wilbur Gingrich, *A Greek-English Lexicon of the New Testament and Other Early Christian Literature* (Chicago: The University of Chicago Press, 1971); Spiros Zodhiates, *The Complete Word Study Dictionary: New Testament,* revised edition (Chattanooga, TN: AMG International, Inc., 1993); *The New Strong's Concise Concordance* & *Vine's Concise Dictionary of the Bible* (Nashville, TN: Thomas Nelson, Inc., 1999).
5. Zodhiates, *The Complete Word Study Dictionary: New Testament,* 605.
6. Henri Nouwen, *The Road to Daybreak* (New York: An Image Book published by Doubleday, 1990), 1–3.
7. Karl Barth, *The Holy Ghost and the Christian Life,* translated by R. Birch Hoyle (London: Frederick Muller Limited, 1938), 22–23.
8. Watchman Nee, *The Spiritual Man,* Volume Three (New York: Christian Fellowship Publishers, Inc. 1968), 81.
9. Ibid., 83.
10. Ibid., 86.
11. Ibid., 87.
12. Susan R. Beacham, "Did You Ever See a King?" Used by permission.

Chapter Eleven
The Holy Spirit and the Big *Es*

1. Hans Küng, *The Church,* trans. by Ray and Rosaleen Ockenden (New York: Sheed and Ward, 1967), 488.
2. H. Richard Niebuhr, *Christ and Culture* (New York: Harper and Row, 1951).
3. "The Lord made Simon alone, whom He named Peter, the 'rock' of His Church. He gave him the keys of His

Church and instituted him shepherd of the whole flock. The office of binding and loosing that was given to Peter was also assigned to the college of apostles united to its head. This pastoral office of Peter and the other apostles belongs to the Church's very foundation and is continued by the bishops under the primacy of the Pope." [*Catechism of the Catholic Church* (New York: Image Book Published by Doubleday, 199), 254.]

4. Douglas R. A. Hare, *Matthew in Interpretation: A Bible Commentary for Teaching and Preaching* (Louisville, KY: John Knox Press, 1993), 190.
5. Ibid., 190. R.T. France, *The Gospel According to Matthew* (Grand Rapids, MI: William B. Eerdmans Publishing Company, 1985), 254. William Hendriksen, *Exposition of the Gospel According to Matthew* (Grand Rapids, MI: Baker Book House, 1973), 647.
6. Paul S. Rees, *Fire or* Fire (Grand Rapids: Zondervan Publishing House, 1953), 5–6.
7. Thom S. Rainer, *Surprising Insights from the Unchurched and Proven Ways to Reach Them* (Grand Rapids, MI: Zondervan, 2001), 34. Gary L. McIntosh, *Three Generations: Riding the Waves of Change in Your Church* (Grand Rapids, MI: Fleming H. Revell, 1995).
8. Thomas Cahill, *How the Irish Saved Civilization: The Untold Story of Ireland's Heroic Role from the Fall of Rome to the Rise of Medieval Europe* (New York: Doubleday, 1995). George G. Hunter III, *The Celtic Way of Evangelism: How Christianity Can Reach the West…Again* (Nashville: Abingdon Press, 2000).
9. Leonard Sweet, *Soul Tsunami* (Grand Rapids, MI: Zondervan Publishing House, 1999), 423.
10. "I Love to Tell the Story" by Katherine Hankey. Public domain.
11. *Dying We Live: The Last Messages of Men and Women Who Resisted Hitler and Were Martyred*, edited by Helmut Gollwitzer, Kathe Kuhn and Reinhold Schneider (New York: The Seabury Press, 1956), 123–132.

Chapter Twelve
The Wind Is Blowing in the Trees

1. The reader should not infer that throughout church history only those people who manifested certain charismatic gifts were the only true Christians or the only people the Holy Spirit used. Rather, this particular emphasis is to show that all the spiritual gifts were available to the church over the past two thousand years and that there have been people who were used by the Spirit in this fashion.
2. Stanley M. Burgess and Gary B. McGee, editors; Patrick H. Alexander, associate editor, *Dictionary of Pentecostal and Charismatic Movements* (Grand Rapids, MI: Zondervan Publishing House, 1988), 417. Many of the insights of this part of the "forest" are taken from Burgess's articles on "The Holy Spirit, Doctrine of: The Ancient Fathers," pages 417–432, and "The Holy Spirit, Doctrine of: The Medieval Churches," pages 432–444. While there are numerous books that provide similar information, these two dictionary articles are a convenient survey for reader interested in more information.
3. Second-century writings include the *Didache* (also known as *The Teaching of the Twelve Apostles*), the *Shepherd of Hermas*, the letters of Clement, Ignatius, Polycarp, Irenaeus, Tertulian, Clement of Alexandria, Origen, Hippolytus and Cyprian. Most Christian bookstores have resources that contain these interesting and important letters from the early church.
4. Jack Deere, *Surprised by the Power of the Spirit* (Grand Rapids, MI: Zondervan Publishing House, 1993), 101.
5. Burgess, ed., *Dictionary of Pentecostal and Charismatic Movements*, 441.
6. William S. Merricks, *Edward Irving: The Forgotten Giant* (East Peoria, IL: Scribe's Chamber Publications, 1983). Also see the article in the *Dictionary of Pentecostal and Charismatic Movements*, 470–471.
7. The open practice of speaking in tongues and prophecies

was soon discontinued in Irving's local church due to confusion among the people, and Irving was forced from the Scottish Presbyterian Church. Irving's experience illustrates that while the general tenor of Protestantism was not accepting of certain spiritual gifts, nonetheless the gifts were evident in the lives of many believers.

8. The material in the remainder of this chapter is drawn primarily from Stanley M. Burgess and Gary B. McGee, *Dictionary of Pentecostal and Charismatic Movements* (Grand Rapids, MI: Zondervan Publishing House, 1988) and Vinson Synan, *The Century of the Holy Spirit* (Nashville, TN: Thomas Nelson Publishers, 2001).
9. Frank Bartleman, *Azusa Street* (South Plainfield, NJ: Bridge Publishing Inc., 1980). This edition includes an introduction by noted Pentecostal historian Vinson Synan and is the complete and unabridged account of Bartleman's *How "Pentecost" Came to Los Angeles—How It Was in the Beginning*, published in 1925.
10. The house at 214 Bonnie Brae has been preserved by the Church of God in Christ and is open to visitors. The original building at Azusa Street has been destroyed, but the location is noted by a street sign between 2nd and 3rd Streets on San Pedro Street in Los Angeles. A historical marker is on the property, which is now the Japanese American Cultural Community Center.
11. The eschatological fever of the revival was partly fueled by the terrific San Francisco earthquake that occurred on April 18, 1906. The loss of life and the property destruction aroused spiritual passion and concern that were similar to that experienced in the United States in the weeks following September 11, 2001.
12. Frank Bartleman, *Azusa Street*, 47.
13. Ibid., 59.
14. See the excellent article on Du Plessis in the *Dictionary of Pentecostal and Charismatic Movements*, 250–254. It should also be noted that Pentecostal theologians and leaders continue to dialogue with a variety of ecumenical

groups around the world. These efforts are not designed for organizational or even theological unity, but primarily to foster better understanding among such groups for the cause of Christ.

15. *Dogmatic Constitution on the Church*, 12, Abbott, 1966, 30. Cited in *Dictionary of Pentecostal and Charismatic Movements*, 111.

16. See Dallas Willard's compelling call to radical discipleship in *The Divine Conspiracy* (San Francisco, CA: HarperSanFrancisco, 1998).

For Further Study

Beacham, A.D. Jr. *Light for the Journey: A Fresh Focus on Doctrine.* Franklin Springs, GA: LifeSprings Resources, 1998.

Bickle, Mike. *Growing in the Prophetic.* Lake Mary, FL: Charisma House, 1996.

Bonhoeffer, Dietrich. *Life Together.* San Francisco: Harper & Row, 1954.

Burgess, Stanley M. and Gary B. McGee. *Dictionary of Pentecostal and Charismatic Movements.* Grand Rapids, MI: Zondervan Publishing House, 1988.

Cannistraci, David. *Apostles and the Emerging Apostolic Movement.* Ventura, CA: Renew Books, 1996.

Cymbala, Jim. *Fresh Power.* Grand Rapids, MI: Zondervan Publishing House, 2001.

———. *Fresh Wind, Fresh Fire.* Grand Rapids, MI: Zondervan Publishing House, 1997.

Jacobs, Cindy. *The Voice of God.* Ventura, CA: Regal Books, 1995.

Deere, Jack. *Surprised by the Power of the Spirit.* Grand Rapids, MI: Zondervan Publishing House, 1993.

Foster, Richard J. *Celebration of Discipline.* San Francisco: HarperCollins Publishers, Inc., 1998.

Hunter, George G. III. *The Celtic Way of Evangelism: How Christianity Can Reach the West... Again.* Nashville: Abingdon Press, 2000.

Nee, Watchman. *The Spiritual Man,* three-volume edition. New York: Christian Fellowship Publishers, Inc., 1968.

Nouwen, Henri J. M. *Here and Now: Living in the Spirit.* London: Darton, Longman and Todd, Ltd., 1994.

———. *Making All Things New: An Invitation to the Spiritual Life*. San Francisco: Harper & Row, 1981.

———. *The Road to Daybreak: A Spiritual Journey*. New York: An Image Book published by Doubleday, 1990.

Pierce, Chuck D. and Rebecca Wagner Sytsema. *The Future War of the Church*. Ventura, CA: Renew Books, 2001.

Pike, Garnet E. *Receiving the Promise of the Father: How to Be Baptized in the Holy Spirit*. Franklin Springs, GA: LifeSprings Resources, 1997.

Roberson, Dave. *The Walk of the Spirit, the Walk of Power: The Vital Role of Praying in Tongues*. Tulsa, OK: Dave Roberson Ministries, 1999.

Smith, Eddie and Alice. *The Advocates: How to Plead the Case of Others in Prayer*. Lake Mary, FL: Charisma House, 2001.

Spurgeon, Charles. *What the Holy Spirit Does in a Believer's Life*. Compiled and edited by Robert Hall. Lynnwood, WA: Emerald Books, 1993.

Synan, Vinson. *The Century of the Holy Spirit*. Nashville, TN: Thomas Nelson Publishers, 2001.

Taylor, John V. *The Go-Between God*. Philadelphia: Fortress Press, 1973.

Wagner, C. Peter. *Apostles and Prophets: The Foundation of the Church*. Ventura, CA: Regal Books, 2000.

Willard, Dallas. *The Divine Conspiracy: Rediscovering Our Hidden Life in God*. San Francisco: HarperSanFrancisco, 1998.

Wimber, John. *Power Evangelism*. San Francisco: Harper & Row, 1986.

———. *Power Healing*. San Francisco: Harper & Row, 1987.

PERSONAL NOTES

PERSONAL NOTES

PERSONAL NOTES

PERSONAL NOTES

PERSONAL NOTES

PERSONAL NOTES

A Totally Practical, Non-Religious Guide to Understanding Your Christian Faith

YOUR JOURNEY STARTS HERE with this bold, convicting, non-judgmental, thought-provoking, one-of-a-kind Journey of Faith series. Each interactive study draws you closer to God's heart where you will find grace and mercy without feeling condemned or overwhelmed. Every page offers you an opportunity to discover an exciting eternal relationship that can grow and go with you for the rest of your life. Take the first step and start your journey here...

ENJOYING YOUR JOURNEY WITH GOD
BY DANIEL BROWN, PH.D.
God delights in you, loves you—and even likes you! Its time to move away from religion and into a relationship with God. You can encounter and examine God close up, through biblical eyes.

CALLED TO RADICAL DEVOTION BY DAVID MORRIS
Get ready for a discovery that will shatter all your myths and misconceptions about worship!

DRAWING CLOSER TO GOD'S HEART BY EDDIE AND ALICE SMITH
Do you know what concerns are on God's heart?

Plugged In to God's Power By Doug Beacham
Explore a non-religious teaching on an extremely spiritual subject.

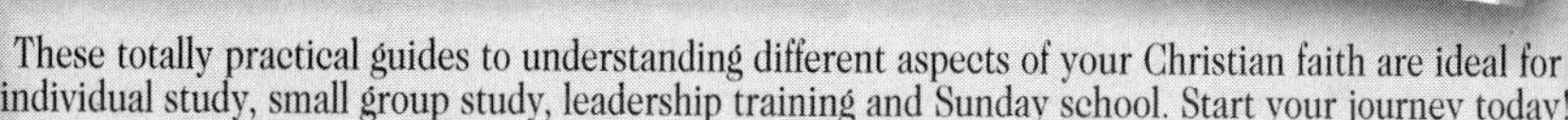
These totally practical guides to understanding different aspects of your Christian faith are ideal for individual study, small group study, leadership training and Sunday school. Start your journey today!

Call Today! 1-800-599-5750

Or visit your local Christian bookstore

www.charismawarehouse.com

A part of
STRANG
COMMUNICATIONS COMPANY

1476B

D1210